Friend *or* Foe?

Friend *or* Foe?

The fascinating story of women's
internment during WWII in Port Erin
& Port St Mary, Isle of Man

Written by the members of Rushen Internment Camp Heritage Action Team
Doreen Moule – Pamela Crowe – Alison Graham – David Wertheim – Sandra Davidson
Jane Saywell and Hugh Davidson

RUSHEN
Heritage Trust
the beautiful south

ISBN 978-0-9932914-4-9

Produced in the Isle of Man by Rushen Heritage Trust.

This book brings together a mix of researched historical fact, internee recollections and personal experience. While every
effort has been made to remain accurate, the passage of time may lead to names and places being mistaken and events
being compressed. The information in this book is true and complete to the best of our knowledge.
The authors and publisher disclaim any liability resulting in the use of information contained within this publication.
While every effort has been made to trace copyright holders, if any have been inadvertently overlooked, the publishers
would be happy to acknowledge them in future editions.

CONTENTS

PREFACE

Sandra and Hugh Davidson

Rushen Camp, in the small villages of Port Erin and Port St Mary in the Isle of Man was the only internment camp for women and married couples in Europe in WWII. Aspects of women's internment in the Island are important for gender studies, military history, treatment of immigrants, and governance, since the Rushen camps were operated not by the military but by civilians from the Home Office. They were a unique form of society. We estimate that at Christmas 1940, over 80% of the population of the two villages – residents and internees who lived together inside a barbed-wire perimeter – were female.

A committed team from the local heritage trust has already run two successful exhibitions on the topic and has now written the first book in Europe specifically covering British women's internment in WWII.

Our volunteer Heritage Action Team (HAT) has, over the past four years, become highly knowledgeable about the topic and has also generated new information through research and local interviews. It has worked closely together and consists of a school teacher, a quantity surveyor, a retired hospice nurse, a former Government Minister and a former Professor of Marketing, a businessman and arts entrepreneur, and a PA/social entrepreneur.

Few people outside the Isle of Man are aware that this holiday Island was chosen for interning 'alien' women during WWII and it is gradually being forgotten by today's Islanders. Much has been written about the internment of alien men on the Island, in both world wars, but it seemed to have been assumed that the women's story was of less interest. Far from it! Among the women were writers, singers, artists, educationalists, scientists and mothers. Our original aim was to tell the story for the local community, and to record local memories, but it has become so much more.

Through our exhibitions, titled 'Friend or Foe', we have reached a much wider audience, not only in the UK, but also in America, Australia, Germany, Lichtenstein, China, and in universities and libraries, as well as the Jewish world. Who knew that Wagner's granddaughter was interned here? That information brought interest from Wagner Societies. The ripples are becoming far reaching. Most of the 6,000 visitors and re-visitors to our exhibitions were moved by the plight of the predominantly refugee families and many urged us to write this book.

With Europe once again overwhelmed with desperate refugees, these stories of endurance and resilience in the face of hardship and injustice are all the more relevant today. The issues of what to do with all the women, children and babies had to be dealt with, then as now.

Where the Rushen internment camp was particularly unusual, however, was that there was eventually a married camp. Husbands interned elsewhere in the Island could join their wives and children, firstly in Port St Mary and finally in Port Erin.

Our HAT – Doreen Moule, Pam Crowe, Ali Graham, Jane Saywell, David Wertheim, Hugh Davidson and latterly me, Sandra Davidson – has unearthed moving stories of these women, and some of their children, and the effect on the local population at the time.

We HAT members didn't know each other before 9th July 2014, when the HAT came into existence, but as we have researched the stories of the 'alien' women we have formed close friendships, and are almost family. We have discovered a love of research, in uncovering human stories and giving them a voice. We have investigated stories of local people who were children at the time and introduced those local people to visiting internees' children coming here to see our exhibitions. Reunions have been made, and more friendships. Out of a dark time and great unhappiness, some good has come.

Each member below has contributed sections to this book. This is our record of the stories we have found and want to share with you.

With many thanks to Culture Vannin, the Gough Ritchie Charitable Trust and Manx National Heritage and Library for their support.

THE AUTHORS

Doreen Moule: Chairwoman of the WWII Internment HAT

Courtesy of Isle of Man Newspapers

Born in Wolverhampton, Doreen grew up in the Black Country and then trained as a teacher in Birmingham, where she taught in a primary school from 1970 to 1999. In 1999, she was fortunate enough to secure a teaching position in Douglas, where she taught for almost 10 years. Doreen and her partner moved to Rushen in 2004 and four years later she retired.

"Prior to becoming part of Rushen Internment Trust and joining the Heritage Action Team (HAT) I had little knowledge of internment in either of the world wars – the history curriculum had let me down! In fact, I had very little interest in 'modern' history, being more entranced by the Ancient Romans, Greeks, Egyptians and the Vikings.

I read Connery Chappell's book, Island of Barbed Wire *as an introduction to the subject and became fascinated. Since then, the research, the outcomes and the continuing links being forged with descendants/families of the internees has become a 'reason d'être' in my retirement".*

Alison Graham

Alison is thoroughly Manx and a qualified Quantity Surveyor, working with her husband Robert in their Quantity Surveying business. She and her husband are also very involved in organising rallies each year.

"Having committed to researching the story of women's internment in Rushen Camp during WWII, our unique journey began. Understandably there were limited numbers of people who were directly involved in this consequence of war with Germany. My own grandmother and mother were directly involved, housing up to 22 women internees during the first year of the internment camp, and receiving married couples the following year in the married camp, but sadly for me they were no longer there to ask them for their reminiscences.

Mona Quillin, a local Port St Mary resident was, at the grand age of 100, able to give an interview which was converted into an information board for our planned exhibition. She had been a next-door neighbour to both my grandmother and my mother. This was the beginning and from here on the momentum to find out more took over.

THE AUTHORS

Trips to the museum and many hours trawling the internet uncovered fascinating people and their stories. Rewarding contacts were made with German and Austrian museums along with the Metropolitan Women Police Association, and many unseen documents have been secured. The information obtained led to more and more avenues, leading to yet more information and so on it went until we realised that, in order to prepare for an exhibition, we had to condense and leave out some of the material in the hope that it could be reintroduced at a later date.

As a result of the two exhibitions, and many requests for the information to be made available in a book, the team has finally pulled it together. Much hard work and long hours have been expended by everyone and, from the early beginnings in 2014, this Heritage Action Team has worked well together. We are not sure yet where we go from here, but the experience of researching this subject has proved that much more information is available relating to Rushen Heritage. It just needs time and motivation, which we have proved we have a-plenty".

Jane Saywell

Jayne is Alison's sister and a multi-talented Manx woman. She is a retired Registered Nurse, having worked for over 40 years in many fields, including intensive care, acute medical, renal, cardiothoracic and Air Ambulance nursing in hospitals and nursing homes in the USA, UK and the Isle of Man.

"My family has also lived immensely varied and interesting lives! I am the granddaughter of May Eslick and daughter of Joan Eslick, who are both featured in this book.

My sister, Alison Graham, and I joined in April 2014, to investigate and research the Women's Internment Camps of WWII in Port St Mary and Port Erin. I had no idea what we were in for: many enjoyable group meetings, researching for information from commissioners' offices, museums, the records office and the internet as well as talking to locals from Port St Mary and Port Erin, including carrying out several live interviews, and now, a book.

This experience has been, for me, an amazing family journey and a big 'Thank You' to Hugh and Sandra, Pam, Doreen, Ali and David for all the support".

David Wertheim

David is a successful international businessman who has lived in both Europe and the USA and has worked in many countries. In 2007 he moved with his family to the Isle of Man where he has become actively engaged in promoting arts and culture, most recently as Vice Chairman of the IOM Arts Council and as a board member of Culture Vannin. He has helped arrange and organise a number of significant art exhibitions in the Isle of Man at the Sayle Gallery and the Manx Museum in cooperation with several leading art institutions. Three of those focused on artists interned in the Island during WWII, and included major retrospectives of the work of both Ernst Eisenmayer (Central Camp) and Kurt Schwitters (Hutchinson Square).

"Although my father was interned in 1940 in Huyton (Liverpool), my awareness and knowledge of the internment of 'enemy aliens' in Britain during WWII was limited. Since I started to study the subject following my move to the Isle of Man my understanding of the very doubtful benefits as well as the disruptive impact of internment on the internees, their lives and their families has grown immensely. Whilst living in Port St Mary I became aware of the then newly established Rushen Heritage Trust, so it was quite natural to offer assistance in researching the Rushen Camp".

Hugh Davidson MBE: Rushen Heritage Trust Board Co-Secretary

After heading up a market-leading American company in Canada and Continental Europe, Hugh co-founded Oxford Strategic Marketing, a consultancy now in its third generation of independent ownership, winning many awards.

He then moved from business entrepreneurship to become a social entrepreneur, with his wife Sandra, applying many of the values and marketing principles embedded in Oxford SM to the H&S Davidson Trust's operations. The Trust has worked on ventures in Vietnam, India and Bangladesh, with Oxfam and Save the Children, enabling over 60,000 people, mainly women and girls, to transform their lives: trebling their income and dramatically increasing their levels of empowerment.

"With others at Rushen Heritage Trust, I became very interested in WWII women's internment. Our home is on the site of a former Victorian boarding house which was occupied by internees, including Ira Rischowski, whose presence is recorded in this book.

This period of the Isle of Man's history is of universal relevance today and contains lessons relating to: gender issues; civil, not military, governance of internees; immigration, because many of the internees were fleeing Nazi oppression; local population and internees living together within a barbed-wire area, which enclosed them both; and women of different nationalities, cultures and viewpoints managing to 'rub along together' – even forming lasting friendships. Could men have done the same? There were emotional conflicts of loyalty: when the news of the death of 42 Manxmen at Dunkirk arrived at the same time as the influx of 3,300 German internees; for Manx landladies with sons in the British army yet hosting Nazi internees; plus the fact that the majority of internees were Jewish and loyal to Britain, living with a minority who supported Hitler.

Another appeal of the topic of women's internment is that it's very under-researched, unlike the story of the male internees – something this book, by an enthusiastic bunch of amateurs with professional standards, is designed to correct".

Sandra Davidson: RHT Board Co-Secretary

Sandra graduated as a mature student in English and Publishing at Oxford Brookes University and was involved in all six of Hugh's books, including the best-selling *Offensive Marketing*. She has also written a book for family and friends based on the lifetime of stories and papers her mother, Joyce Gott, had written.

Sandra is a trustee of the H&S Davidson Trust, a member of both the Inner Wheel and Save the Children IOM, and a volunteer in the Save the Children shop in Port Erin. She has travelled with Hugh to Vietnam, India, and Bangladesh to visit projects with Oxfam and Save the Children.

"I have found this whole project immensely eye-opening. Parallels from the rants of the press in wartime Britain are being echoed in the rants in the press today. Is it harder to be a refugee today than it was then? Yet there was then, and is now, humanity to be found. It just doesn't receive as much attention. No doubt in Rushen Camp there were resentments between locals who felt the internees were getting things they could not, and internees who felt a keen sense of injustice at being deprived of their freedom. Despite this, tolerance and even friendship was able to grow".

Pamela Crowe

Pamela was Co-Director of a wholesale and retail booksellers and newsagents for 25 years. On retirement she was elected to Tynwald, the Isle of Man Parliament, where she served for 13 years in a number of roles. She is now a fundraiser for charity and a keen researcher.

"My grandfather, a founder member of the Liverpool Scottish Regiment, furious at being told he was too old to fight in WWI, volunteered and was one of the first guards in the internment camp established in the Isle of Man, first in Douglas and then at Knockaloe.

I listened to my mother's tales of WWI on the Island, and after marrying into a large southern Manx family I heard stories from my mother-in-law about the WWII internment camp in Port Erin. Many of my husband's family, cousins, aunts and uncles, housed internees – from the largest hotel in Port Erin to the small hotels. All had interesting tales to tell.

The people I have written about have become a part of my life. The much-maligned Dame Joanna, a devoted and caring nurse and a skilled organiser, was determined to protect her charges and I hope my admiration for Dame Jo shines through every line in her story.

I traced the family of Wanda Wehrhan to the USA and talked at length with her great-granddaughter. Wanda kept a copy of every letter she had written asking for help for others and, unlike many who had cast her as the Nazi leader of the camp, what I found to my surprise was a true love story with the saddest of endings.

A bible in the Manx Museum library led me on a search across Europe. After finding Eva Rieger, the owner of the bible in Lichtenstein and now an expert on Wagner, our contact culminated in a wonderful weekend reunion in Port Erin with her friends and relatives.

The Lutherans in the camp played a pivotal role and Sister Anna Jochman became the leader of the camp. All of them had a connection with Bethel, a seminary and Deaconess training facility with specialist nursing and village community hospital for epileptics. Their archivist, Sister Gabriel, has been most helpful and interested in our research.

Cyril Cuthbert, who was appointed as Commandant of the much-depleted camp in 1941, was an enigma. There are few stories of his time as Commandant but I did uncover some interesting facts.

I have so enjoyed being a member of the team and I am continuing with my research".

PART 1: HOW THE CAMPS BEGAN AND EVOLVED

FROM FRIEND TO FOE

CHAPTER ONE

Europe and Britain by 1939 – The crisis for refugees across Europe

In 1933, when people, particularly Jews, in Germany began to be pressurised by the new political regime, between 37,000 and 38,000 people fled to neighbouring countries. This level of emigration declined from about 1933 to 1935, partly because the situation in Germany stabilised, but also because the immigration laws in the United States were being strictly enforced. In addition to that, European and British Commonwealth countries were becoming increasingly disinclined to take additional Jewish refugees.

However, 1938 saw a pronounced increase in applications for visas. This was a result of a combination of:

* the German annexation of Austria in March,
* the increase in attacks on Jews in the spring and summer,
* '*Kristallnacht*' (the Night of the Broken Glass) on 9th/10th November 1938, when the Nazis attacked the Jewish people, destroying approximately 200 synagogues, 8,000 plus shops and businesses with tens of thousands of Jews being sent to concentration camps and
* the ensuing confiscation of Jewish-owned property.

In spite of the difficulty in finding a guaranteed destination, about 36,000 Jews left Germany and Austria in 1938 and a further 77,00 in 1939.

This was a major international refugee crisis. A conference was called in Evian, France, by President Franklin D. Roosevelt, which was attended by

Above: 1939 Adolf Hitler with Rudolph Hess at a rally. (/AFP/Getty Images)

Jewish children from Berlin and Hamburg arrive at Waterloo Station in London. (Courtesy of Austrian National Library)

delegates from 32 countries including Australia, Canada, France, the United States and Great Britain, but the only country that agreed to take additional refugees was the Dominican Republic.

During 1938–1939, the UK accepted 10,000 unaccompanied Jewish children (*Kindertransport)* on an emergency basis. By 1939, Czechoslovakia had also been annexed by Germany and Czech Jews were added to those applying for visas. The quota for the United States for that year (which was filled) was 27,000, but this did not scratch the surface of the demand, by the end of June 1939, for 309,000 places.

By the outbreak of WWII in September 1939, an approximate total of 282,000 Jews had left Germany and 117,000 had left annexed Austria. About 40,000–60,000 emigrated to Great Britain from Germany, Austria and Czechoslovakia (mostly Jews, non-Aryans and left-wing opponents of Hitler), with large numbers going also to the United States, Palestine and Central and South America.[1]

At the end of 1939, approximately 202,000 Jews were left in Germany and 57,000 in annexed Austria. Many of these people were elderly. Jewish emigration was officially forbidden in October 1941 and by that time about 163,000 Jews were left in Germany. Most of those died in the concentration camps during the Holocaust.

Bearing all this in mind, it is important to remember that in 1939, Britain (and most of the rest of Europe) was still recovering from the effects of WWI and the Great Depression, but it was clear that war was yet again looming and

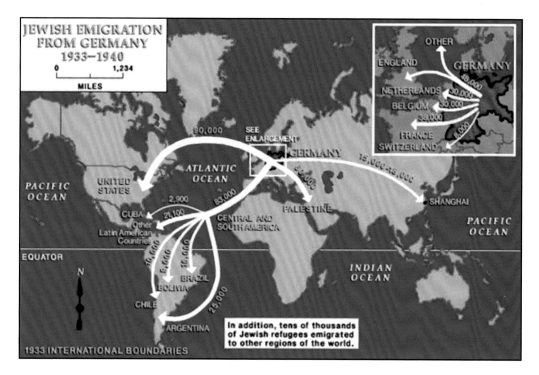

JEWISH EMIGRATION
FROM GERMANY
1933–1940

that Germany had the strongest military power, with Britain needing another couple of years to catch up.

Jewish emigration from Germany (Aubrey Boag, jackwhite.net/quakers)

How and why WWII internment happened

'**Enemy aliens**' – definition: 'a native, citizen or subject of one country living in another country with which it is at war, and viewed as suspect as a result' (*Collins English Dictionary*).

At the outbreak of war in 1939, there were approximately 70,000 enemy aliens in Britain. A major concern was that some of them might be spies or willing to collaborate with the enemy in the event of an invasion. As a result, all Germans and Austrians, between the ages of 16 and 70, had to attend special Home Office tribunals at which panels of people such as judges, magistrates, Justices of the Peace and civil servants categorised them into one of three groups:

> **Category 'A'** – 569 pro-Nazi supporters immediately interned as *high security risks.*
> **Category 'B'** – approximately 6,700 who were subject to restrictions and supervised as *doubtful cases.*
> **Category 'C'** – about 66,000 (90%), who were free to continue their lives as *no security risk.* About 55,000 of category 'C' were acknowledged to be 'refugees from Nazi oppression' and most of these were Jewish.

There were 120 tribunals set up in September 1939 in different regions around Britain. The majority were in London, where the highest concentration of Germans and Austrians were living, with 11 tribunals in north-west London alone. In line with the Registration of Aliens Act 1914, all enemy aliens had to register their details with the police and regularly notify them of any changes. The police were responsible for providing this information to the interview panels at the tribunals, thus giving them relevant background knowledge. The tribunals had completed their work by February 1940, having assessed 73,000 individuals of whom only 569 were sent for internment.

Category 'A' internees were sent to camps set up around Britain, including Glasgow, Manchester, Bury, Liverpool, Huyton, Kempton Park, Lingfield, Sutton Coldfield, Seaton and Paignton, but the majority were sent to the Isle of Man, where the men were held in Peel and the women in Rushen.

Other internees were initially sent to places such as Holloway Prison (female) in the London Borough of Islington, and Huyton (male), outside Liverpool. Additional places, such as race courses and empty housing estates, were pressed into use as internment or transit camps, with the quality of conditions varying greatly. Some were considered to be primitive, while others provided all basic needs. After a few weeks, the majority of the internees were transferred to the Isle of Man.

In the spring of 1940, after the failure of the Norwegian campaign, there was increased antagonism towards enemy aliens because of the heightened fear of spies. By May 1940 the war was at a critical point: Britain was vulnerable to invasion and the war was being lost. Operation Dynamo was underway and the evacuation of French and British troops from Dunkirk had begun. Warships, ferries, pleasure boats, fishing boats and every type of small craft sailed to Dunkirk to reach the stranded troops. The Isle of Man sent the best of its ships, bringing out 24,669 troops and losing three ships in the process. One man in every 14 who escaped from Dunkirk reached England in a Manx boat.

The risk of a Fifth Column in Britain arising from the freedom of thousands of

Holloway Prison – many internees were held here before being sent to the Isle of Man. (Private collection)

enemy aliens was now considered to be a real possibility. In response to public pressure, and despite the earlier tribunal results, the government began to intern all male Germans and Austrians between the ages of 16 and 60, including Category C refugees. Consequently, a further 8,000 enemy aliens were apprehended.[2]

When Britain and Italy did go to war, in June 1940, Winston Churchill reputedly said, 'Collar the lot!' thus ordering that the 19,000 plus male Italians in Britain should all be detained regardless of the fact that most of them had lived in Britain for several decades. It also included foreign nationals who happened to be travelling or studying in Britain. For refugees, who had fled Nazi Germany and who considered Britain to be a safe haven, the future was once again uncertain.[3]

Why was the Isle of Man chosen for the internment camps?

When, in January 1940, plans were suggested for internment of enemy aliens, Sir John Anderson, the Home Secretary, declared that there was nowhere in the British Isles, sufficiently removed from areas of military importance, that could be used to house large numbers of internees.

The authorities were reminded by the Manx Chamber of Trade that some 23,000 male internees were housed in the Isle of Man during WWI. As a result, decisions were taken in London to set up internment camps in the Island yet again.

Key events September 1939 – June 1940

The first eight months of WWII were largely uneventful for people living in Britain. The period until the end of April 1940 was known as 'The Phoney War' for that reason. Since September 1939, when Britain declared war on Germany, there were only a few minor skirmishes in France and little activity in the air, since most of the German army was engaged on the Eastern Front with Poland.[4]

However, in May 1940, the month of the internees' arrival in Port Erin, the picture changed dramatically, with some seismic events, as follows:

10th May. Neville Chamberlain resigned as British Prime Minister and was succeeded by Winston Churchill. On the same day, Germany invaded Belgium, Holland and France.
13th May. Churchill's famous 'Blood, sweat and tears' speech.
15th May. Holland surrendered to Germany.
26th May. Calais surrendered to Germany.
28th May. Belgian army surrendered.
26th May to 4th June. Evacuation of 338,000 Allied troops to England from Dunkirk (one-third were French). This was the biggest military evacuation in history.
10th June. Italy declared war on Britain and France. Norway surrendered to Germany.
14th June. Paris occupied by Germany.
25th June. Surrender of France.

From July onwards the situation improved slightly for the Allies, notably with their success in the Battle of Britain, which lasted from 10th July to 31st October 1940. Over this period, the RAF lost 915 aircraft, but the Germans lost almost twice as many – 1,733. Hitler had planned to invade Britain on 15th September 1940 but, influenced by the result of the Battle of Britain, he decided to postpone this until spring 1941.

There was heavy bombing of British cities, including London, Manchester, Liverpool and Coventry. On 21st October 1940, Liverpool was bombed for the 200th time and some of the fires could be seen from Port St Mary.

Another important event, which directly affected the families of some landladies, was the conscription of British males aged 21 to 35 years. This was announced on 17th September 1940.

In summary, 1940 saw the Allies struggling, while the Axis powers achieved successes in Europe, Africa and Asia.

The impact of Dunkirk on Manx people, 29th May 1940

The British government's plan at Dunkirk was to rescue 45,000 members of the armed forces. In the event, 338,000 were rescued, which is why this retreat was considered a triumph. Of those 338,000, about 7%, or 24,000, were taken back to England in Manx ships, staffed mainly by sailors of the Isle of Man Steam Packet Company (IOMSPC).

Eight IOMSPC ships were involved and made many journeys across the English Channel, fully laden with troops. Sadly, three were sunk.

The 29th May 1940 has been described as the blackest day in the history of

British and French troops waiting among the dunes of Dunkirk beach for their evacuation. (ullstein bild/ullstein bild via Getty Images)

the Isle of Man Steam Packet Company. At 5.30 a.m., during her second journey into Dunkirk, the *Mona's Queen III* struck a magnetic mine. It broke her back and she sank very quickly with the loss of 24 crew. In the afternoon, the *Fenella II* was bombed during her first run to Dunkirk while taking on troops at the stone jetty. In the late evening, the *King Orry IV* was bombed.[5]

In total, 45 men lost their lives that day and most of them were Manx, mainly from Douglas. Two were from Port St Mary, one from Port Erin and one from Colby.

It is a remarkable coincidence that this tragic day for the Isle of Man, and for the Manx friends and relatives of those who died, was also the day on which the first women internees arrived. Both locals and internees had their own personal troubles.

The sinking of the Arandora Star

Just as tragedy at sea struck Manx inhabitants at the end of May 1940, so it affected internees at Rushen Camp when the Blue Star liner *Arandora Star* was sunk by a German U-boat on 2nd July 1940.

It had sailed from Liverpool at 4 a.m. on 1st July, bound for Newfoundland, with 1,200 German and Italian male internees on board. The ship zigzagged along the Irish Sea, past the Isle of Man, but despite this evasion tactic was sunk by a German torpedo in the Atlantic, 75 miles from Bloody Foreland, off the coast of Ireland. Of the lives lost, 486 were Italians and 175 Germans, some married to women interned at Rushen Camp. A bad situation was made worse by the lack of information and women, who knew their husbands had sailed on the *Arandora Star*, spent agonising weeks not knowing whether they were alive or dead, but fearing the worst.

As Connery Chappell put it:

"What was to cause so much public distress after her loss was the doubt about the identity of who, and who was not, aboard her, for to keep father with son or

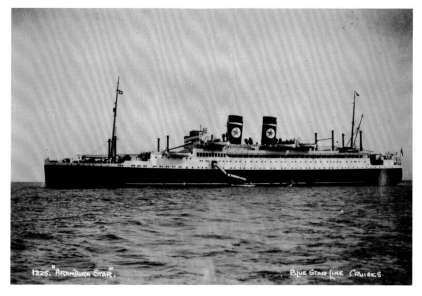

Blue Star liner *Arandora Star* sunk by a German U-boat while transporting internees to Canada. (Camrose Media)

pal with pal, men had swapped place with place in the camps from which the internees were being transferred, some wanting a transfer to they knew not where, while some were frightened of the unknown and only too anxious to stay put. 'Identities' were temporarily exchanged; Pedro was called but Castellani turned up. Officialdom was too busy to do more than count heads.[6]

The survivors of the *Arandora Star* were picked up by the Canadian destroyer *St Laurent* and taken to Greenock on the Clyde.

THE ARRIVAL OF THE WOMEN INTERNEES IN THE ISLE OF MAN AND LOCAL REACTION

CHAPTER TWO

For the first half of 1939 life on the Isle of Man went on more or less as normal. Tourists arrived, the TT races came and went, with many competitors from Europe, and the only families who were really aware of the impending war were those who had members in the armed forces.

However, when war broke out ferry and air services were severely cut and, within a few days, it became compulsory for passengers on the Manx boats to have landing permits at the Liverpool landing stage. The Manx people bitterly resented the imposition of passports and permit cards for journeys between Liverpool and Douglas. Editorials in the local newspapers called it 'Hitlerism', and by the 6th October 1939, the requirement for travel documents had been revoked.[1]

In 1940 the visitors once again arrived, but not those expected. Events moved very quickly that May, one of the pivotal months in WWII. In mid May, the Port Erin Town Clerk, Alec Clague, was told that the British Home Office intended to set up a women's camp in Port Erin. He toured the boarding houses and hotels, asking the owners if they would take in internees, paid for by the government, but at a much lower rate than for tourists. It was a guinea per person per week (just over £1). Most agreed. But it was not until 24th May 1940 that the War Cabinet decided to intern large numbers of German and Austrian women on the Isle of Man. Even then, there were rumours that the expected new arrivals would be young evacuees from Liverpool.

The first women internees arrived on 29th May 1940 and disembarked at

Arrival – Women aliens entering Douglas railway station to entrain for the charming resort of Port Erin which is to be their place of detention until Germany is humbled (Image courtesy of Manx National Heritage)

Port Erin's New Role

INTERNMENT CAMP FOR WOMEN ALIENS

Disembarkation Scenes At Douglas

PORT ERIN, one of the Island's most delightful resorts, is now the temporary home of about 3,500 women aliens who have been placed there under open internment.

News that the district was to be used for this purpose was known to us last week, but its publication was prohibited by the Censorship Department of the Manx Government.

On Monday, however, the information was disclosed to the world by the B.B.C., which broadcast the following official statement issued by the Home Office :—

"The Home Secretary has authorised the temporary internment throughout Great Britain of all German and Austrian women over 16 and under 60, whose present classification is B ; that is to say, those who, though exempted hitherto from internment, have been required to comply with special restrictions.

"Arrangements have been made for the internment of these women in the Isle of Man. They will be allowed, if they so desire, to take with them their children under the age of 16."

Local report about the opening of the internment camp. (Image courtesy of Manx National Heritage (*Isle of Man Examiner*, 31st May 1940, p. 5))

Douglas at around 7 a.m. from the Belgian cross-Channel ferry the *Princess Josephine Charlotte*. Isle of Man Steam Packet ships *Victoria*, *Snaefell*, *Rushen Castle* and *Ben my Chree* were also used in the transportation of internees, and the passenger lists would simply note internees and their total number.

Internees were accompanied by members of the Quaker community in Britain and, from the pier, they walked to Douglas railway station and the bus station for onward transportation to Port Erin. Many who were to be transported by bus were suspicious and wanted to go by train, because they were afraid that they were going to be separated from others that they knew. The train was crowded and one young Manx boy, John Corkish, who was on Port St Mary Station platform, says that the train had *three* engines – front, middle and rear – because of the load.

Once at Port Erin Station, they were escorted to St Catherine's Church Hall where they were issued with registration cards and given details of where they were to be billeted. Their accommodation was the various hotels and boarding houses in Port Erin and Port St Mary.

The local newspaper reported the arrival of the women (above left).[2]

Who were the internees and where did they come from?

As previously mentioned, most of the enemy aliens were from Germany and Austria, but there were a number from Italy and the countries neighbouring Germany and Austria.[3]

Many of these people had come to Britain soon after WWI, to begin a new life. Over the years some had set up their own businesses and all were settled into the communities they had joined and had brought up their families as British. They were not expecting further conflict and had not felt it necessary to become British citizens.

Others were comparatively recent arrivals, fleeing Germany after Hitler came to power in 1933. Many of these people were Jewish and, as the persecution of Jews became progressively intense and widespread, those who had realised what was happening and could leave easily did so.

Refugee numbers dramatically increased from 1938 as the urgency to flee the persecution increased. Many refugees who came to Britain had been used to a comfortable standard of living and had to deal with the practical difficulties of being in exile as best they could.[4]

For the lucky ones who were permitted to work, they had at least some control over their accommodation and general living conditions. The largest group of women immigrants, over 20,000, arrived on domestic permits in 1938 and 1939, since these were the easiest type to obtain. They were, in many cases, totally unfamiliar with this type of work. Teachers, medical students and other qualified women were engaged as 'maids' or 'domestic servants'. By September 1939 the doors were effectively closed and only a trickle of refugees reached Britain from Europe.

At the outbreak of war, some 8,000 foreign 'domestics' were sacked by their employers, who feared that they might be employing 'enemy aliens'. With the loss of their jobs, and also their homes, the situation was only saved by the refugee organisations, which came to their rescue.[5]

By May 1940 when it had been decided to intern the 'enemy aliens', arrests began. The internees were given very short notice, in most cases 24 hours, to gather their belongings together into one suitcase before they were arrested and taken to the nearest police station. Some were arrested at home, others at their place of work.

Many children of the internees were collected by police officers from their classrooms without warning and taken to join their mothers. Some internees had to arrange for their children to be cared for by family and/or friends and the children joined them later.

From the police stations, they were taken, as mentioned in Chapter 1, to internment/transit centres around the country. In some cases, the internees were at these detention centres, such as Holloway Prison, for 2–3 weeks before being transported to Liverpool for onward passage to the Isle of Man. As they were taken to board the boats at the docks they were jeered by the crowds and some people spat at them.

As mentioned above, they travelled by boat to the Island and then by train and bus to Port Erin and Port St Mary, where the arrival of approximately 3,500 internees into a community of less than 2,000 local people, at very short notice, put a considerable strain on resources and residents.

Dame Joanna Cruikshank to the rescue

Sir John Anderson had earned his nickname 'The Home Front Prime Minister' by his actions: nearly two million people benefited from an Anderson shelter in their gardens, built to protect them from German bombing. It was his role to establish which foreign nationals living in the UK at the outbreak of war needed to be confined. He established tribunals that worked to a clear sighted, logical and consistent policy, interviewing 73,353 aliens of which only 569 were initially sent to internment camps.

Sir John was furious when the new Prime Minister, Winston Churchill, fearing immediate invasion of the British Isles after the fall of France, allegedly pronounced 'Collar the lot'. A policy to intern all aliens living in the British Isles was speedily implemented. The Isle of Man had a history of managing prisoners of war and men's camps had already been planned for the Island, but Sir John had now to intern women.

The southern tip of the Island, the sheading of Rushen, was chosen as a possible site. A Commandant was identified – Dame Joanna Cruickshank, a heroine of WWI, who had established the RAF Nursing Service and military hospitals throughout the world. She had volunteered in WWII and was asked to be Matron in Charge of all auxiliary nursing and ambulance services throughout the UK, but had recently stepped down due to a recurrence of pernicious malaria. Sir John was reluctant to write to her, knowing that despite the recurrence of the pernicious malaria that she suffered from she would find a formal approach difficult to refuse, but Sir John's Private Secretary suggested that he should perhaps approach this highly experienced Matron of WWI informally.

Dame Joanna Cruickshank readily agreed to establish the Women's Internment Camp. No formal letter was ever sent and we do not know whether she was ever paid to take on, at the age of 64, what surely must have been one of the most onerous tasks that she had tackled in her illustrious career.

With a staff of just five and the help of the local clergymen's wives, the Commandant had, in two days, requisitioned hotels and rooms in private houses, set up her own office and a small hospital at the Hydro Hotel and put in place a registration system. But no one was expecting the influx of internees on 29th May 1940. Inspector Cuthbert, who later took over from Dame Joanna, estimated the figure as close to 4,000, but we rely on the registration numbers of 3,500. Nevertheless, all were housed by nightfall, a remarkable feat of organisation.

How the landladies coped

For the landladies this new experience must have been a considerable challenge. They were all experienced in looking after tourists, but only in the summer and not all day. Most of their accommodation offered bed and breakfast and high teas, but this was supervision of a very different kind. There were rations to be ordered, rotas to be organised, rules to be observed and curfews to be controlled and there was no doubt that they rose to these challenges.

However, there must have been a certain amount of animosity towards what the local people perceived as 'the enemy', especially as they arrived on the very day when three Manx ships were attacked at Dunkirk, with two being sunk and the third sinking the next morning. Nevertheless, most people put their own feelings to one side and treated the internees, as they had been asked to do by the Commandant, 'with kindness'.

HOW THE CAMPS EVOLVED 1940–1945

1940

By His Excellency Vice Admiral The Right Honourable The
Earl Granville, C.B., D.S.O., Lieutenant Governor of the
said Isle,   &c.,   &c.   &c.

THE DEFENCE REGULATIONS (ISLE OF MAN) 1939.

THE ALIENS RESTRICTION ACT, 1922.

CONTROL OF HIGHWAYS – PORT ERIN.

I, the said Lieutenant Governor, in exercise of
the powers vested in me by the Defence Regulations (Isle of
Man) 1939, and the Aliens Restriction Act, 1922, and all
other powers me in that behalf enabling DO hereby make the
following Order :

1.   All highways or rights of way leading from the area
comprised within the Village District of Port Erin to other
parts of the Island, except the Main road leading from Port
Erin to Douglas, shall be forthwith stopped up and the
exercise of any right of way or the use of any such highways,
except the aforesaid main road, is hereby prohibited.

2.   Persons may only leave or enter Port Erin by the aforesaid
main road or by the Isle of Man Railway.

3.   Persons entering or leaving Port Erin must produce their
National Registration Identity Cards to an officer of Police
or other authorised officer.

4.   No British subject shall enter Port Erin unless he or she
is a resident in that village district or has cause for
entering the said district for business purposes.

5.   No alien shall proceed out of Port Erin without first
having obtained a permit issued under the authority of the
Chief Constable.

AND I DO HEREBY give authority to Bertram Edward
Sargeaunt, Government Secretary, to take all such steps as
appear to him to be necessary and expedient in connection
with the stopping up of such highways or rights of way

GIVEN under my hand this 29th day of May, 1940.

Granville

Lieutenant Governor.

1940/148
The Defence
Regulations (Isle of
Man), 1939
The Aliens Restriction
Act, 1922
Control of Highways –
Port Erin, Port St Mary
and Parish of Rushen
31.05.1940.
(Reproduced by
permission of the
Treasury of the Isle of
Man. ©Crown
copyright reserved)

At very short notice, 3,500 women and children were expected to arrive in
Rushen Camp on 29th/30th May 1940. It was clear that arrangements needed
to be made for controls and boundaries to be set up, so orders (illustrated
overleaf) were signed by the Lieutenant Governor, His Excellency Vice Admiral
The Right Honourable The Earl Granville, CB., DSO and dated 29th May 1940.

The area covered by the orders was extensive and covered all the properties

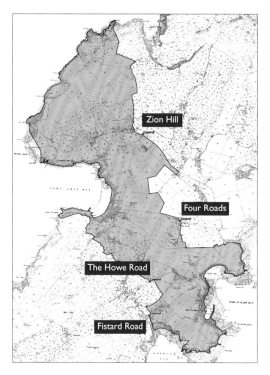

Map 1: The position of the main control points as outlined in the Order for Control of Highways. (Reproduced by permission of the Treasury of the Isle of Man. ©Crown copyright reserved)

that were being used to accommodate the internees. This arrangement was unique and meant that, in practice, the residents and the internees were interned together as a joint community behind the barbed wire. It provided control points where local people could move in and out of the camp with their identity cards and it also meant that the internees had some freedom to go for walks and use the beach. In the early days some of the internees were indulging in nude bathing on Port Erin beach, which shocked the local people. This was stopped, but whether by order or local disapproval is not known.

Map 1 shows the area covered by the orders with the original control points marked. The main control point, at that time, was at Four Roads, Port St Mary.

According to this map, other control points were established at Zion Hill, The Howe Road and Fistard Road. However, by 2nd August 1940, additions had been made to these control points and set hours had been identified for their use.

Up to this time, the internees had been allowed considerable freedom to walk the hills and valleys between Port St Mary and Port Erin, but the decision was made to restrict this freedom.

An extract from the *Closing of Highways – Port Erin, Port St Mary and Rushen* dated 2nd August 1940, reads as follows:

Persons may only enter the enclosed area by the Isle of Man Railway or by the following road entrances:

The Four Roads   (24 hours of the day).
The Howe Road   (24 hours of the day).
Zion Hill   (7 a.m. to 11 a.m. and 3 p.m. to 6 p.m. daily).
Fistard Road   (9 a.m. to 1 p.m. and 5 p.m. to 9 p.m. daily).
Daragh Road   *(Open daily from 7 a.m. to 12 noon and*
Ballahane Farm Road   *} from 3 p.m. to 6 p.m., if required in*
Glendown Farm Road   *connection with farming operations only).*

Once it had been established that many of the internees were no threat to Britain, considerable numbers were released to the mainland and by October 1940 the extent of the area covered by the camp had changed, as can be seen on Map 2.

Updated information from the *Control of Highways – Port Erin, Port St Mary and Parish of Rushen* (11th October 1940) reads as before, but with the additional controlled entrances at Spaldrick Hill (Port Erin) and Ballacreggan (Port St Mary), which were open between 7 a.m. and 11 p.m. daily.

During the latter part of 1940, the Home Office having had time to consider the actions taken earlier in May, began to review and re-evaluate the threat posed by the internees. The internees themselves had made many requests to the authorities for their release and also to be able to meet with their male relatives who were interned in various camps throughout the Island.

After much protesting to the camp authorities by separated married couples, by the end of July 1940, the wives of male internees were permitted to meet once a month. This meeting (see poster) was at the Ballaqueeney Hydro, but other meetings were to take place later when husbands were brought, always under escort, to Collinson's Café in Port Erin or wives, again under escort, were taken by train to Douglas and then coached to Derby Castle.

1941–1943

In May 1941 the situation changed again, with the opening of the mixed/married camp in Port St Mary.

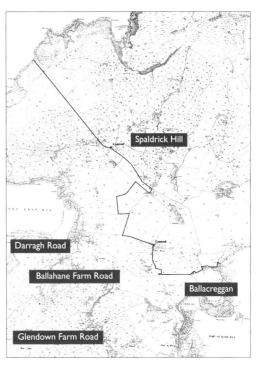

Map 2: 1940/332
The Defence (General) Regulations (Isle of Man), 1939
The Protected Area (Rushen Internment Camp) Order (No.2) 1940
02.08.1940.
(Reproduced by permission of the Treasury of the Isle of Man. ©Crown copyright reserved)

The single internees and those married internees who were not to be reunited, were moved to Port Erin. The Golf Links Hotel which had earlier been occupied by mainly Jewish refugees who had since been released, now housed the internees classified as loyal to Germany and the Windsor House Hotel accommodated the majority of the German Nursing Deaconesses. Internees in these hotels had all signed a request for repatriation

The Ballaqueeney Hydro and boarding houses on Port St Mary promenade, plus some pockets of accommodation elsewhere in the port/village, were taken over as married quarters for those internees whose husbands were brought from camps elsewhere in the Island to be reunited with their families.

Once more the map changed (see Map 3).

Internees whose husbands remained in the men's camps continued to apply for visiting permits and regular meetings were held at Collinson's Café in Port Erin.

With the opening of the married camp came the new Camp Commandant, Inspector Cyril Cuthbert, who was installed on 3rd June 1941.

At this time too, permission was given for the internees to establish small industries and, in Port Erin, internees were able to prepare and sell chicken feed manufactured from the kitchen waste of houses and hotels. The internees were also given permission to set up a piggery.

By now the numbers of internees were greatly reduced, but, where possible, workshops and classes set up during the first year of the camp, for both adults and children, continued. Recreation included two shopping days a week, visits

Poster giving details of a meeting between husbands and wives. (Courtesy of the Leo Baeck Institute, New York)

to the Strand Cinema in Port Erin, musical and theatrical nights and the use of the beach for swimming and physical education, but always, beneath the surface, there was the longing for notification of their release.

The Married Camp in Port St Mary closed in 1943 and moved to Spaldrick at Port Erin, leaving Port St Mary 'open for business' once more.

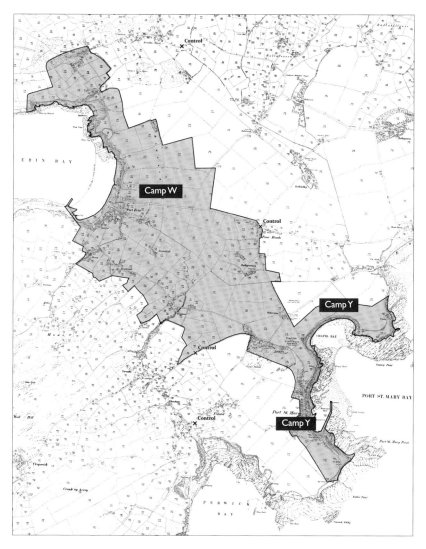

Map 3: The Married
Camp (Camp Y) and
Camp W for the
unmarried women and
those not to be
reunited with their
husbands.
1940/377.
The Defence (General)
Regulations (Isle of
Man) 1939
Control of Highways –
Port Erin, Port St Mary
and Parish of Rushen,
11.10.1940.
(Reproduced by
permission of the
Treasury of the Isle of
Man. ©Crown
copyright reserved)

1944

By August 1944 most of the internees had been released and returned to the mainland and only those who had requested to be returned to Germany were left.

At this point, changes were made to *The Protected Areas (Port Erin and Rushen and Arbory) Orders*. On 31st August 1944, the Lieutenant Governor signed the revised orders. These orders came into force on the 9th September 1944 and were the first revisions since 1942.

The new orders, which remained in place until the camp closed in September 1945, read as follows:

The Protected Area comprises the Port Erin Internment Camps for the detention of interned persons, being that portion of the Village District of Port Erin bordered red on the plan attached to the order made by me, dated the 31st of August 1944, controlling highways and rights of way leading from the said area to other parts of the Island.[1]

Map 4 shows the area designated by these orders:

By the time the camp closed there were just a couple of hundred internees remaining. They left the Island on 8th September 1945.

Map 4: The reduced size of the Camp in Port Erin. 1944/289. The Defence (General) Regulations (Isle of Man), 1939 The Protected Areas (Port Erin and Rushen and Arbory) Orders Amendment Order, 31.08.1944 (Reproduced by permission of the Treasury of the Isle of Man. ©Crown copyright reserved)

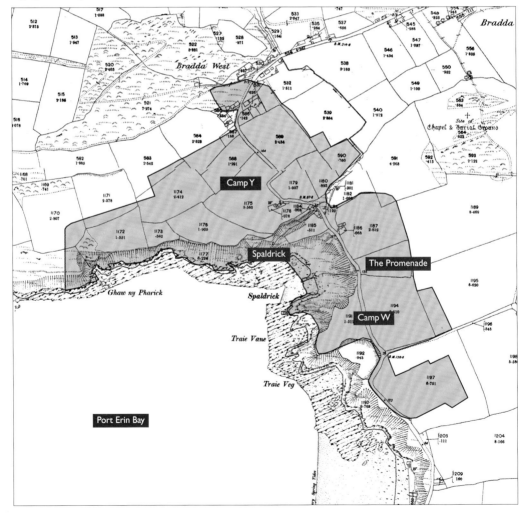

TWO VERY DIFFERENT COMMANDANTS: CRUICKSHANK & CUTHBERT

Dame Joanna M Cruickshank DBE, RRC (1875–1958). Rushen Camp Commandant – May 1940–May 1941

Dame Joanna Cruickshank, known always to her family as Margaret, was born on 28th November 1875 in Murree, India (now Pakistan). She was the daughter of Aberdeen-born William Cruickshank and was the second of five children, all of whom were born in India where their parents had settled. After showing an early interest in nursing, she came to England in 1907 to enrol as a probationer nurse at Guy's Hospital at the relatively late age of 31. She completed a general nursing course and then gained diplomas in both massage and midwifery. In about 1912 she returned to India where, in 1914, she was a sister with Lady Minto's Indian Nursing Association (INA) and stationed in Burma.

In 1917, with British and Indian troops fighting on the North West Frontier and in the Middle East, she joined Queen Alexandra's Imperial Nursing Service, caring for the injured soldiers. Like many of the troops she contracted falciparum malaria, the most dangerous form of the disease. She initially sought

Dame Joanna Margaret Cruickshank by Bassano Ltd. (© National Portrait Gallery, London)

relief from the debilitating fevers in the cool hills of the Punjab, but, by then 42, she was invalided back to England in March 1918 for convalescence where the climate was even cooler. This journey proved hazardous as she later recalled:

"The culminating point was when the ship was torpedoed in the Mediterranean. We had of course been aware of the danger, but none of us knew what it would feel like. Even now … that moment when the ship was struck is as vivid in my memory as when it happened. We had to take to the open boats and after a few hours at sea we were picked up by a Q-boat and sent home overland through Spain. We expected at any time to be detained as prisoners of war".[1]

Princess Mary's RAF Nursing Service

In October 1918, Joanna Cruickshank joined the recently formed Royal Air Force Nursing Service (RAFNS) as a Matron. The RAF had only come into being on 1st April 1918[2] and by June acquired its own nursing service. The first Acting Principal Matron, Miss L. E. Jolley, was appointed in July 'for the duration of the war'. However, when the war ended, the future of the RAFNS was in doubt with the Royal Navy urging its disbandment. The Chief of Air Staff, Sir Hugh Trenchard, opposed this, but the uncertainty led to Miss Jolley's resignation. On 25th November 1918, a few days before her 43rd birthday, Joanna Cruickshank was appointed as her replacement as Acting Matron-in-Chief of the fledgling service. Uncertainty about the future of the RAFNS continued throughout 1919 and it is recorded that at a meeting in July heated exchanges took place between Joanna Cruickshank and her army counterpart.

It was not until January 1921 that the future was assured by the grant of a royal charter by King George V. On 14th June 1923, with the King's approval, his daughter Princess Mary, who had commenced nursing training in 1918 at the Great Ormond Street Hospital for Sick Children, but in 1922 married Viscount Lascelles, became president of the service. It was renamed in her honour the Princess Mary Royal Air Force Nursing Service (PMRAFNS).

Dame Joanna in Lady Minto's Nursing uniform. (Courtesy of Princess Mary's Royal Air Force Nursing Service (PMRAFNS))

Soon after its creation, the PMRAFNS established three hospitals: at Finchley, North London (1919), Cranwell, Lincolnshire (1919), and Halton, Buckinghamshire (1920, rebuilt 1927). In 1923 an RAF hospital was built at Hinaidi near Baghdad to support RAF operations in the Middle East. In 1926 the RAF established a hospital on the site of an old army hospital in Ludd, in Palestine, and in 1928 another RAF hospital was established in Aden. Joanna Cruickshank held responsibility for all of them and helped design the nurses' uniforms.

In recognition of her organisational and managerial skills, she was awarded a CBE in 1927.

In November 1930, Joanna Cruikshank, having reached the mandatory retirement age of 55, was faced with retirement from the PMRAFNS. The minutes of a meeting of the Nursing Services Advisory Board record:

"… high appreciation of the way in which Dame Joanna

Cruickshank had discharged the duties of Matron-in-Chief during her long tenure of office. She had the responsible task of creating the Nursing Service, and the board consider that its present state of high efficiency is largely due to her ability, guidance and example."[3]

On leaving, Dame Joanna presented a silver rose bowl for the annual inter-hospitals tennis tournament, which was named after her as the Dame Joanna Cruickshank Tennis Tournament. For her services to the PMRAFNS Joanna Cruickshank was, in 1931, awarded Dame of the British Empire (DBE) to add to her CBE.

British Red Cross

In 1938 Dame Joanna accepted the post of Matron-in-Chief of the British Red Cross Society and in 1939 was appointed Matron-in-Chief of the Joint War Organisation of the British Red Cross and the Order of St John of Jerusalem, a position she was forced to relinquish in early 1940 due to a recurrence of ill health. Dame Joanna received the rarely awarded Royal Red Cross Medal for exceptional service in military nursing, an honour shared with Florence Nightingale.

Style of uniform used by Queen Alexandra's Nursing. (Courtesy of Princess Mary's Royal Air Force Nursing Service (PMRAFNS))

Rushen Internment Camp

However, Dame Joanna was to have one final and very important role. In 1940, she was approached informally by the Under-Secretary of State for the Home Office, Sir John Moylan, and asked to help establish an internment camp in the Isle of Man for women arrested as enemy aliens in the UK. She was already 64 years old.

In May 1940, although still unwell, she arrived in the Isle of Man, as the Commandant for the Home Office, with just a few days to establish a facility for women and children in the villages of Port Erin and Port St Mary.

Working tirelessly with her unrealistically small team of five assistants to deal with the several thousand internees who soon arrived, she requisitioned hotels, spare rooms in homes and the use of church halls. Conditions in the camp were, at first, disorganised, but her combination of military and nursing training and experience served her well. Requiring householders to house people they thought were the enemy was not easy, but time did not allow for excuses or arguments, as billets had to be found for an unknown number of women and children. Her only instruction to these reluctant landladies was that they were to treat the internees with kindness.

The first internees arrived on 29th May 1940. A registration office had been set up in St Catherine's Church Hall in Port Erin and the wives of the local clergy helped register the internees and escort them to their billets. More internees arrived the next day. The hotels and guesthouses were soon full and private homes were filling up. Among the influx were over 300 pregnant women and the need for a medical facility was critical. Dame Joanna's solution to this was simply to convert the ground floor rooms of the Hydro Hotel, where she had established her office, into a temporary hospital with beds and screens soon assembled.

Within a few days the first wave of some 3,000 internees had all been housed, generally two to a bed, as most hotels had very few, if any, single rooms. The local people slept uneasily, outnumbered by women they thought were Nazis. One hotelier who claimed they had housed all Nazis, when asked how they knew, had simply responded that they all spoke German. There was a failure to understand the majority were German-speaking refugees escaping Nazism.

Order out of chaos

From the initial chaos, order was soon established, and the necessities of daily life addressed. Landladies would not allow washing in the rooms. Many just had a cold water tap and sink. Washing machines were ordered and installed in a central area and the babies' nappies were soon drying in the fresh sea air. The maternity unit was staffed and dealing with the pregnant ladies. A leader was appointed in each house to meet with the Commandant each week to exchange information and complaints. Books were donated, and an interned Scottish bookseller organised and ran a library which proved very popular. Numerous choirs were formed and professional singer Jeanette Simons, almost from the first week, held musical evenings.

The Quaker Germany Emergency Committee was one of the first welfare organisations to arrive at Rushen Camp. Acting on their recommendations invitations were quickly extended to two volunteers from the Jewish Refugee Committee, and three further Quaker volunteers were sent to assist[4]. Among them was Margaret Collyer, a German speaker who had worked with the Quaker German Emergency Committee in both Berlin and Amsterdam. The Committee's general secretary, Bertha Bracey (see Chapter 14), also visited the camps and quickly called for an improvement in the conditions. By the time the camp had reached its peak number of around 4,000 internees in November 1940, Dame Joanna's staff had risen to about 25 and most of the volunteers could be released to return to the mainland. It was agreed that Margaret Collyer would remain.

A major problem in the camp was boredom, and to help combat this, in September, on the recommendation of Margaret Collyer, Dame Joanna approved internee economist Ruth Borchard's plan to establish the Service Exchange (see Chapter 8). Also, morale had recently improved with the arrival of some 50 children, including two small babies who had not been allowed to travel with their mothers when they were interned. It was realised that the older children needed schooling and Dame Joanna agreed to the establishment of a kindergarten school[5]. Initially there were no qualified teachers, but when experienced Montessori teacher, Dr Minna Specht (see Chapter 12) arrived as an internee from Holloway Prison, she took over the running of the school and also opened a kindergarten and school in Port St Mary.

Dame Joanna was proud of the quality of health care in the camp. She had appointed a health superintendent in each of Port Erin and Port St Mary supported by internee doctors and nurses. There was both an adult and a paediatric clinic. Quoted in *The Manchester Guardian* in the only interview she gave to the press while Commandant[6], Dame Joanna, whom it should be remembered was a trained midwife, claimed:

Recognition

There were setbacks, but when Bertha Bracey returned six months after her initial inspection, she published this report in *The Manchester Guardian* on 21st February 1941:

ISLE OF MAN INTERNMENT CAMPS
The Great Improvement Made in Six Months By Bertha Bracey

It has been my privilege, as chairman of the Central Department for Interned Refugees as well as general secretary of the Germany Emergency Committee of the Society of Friends, to pay a number of visits to the camps in the Isle of Man. There are certain observations and comments which I can make without discussing the general policy.

THE DIFFICULTIES

It should not be forgotten that the difficulties of those who have had to carry out this policy have been very great – taking over large bodies of internees at short notice, trying to obtain equipment in war-time, having to satisfy three Government departments (the War Office, the Home Office and the Manx Government), – and dealing with a human problem arising out of a confused situation of refugeedom and war has been anything but simple. It has been a matter of great interest to watch the progress made during the last six months. Unsatisfactory camps on the mainland have been closed down, and the main concentration of refugee and other civilian aliens is now in the Isle of Man. The men on the spot, who had no hand in the formation of the policy of internment, struggled from the beginning against very difficult conditions. Greatest of all, perhaps, was the state of mind of the internees. This had two main elements, sheer bewilderment and a rankling sense of injustice. Few could be expected to see that, with German invasion as a really imminent threat to this country, the basis on which tribunals had worked was not entirely adequate to the new situation. It is greatly to the credit of the British officers in charge of the camps that, on the whole and in one or two outstanding instances, they showed a quick and generous appreciation of the psychological reaction of the internees.

Look for a moment at the position as it faced the commandant of the women's camp in May 1940. Within 48 hours of arriving at the Rushen peninsula she, with five helpers, had to receive about three thousand women and children. Not even

WOMEN INTERNEES IN ISLE OF MAN

Interview with Dame Joanna Cruickshank

From our London Staff

FLEET STREET, FRIDAY.

So far about 360 of the women interned in the Isle of Man have been exempted from internment by the tribunals which are meeting daily. Where the women have husbands they come before the tribunal at the same time. The tribunals deal with about twenty women each day, and go so thoroughly into each case that, while they are doing their best to hasten the task, it will probably take six months to complete it. Two weeks ago the number of women interned was about 3,820. Some women are released on health grounds, the others under ordinary release regulations.

The commandant of the women's camps is Dame Joanna Cruickshank, former Matron-in-Chief of the British Red Cross as well as of Princess Mary's R.A.F. Nursing Service. Dame Joanna, who is spending a few days in London, tells me that the larger number of the women interned are Jewesses who will not claim their German or Austrian nationality, and many are refugees who have suffered from the Nazis. Some women have been in this country for some time, visiting Germany occasionally or having relatives there. Others, classified as British born, may be partly of German parentage. The thousands of women at Port Erin and the smaller number at Port St. Mary are living in hotels and boarding-houses whose proprietors remain in charge and receive a Government allowance per head.

Health Record

The camps have a wonderful health record. There has been a great improvement in the health of the women, many of whom arrived as chronic cases. Those children, too, who were unhealthy when they came, many of them suffering badly from malnutrition, now seem to be bursting with health and happiness. Dame Joanna declares that one would not see bonnier children anywhere.

The health superintendent in each district is assisted by internee doctors and nurses. There is a clinic for children, and another for children, each attended by doctors and nurses, and during six months there has been only one death in the camps. That was a bad heart case. Our own people would have to pay a high price for the treatment that maternity cases from the camps are receiving. The mothers' health is greatly improved.

The large number of children living happily with their mothers under internment conditions are, of course, not internees. The younger children attend schools, two of which have Froebel-trained teachers, while the schools for older children are directed by German teachers. From eleven years onwards the boys are under the instruction of island teachers with a long experience of youth and highly recommended by their Government.

Permits are given to women science students to work in the marine biological

station at Port Erin, and its hall is open daily for an hour for the older children, who listen to lectures, while younger children inspect exhibits.

Occupations for the Women

A variety of occupations arranged for the women include lessons in languages, English being the most popular, and by experts in music, arts, handicrafts, dressmaking, cookery, and other domestic work. A talented Austrian sculptor holds clay-modelling classes, and her pupils are doing good work. There are indeed so many classes that it is difficult to accommodate them all.

With the help of internees Dame Joanna has organised an interchange of services between the women, many of them highly skilled. They make frocks for each other, dress their hair, wash or mend their clothes, and so on. Large quantities of clothes and of materials sent to the island are remodelled or made up by the internees in the styles they prefer under expert direction. Payment is made by coupons, and when the worker has earned twenty-four she exchanges eight coupons for cash, while the rest pay for interchange of services. Since the women are being fitted for future employment their time is profitably spent. They also knit for the men, who in return mend their shoes or do carpentry or other jobs for them.

Dame Joanna says that, while there have been little personal quarrels between Nazi women and some of the others, investigation has always shown them not to be serious. In six months there has never been any real trouble. When women are identified as Nazis they are put in quarters apart from the others. The Kosher Jewesses have their own house.

Married Camps Projected

The Government is considering, and hopes to establish, married camps. Meantime wives meet their husbands once a month for two hours in a hall large enough to let them move about as they choose and talk in privacy. Other visitors and people from the mainland have their conversations with internees in the presence of one of Dame Joanna's staff.

"If you curtail people's liberties there will always be grievances," said Dame Joanna, "but the authorities are doing their best. They have no desire to keep anyone on the island unnecessarily, and there are very few restrictions. The women are free to go anywhere in the wide area where the two camps are situated. They can go to the shops, to the cinema, and attend churches of their denominations. They are free of the beaches, and many of them enjoy bathing. Curfew varies with the season —at present it is at 8 p.m. The islanders, including their hosts, are very good to the women and get on particularly well with the Jewish women, who are very amenable to advice."

the names of the internees were known to her, still less any information about ages, family units, state of health or status. Hotels, boarding-houses and private houses had arranged to receive differing numbers of internees. With the help of some of the local clergy, women and children were counted out, ordered in groups and sent off to billets. The double bed seems to be a system throughout the Isle of Man, so it was no fault of the commandant if sick and healthy, Nazi and anti-Nazi, women and children were found sharing rooms and even beds. The commandant's office, by the way, was hopelessly inadequate.

It was soon discovered that there were no fewer than about three hundred expectant mothers, while there were some serious cases of infectious disease. Some mothers had brought their children; some had not and wished to have them. Two local doctors were asked to give part time service to the internees by arrangement with the two trained nurses who were sent to act as medical superintendents to the two districts, Port Erin and Port St Mary.

The situation as I found it in the first week in January 1941, is this. The staff has been increased to about thirty. The commandant now has a good office with the necessary equipment. There is a resident woman medical officer, two clinics and a nursing home and in these, internees with nursing and medical qualifications assist the British staff. Surgical, mental and complicated medical cases are sent to island hospitals outside the camp. Women who require kosher food are in one house and one or two houses have been set aside for Nazis. There are two schools, one in Port St Mary and one in Port Erin, staffed by internee teachers.

BARTERING SKILLS

A golf clubhouse has been turned into a small kindergarten (incidentally still in need of small chairs and tables and other equipment), and a café has been made into an occupational centre which also houses the library. Here there are classes in modelling, making of felt toys, dressmaking, lingerie, musical appreciation, &c. A service exchange scheme, thought out by one of the internees and sanctioned by the commandant, has been in operation for several months, and by this, dressmakers, darners, children's nurses, hairdressers, knitters, and so on, earn tokens which they can exchange for any of the other services and, under certain conditions, for cash which they can spend in the local shops. The exchange scheme does not yet reach all the women and the link with normal currency is causing some complications. Each house or group of smaller houses has an internee representative, who brings matters requiring attention or suggestions to the district supervisor. There are four such supervisors in charge of districts and they in turn bring matters to the attention of the commandant.

The commandant has regular meetings with the house representatives, the district supervisors and the householders. There are considerable possibilities of development in this system.

No one who has not been in a position to watch these developments will ever quite realise at what cost to the small body of original workers these improvements have been carried through. It has meant long hours and unremitting devotion all day and every day, including Sundays. The camp is to be congratulated on having a staff which is so keen, hard-working, sympathetic and capable. But past rigours take their toll, and it will probably be months before some of the workers can sit back and take breath and see the whole, with all its possibilities.

The men's camps differ very much in sites, basic physical possibilities and the energy and initiative shown by the commandants and their officers. Hutchinson, Onchan and Peel have been some of the most favoured in all these ways, and there are few educational settlements in this country which would not be proud to be able to turn out work of the same high quality as is being done at Hutchinson. The wireless programme, which can be turned on in one room in each house, is well selected and made me feel I had not in the past done justice to the B.B.C. The work of the artists and of the technical school is of outstanding quality.

Onchan has a large football ground, allotments, five acres ready for potatoes, rabbits, poultry, and will shortly have started with pigs. The inter-camp football league causes much excitement and matches are very popular. Considering the difficulty of getting materials and equipment, a great deal has been done towards providing occupation in all the camps, but really positive large-scale developments along this most important line are almost impossible, while no one knows what the numbers and varying skill of the internees remaining in the camps are likely to be in a month or two.

Dame Joanna had something of a reputation as a martinet as well as having difficulty working with men. This latter seems somewhat surprising given her success in establishing the PMRAFNS and throughout her highly successful career, working in a world and at a time where women often were forced to adopt a subordinate role. She was a highly experienced and successful trained nurse as well as being a 'no-nonsense' hospital administrator who had achieved her success remarkably quickly. In this, her last professional role as Camp Commandant she was once again successful under very difficult conditions.

Dame Joanna faced criticism for her failure to understand the complexities of the German situation and the tensions between the Jewish refugees and the Nazis as well as having favoured some of the Nazi internees. Though this may have been the case, she saw her role as the efficient establishment and running of a camp for internee women. It is unlikely that she saw reasons to differentiate between them other than on ability. Only if political and personal differences interfered with the efficient running of the camp it seems would she have been willing to act. Undoubtedly there were those who were jealous of her success and abilities.

Dame Joanna's resignation reported in the local press. (Image courtesy of Manx National Heritage (*Mona's Herald*, Tuesday 27th May, 1941, p.1)

Resignation

The ceaseless work and pressure took its toll on the by now 65-year-old Commandant and the married camp was planned to open in Port St Mary on 8th May 1941. One of her deputies, Miss Wilson had put into place the arrangements for this. Dame Joanna felt sure that a woman would be chosen to replace her.

She knew her ill health was showing signs of returning when she wrote her resignation letter in which she mentions that she had never been formally appointed, so perhaps she never received any remuneration. It is touching to see in the letter that, ever the

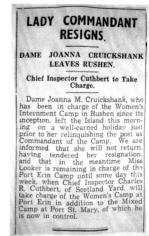

LADY COMMANDANT RESIGNS.

DAME JOANNA CRUICKSHANK LEAVES RUSHEN.

Chief Inspector Cuthbert to Take Charge.

Dame Joanna M. Cruickshank, who has been in charge of the Women's Internment Camp in Rushen since its inception, left the Island this morning on a well-earned holiday just prior to her relinquishing the post as Commandant of the Camp. We are informed that she will not return, having tendered her resignation, and that in the meantime Miss Looker is remaining in charge of the Port Erin Camp until some day this week, when Chief Inspector Charles R. Cuthbert, of Scotland Yard, will take charge of the Women's Camp at Port Erin in addition to the Mixed Camp at Port St. Mary, of which he is now in control.

nurse and midwife, she comments that a baby was delivered unexpectedly that evening.

Whatever the reasons, it seems Dame Joanna saw this as a timely opportunity to tender her resignation and the establishment of a married camp in Port St

HEADQUARTERS
WOMEN'S INTERNMENT CAMP,
PORT ERIN,
ISLE OF MAN.

Ref. No. JMC

May 10th 1941.

Sir John Moylan, C.B., C.B.E.,
Scotland House,
Westminster, S.W.1.

Dear Sir John,

I am inexpressibly relieved to get your kind letter of May 6th and to know that you have immediately grasped the hint that I gave that I should be glad if I might be allowed to relinquish my work here; as you know better than most, it has been a more difficult task than one could well imagine and I must confess that if I had foreseen one half of the strains and stresses it was to involve my courage would have failed me at the outset and I could never have undertaken it, even though, in those grim days of May last year there was nothing one could refuse to do if it was likely to help, even in the smallest way, the government and the country. If I had not had devoted and loyal help from my colleagues I could not have done it and there have been many times during the past twelve months when I thought I could not go on, and many times, I fear, when I have threatened to go, but until now there has always been the feeling that having put my hand to the plough, however hard the furrow, I must not look back.

Now, however, as you suggest, we have come to the end of a furrow and before we start another it would be wise to look round. Miss Looker and I have often said to each other lately that as the releases end and only the less friendly internees are left the whole character of the camp must probably change; and, more especially since we have known that it might be the intention of the Home Office to send the 12(5A)s and 18B. cases here we have agreed that we neither of us have the right kind of training or experience, and I think I may add, temperament or inclination to carry out a policy which may I suppose be increasingly repressive and where 'security' and 'intelligence'

/will

the
will be more and more/important side of the camp administr...
We have no doubt in our own minds that we would not only ...
much rather not have to be responsible for work of this k...
for which we have no training or aptitude but also that we
could be more useful in the national effort on the mainland
doing work in which we are more experienced and for which we
have better qualifications.

You will understand therefore that your letter received
last night came as a very great relief as it shows that your
mind has been working in the same direction. and. I now feel that
I can ask you to find another Commandant as quickly as possible
without seeming to shirk responsibility or to be weakening in
determination to take my part in the way I have been asked in
the war effort.

Now that I know I am shortly 'to be exempted from internment' I realise how anxious I am to get away and to be once
more working among my own people on the mainland and I do
earnestly ask that my successor be appointed as quickly as you
conveniently can. I think it will be far wiser if the 18 B.s.
and others do not come until the new Commandant is installed as
then she can make whatever arrangementssshe thinks best for them.
It will probably also be wiser if the axe-ing of the establishment is postponed until she is able to choose which, if any, of
the present staff she wishes to retain. Our numbers this week,
with the transfer to the married camp fall for the first time
below two thousand and I suppose the axe-ing will not be long
delayed. If the 18 B.s need not come immediately I think it may
be as well if I go on leave, from which I do not come back,
shortly. At the moment apart from the questions connected with
the arrival of these people and the question of what our establish
ment is to be things are quieter than they have been and I could
get away more easily. Minor problems of course are always with
us; last night though it was the first for several without an
'alert' we had a baby born rather unexpectedly in the early hours
of the morning in the Hydro!

I do not know whether as I have never been 'formally'
appointed you will require from me a 'formal' letter of resignation?

Yours sincerely,

(Signed) JOANNA M. CRUICKSHANK.

Opposite and above: Dame Joanna's 'official' letter of resignation to Sir John Moylan. (Courtesy of the National Archives)

Mary under a separate Commandant, coincided with her announcement on 22nd May 1941 to retire; both she and her Deputy, Miss Looker, left for London the same day. It was almost exactly one year after she had taken on the challenging role of Internment Camp Commandant. She was congratulated by the International Committee for Refugees in Europe on the quality of care for the internees.

Retirement

In retirement Dame Joanna regularly attended reunions of the PMRAFNS and the annual inter-hospitals tennis tournaments. Dame Joanna never married. She died on 16th August, 1958, aged 82.

***

FROM CONSTABLE TO COMMANDANT –
The enigmatic Cyril Roy Mitchell Cuthbert (1902–1984)
Rushen Camp Commandant, May 1941 to closure in 1945

An enthusiastic amateur forensic scientist, Constable Cuthbert was keen to establish a more scientific method of crime detection at the Metropolitan Police HQ. He had some medical and dental knowledge and, after taking evening classes in chemistry, he invested in a 35-shilling second-hand microscope and set himself up as 'the scientific policeman'. However, his superiors viewed his activities as highly inappropriate and he came close to losing his job.

Lord Trenchard, the Metropolitan Police Commissioner during the 1930s, on an official visit to the offices of the Metropolitan Police spoke to Cuthbert, who had hastily acquired a white coat from the kitchen staff and set up his microscope, and was persuaded by the young Constable that a forensic unit was desirable. Some of Cuthbert's colleagues felt that the ambitious Cuthbert had prompted Lord Trenchard to this course of action for his own ends, perhaps aware that the Lord had initiated the Police Training College at Hendon to produce leaders from the ranks.

The Chief Financial Officer of the Metropolitan Police at the time was senior civil servant John Moylan, who was involved with the financing of this unit – a man whose path Cuthbert was to cross again when Sir John was the Parliamentary Secretary to the Home Office Minister responsible for internment.

Professional scientists were employed and a laboratory was established. Sgt. Cuthbert became the Forensic Unit Clerk and the Liaison Officer. He was fascinated by the procedures, watching closely and making notes as the famous scientists in the unit solved crimes with their forensic investigative skills.

At the outbreak of war, Cuthbert, now an Inspector, was transferred as clerk to the alien tribunal at Bow Street Magistrates Court in London and, in September 1940, he applied to be transferred to the tribunal administration team in Douglas, Isle of Man. His wife, Barbara, became a land girl, living at Ballacreggan Farm at Port Soderick.

The need for tribunals was declining rapidly and Inspector Cuthbert saw an opportunity to transfer to Port St Mary, where a married internee camp was being established. Miss D. J. Wilson was appointed as his Deputy. He worked alongside Miss Wilson, a former prison Governor, who had single-handedly progressed Dame Joanna Cruickshank's vision for a married camp. Dame Joanna must have felt frustrated at the establishment of the women's camp, as she could not acquire single beds when establishing the camp and the double beds now required for the married camp were equally elusive.

Inspector Cuthbert moved into the Ballaqueeney Hydro as Commandant in charge of the 300 internees now settled in Port St Mary. On 8th May 1941, some 162 reunited couples moved into married quarters.

When rumours surfaced that Dame Joanna was unwell and was retiring, it prompted Cuthbert to write to Sir John Moylan at the Home Office to say, as he was already involved with the married camp, he would be ideally placed to take command of both camps along with Miss Wilson; the Home Office agreed.

Cuthbert at work. (Courtesy of Manx National Heritage)

Dame Joanna's resignation letter had clearly referred to the new *female* Commandant, but Miss Wilson, the woman who had been such a valuable Deputy to Dame Joanna, was to be second in command to Inspector Cuthbert. After questions in Parliament about the suitability of a man in charge of the women's camp, 'women's interests' were to be the responsibility of Miss Wilson in her capacity as Deputy Commandant.

Cuthbert certainly won over the local landladies. They described him as a 'ladies' man'. Some even thought he had been a film actor (*because of his good looks?*). He had an excellent assistant (Miss Looker) who arranged children's parties and many other activities, leaving time for the Commandant to continue collecting every newspaper cutting from the beginning of the camp. Despite his charming manner with the local landladies, the Home Office had sent him a stern reprimand for altering official orders referring to 'internees' to read 'Aliens', reminding him that many of the children had been born in Britain.

By August 1942 the internee numbers were so dramatically reduced that the married camp was moved to Spaldrick, Port Erin. Inspector Cuthbert moved into a furnished house in St Georges Crescent, Port Erin and the married camp was moved in one day from Port St Mary to Spaldrick; it seems to have been a carefree day, everyone cooperating in loading and unloading the lorries.

The married camp and the women's camp were separated by a barrier and guard hut, and a simple tally system. Married camp internees had to pick up a tally from the guard on the way to the village, to be returned when they came back through the barrier.

In September 1944 Cyril Cuthbert became a proud father of a son, John Anthony, who was baptised in St Catherine's Church, Port Erin, although it

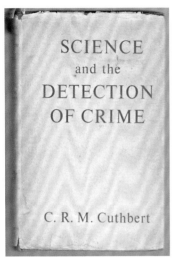

SCIENCE
and the
DETECTION
OF CRIME

C. R. M. Cuthbert

would seem that his wife and son returned to England where his son died tragically as a result of a road accident.

In his office in Victoria Square, Port Erin, Cyril spent many hours collating the newspaper cuttings which he compiled into a report. *The Cuthbert Report* appears to be an actual report of the camp, but many observations of his own that are in the report have been disputed by local residents who lived in Port Erin at the time. Maybe it was a blueprint for the organisation of an internment camp in the future. There does not appear to be any request for such a report from the Home Office, but they did acknowledge that they had received it.

Cuthbert remained in Port Erin until the camp closed in 1945; he then returned to London and assumed his liaison responsibilities at the Metropolitan Police Forensic Laboratory. He lectured to many police departments on the subject of forensic criminal investigation. He was an eloquent speaker, giving informative talks on the cases he had seen and investigated, and after one such lecture to the Medico-Legal School of Harvard University in 1950, he became an honorary fellow of the University.

After receiving the King's Medal for Distinguished Service and his promotion to Detective Superintendent, he retired from the police service in 1951. Thereafter, he travelled the world selling British scientific instruments to India, Pakistan, Ceylon and Malaysia.

In 1958 he wrote a well-received book, *Science and the Detection of Crime*,[1] detailing the fascinating cases he had seen while observing the work of the team of scientists at the Metropolitan Forensic Investigation Department.

He died in 1984 in Haywards Heath, Sussex aged 81.[2]

OBITUARY

MR CYRIL CUTHBERT
Former head of Metropolitan
Police Laboratory

Mr Cyril Cuthbert, who died aged 81 at his home in Haywards Heath on May 5 had a distinguished and varied career firstly with the Metropolitan Police and subsequently as a hospital administrator.

He was educated as a cathedral scholar at Winchester, and then went to University College, Exeter with the intention of studying medicine. After successfully passing the pre-clinical examinations however his medical studies had to be abandoned because of the death of his father in 1923.

The following year he joined the Metropolitan Police and served at New Scotland Yard between 1925 and 1928 and again, as a sergeant, from 1932 to 1935. He was an instructor at the Police College, Hendon from the date of its inception in 1935 until the outbreak of war in 1939, and during this same period was administrative head of the Metropolitan Police Laboratory at New Scotland Yard, being credited with its virtually single handed creation.

In 1938 he planned and built up the instructional museum at the Metropolitan Police College at Hendon and this was to be a permanent feature of the training of detectives for many years.

Following a period as Secretary of the Enemy Aliens

Tribunal and other associated committees in 1939 and 1940, he was promoted Chief Inspector in 1941 and appointed as Commandant of the Married Enemy Aliens Internment Camp and Commandant of the Women's Internment Camp in the Isle of Man until the end of the war.

He was appointed as Chief Liaison Officer of the Metropolitan Police Laboratory in 1946 and was promoted Superintendent in 1951. He was one of the very few people awarded both the King's Police Medal and the King's Fire Service Medal, and retired from the Metropolitan Police in 1951.

He was a member of the Medico Legal Society of Great Britain and a Fellow of the Institute of Police Science, Harvard, USA, and lectured widely on forensic science and Police matters throughout Britain and the world.

Following a few years in export administration, he was appointed in 1956 as Secretary of St George's Hospital Medical School and spent the next fourteen years at Hyde Park Corner where in tandem with the then Dean, Dr Alastair Hunter, he became known to generations of medical students and academic staff as an able administrator and a pillar of the institution.

Top left: Book about forensic science written by Inspector Cuthbert in 1958. (Courtesy of Manx National Heritage)
Left: Obituary C. R. Cuthbert (1902–1984). (Courtesy of Manx National Heritage)

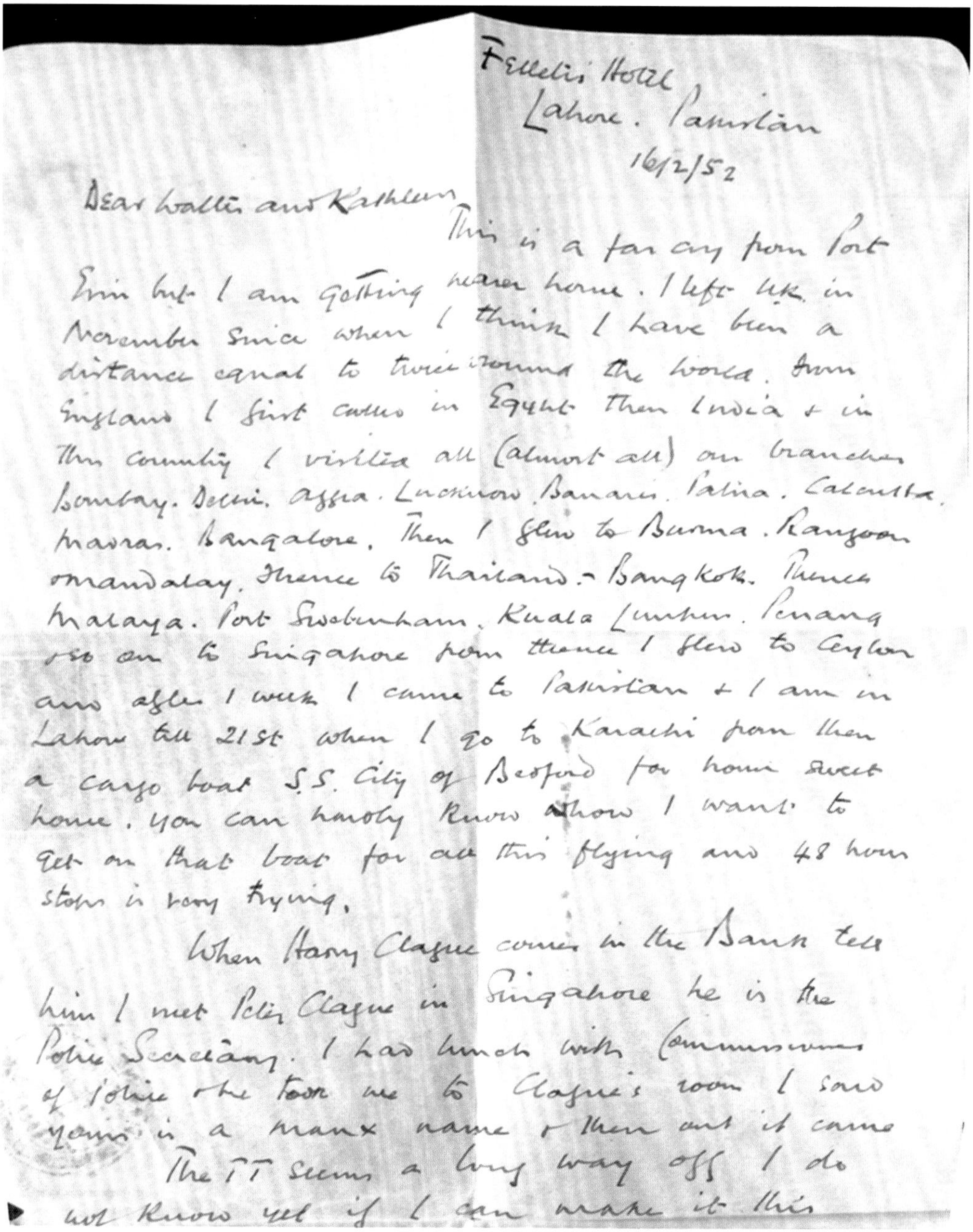

Felletis Hotel
Lahore. Pakistan
16/2/52

Dear Walter and Kathleen,

This is a far cry from Port Erin but I am getting nearer home. I left U.K. in November since when I think I have been a distance equal to twice round the world. From England I first called in Egypt then India & in this country I visited all (almost all) our branches Bombay. Delhi. agra. Lucknow. Banares. Patna. Calcutta. Madras. Bangalore. Then I flew to Burma. Rangoon Mandalay. Thence to Thailand – Bangkok. Thence Malaya. Port Swebenham. Kuala Lumpur. Penang so on to Singapore from thence I flew to Ceylon and after I week I came to Pakistan & I am in Lahore till 21st when I go to Karachi from then a cargo boat S.S. City of Bedford for home sweet home. You can hardly know how I want to get on that boat for all this flying and 48 hour stops is very trying.

When Harry Clague comes in the Bank tell him I met Peter Clague in Singapore he is the Police Secretary. I had lunch with Commissioner of Police who took me to Clague's room I said yours is a Manx name & then out it came

The TT seems a long way off I do not know yet if I can make it this

Above and overleaf: Cuthbert's letter from Lahore in 1952. (Courtesy of A. Wilson)

By all accounts you have had awful weather this winter for my part I have been fried & re fried till a little cold weather seem desireable.

Very best wishes to you all & hoping Ann & Richard are both

Yours

Cyril Cumbert

Second page of Cuthbert's letter from Lahore in 1952. (Courtesy of A. Wilson)

THE MARRIED CAMP 1941–1945

Locals say, not in Port St Mary

"We the undersigned rate payers hereby desire to register our protest against the Village being turned into a mixed alien camp."[1]

This was the reaction of the local residents of Port St Mary when they were made aware of the intention to establish a married camp within the town. Their letter to Port St Mary Commissioners continued:

"We do not consider that their influence will be good for the native population, especially the younger people and children, and also object to male aliens being billeted on our women-folk while the majority of the male population are absent on their various War duties."

Known officially as 'The Mixed Alien Internment Camp' and colloquially as 'The Married Camp', when the idea was first floated there was local opposition. The residents of the town had already seemingly come to terms with the billeting of women and children 'aliens' for the previous 12 months, but the housing of husbands of the women aliens would not be tolerated.

A married camp was being considered as early as January 1941 and a deputation of Port St Mary Commissioners was appointed to review this matter with the then Camp Commandant, Dame Joanna Cruickshank.

In March 1941 the Port St Mary commissioners received information from Dame Joanna that the camp for married aliens would be in Port St Mary. Soon after, Dame Joanna relinquished her position as Camp Commandant.

"Dear Mr Clague, You will have seen in the press that I am relinquishing my appointment as Commandant of this Camp, and I write to ask you whether you will kindly convey to the Commissioners my sincere thanks and appreciation for the help and support they have given me during the past twelve months.

The task has been a difficult one, and without the help I have been given by the Commissioners and also by the householders, it would have been almost impossible to have carried on."[2]

New Commandant for the Married Camp – May 1941

Dame Joanna anticipated a female would take over her position of Camp Commandant; the Home Office and Isle of Man Constabulary obviously decided otherwise.

The Board of Port St Mary Commissioners met with New Scotland Yard Chief Inspector Cyril Cuthbert, newly appointed to the position

Dame Joanna's letter to Port Erin Commissioners, dated 29th May 1941.

CHAPTER FIVE

Above: Appointment of Inspector Cuthbert to Commandant. (Courtesy of Manx National Heritage)

Below: Painting of Port St Mary Promenade taken from Christmas card presented to Commandant Cuthbert - December 1941. (Courtesy of Manx National Heritage)

of Commandant of the proposed married camp, Miss D. J. Wilson of the Prison Commission Service and Deputy Commandant, and Mr Latham from Government Office. The question of the married camp for Port St Mary was fully discussed and particulars of the rate payers petition given.

Government Office then forwarded a letter to the Port St Mary Commissioners advising:

"Sir, I have to inform you that the Home Office desire that a camp for married internees and their families shall be opened at Port St. Mary early in May, and they have appointed Chief Inspector Cuthbert of the Metropolitan Police to be Commandant of the Camp.

It is proposed that this camp shall be confined to the houses on the Promenade at Port St. Mary and the fence will include two fields in the rear of the Promenade houses and will run out to the Point".[3]

Married Camp officially opened

The first of April 1941 officially saw the opening of the married camp in the boarding houses and Ballaqueeney Hydro along Port St Mary promenade. On hearing the news that a married camp was being created in Port St Mary, one male internee held in the Onchan camp wrote the following entry into *The Onchan Pioneer*, a compilation of documents and drawings held in the iMuseum, Douglas[4].

Taken from the
Onchan Pioneer.
(Courtesy of Manx
National Heritage)

PORT ST. MARY

On Monday and Tuesday 114 brother-internees are leaving our camp. Not since July 1940 have we witnessed so many comrades leaving us at the same time. But as the circumstances leading to the departure were ten months ago, when hundreds were transported overseas, this time their faces are joyous in expectation of their reunion with their wives and children in the Married Camp at Port St. Mary.

For one year members of families interned on the Island were separated except for 8 meetings of 18 hours all in all. Only very intimate English friends of ours can feel and understand what reunion with our families means to us, when they remember that in many cases we German and Austrian Refugees found refuge in this country after hardships under Nazi oppression which deprived us of brothers, and sisters, who are scattered all over the world and whose fate often is unknown. We are happy to know, that our friends will live together with their wives and children while they are waiting anxiously for their release from internment – to do whatever useful work they can, ready to share hardships and danger with everyone outside.

They will not be idle either while still confined in internment. The majority was already engaged in agricultural or other work in our camp and they hope to be given similar opportunities at Port St. Mary.

There are still over 60 comrades left behind who have their families at Port Erin and who are waiting with anxious hearts for their reunion to come. We are aware of the initial difficulties when opening a new camp on new lines. We are confident that the fortunate members of the first selection will do all in their power to assist their Commander to build up that new camp in the same productive and constructive spirit with which we are all working at Onchan. It rests with them to shorten the time of waiting for their friends with whom they and their families have spent so many months together at Onchan or Rushen.

All good wishes are accompanying you, our friends. May you find, and give, comfort in your common life with your dear ones during these trying times. To many of you the camp owes gratitude for work done. Many of you leave friends behind who are waiting for happier days to meet you again.

Good luck to you, your wives and children,

for: ONCHAN INTERNMENT CAMP,

W. J. Jackmann,
CAMP SUPERVISOR

All change

Single and married women internees billeted in Port St Mary, who were not to be reunited with their husbands, were moved into the women's internment camp, which remained in Port Erin, effectively creating two separate camps and a 'neutral zone'. A barrier was positioned at the entrance to the Port St Mary promenade and the main road junction where a control officer was stationed. A further barrier was set up enclosing the compound at the entrance to the promenade, leaving access and amenities open for locals and visitors once again. With the exception of the promenade, Manx residents were now able to visit and stay in the unenclosed area of Port St Mary on production of their National Registration Identity Card.

The port was now also open to receive and welcome visitors from across the water, but they were required to write to the Chief Constable, Major J. W. Young, in Douglas stating that they wished to reside in Port St Mary on holiday and obtain a police permit.

Similarly, residents of Port St Mary wishing to enter Port Erin Camp, and residents of both Port Erin and Port St Mary who wanted access to Port St Mary promenade and Chapel Beach, also required a police permit card. The *Isle of Man Weekly Times* reported various hardships the barriers were creating for the locals. On 8th Feb 1941 they wrote:

"A deputation from the Port Erin Commissioners has interviewed the Government Secretary on the restrictions placed on entry from Bradda into Port Erin, which mean the people of Bradda are deprived of the amenities of the village district after 6 p.m. A petition of protest, signed by 58 residents, was sent to the Commissioners. The Isle of Man Weekly Times was informed by a Bradda resident that a number of people had written to the Chief Constable, asking for passes into the internment area so that they might go to the pictures. He replied that passes were not issued for this reason, but could be had for legal business."[5]

On 1st March 1941 they reported:

"Port St. Mary Commissioners had received a letter from the Government Secretary confirming arrangements will be made under which the Chief Constable will issue permit cards to bona fide residents within a two miles' radius of the perimeter of the camp. Application should be made to the Chief Constable for a permit card."[6]

Local shopkeepers had benefited greatly from the requirements of the internees during the first year of the camp, so the reduction in the numbers of internees and being no longer within the boundary of the new camp created some hardship. Local shopkeepers in Port St Mary, Miss M. E. McNeill, Miss D. Cubbin, Miss C. Skelly and Mrs E. M. Walker wrote a letter to the Port St Mary Commissioners objecting to their premises being placed outside the camp barrier.

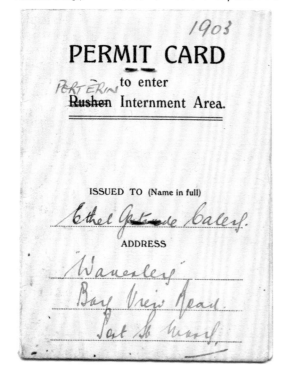

Police Permit Card. (Courtesy of Manx National Heritage)

1903

PERMIT CARD

PORT ERIN to enter

~~Rushen~~ Internment Area.

ISSUED TO (Name in full)

Ethel Gertrude Caley.

ADDRESS

"Waverley"

Bay View Road.

Port St Mary

The Commissioners referred their letter to the new Commandant, Cyril Cuthbert, and advised the ladies they would be informed of any action taken. Commandant Cuthbert discussed the matter with those affected and arranged for the internees to visit the shops on a Monday and Wednesday from 2.30 p.m. to 4.30 p.m. Male internees were permitted to spend up to 10 shillings per week and women up to 5 shillings.

During May 1941, with the arrival of contingents of male aliens from the internment camps at Douglas and Ramsey, around 150 families had been reunited in the married camp on the promenade with a total number of 387, which included 67 children. The married camp was expected to be increased to 300 families, eventually to hold around 700 internees, but these numbers were never reached.

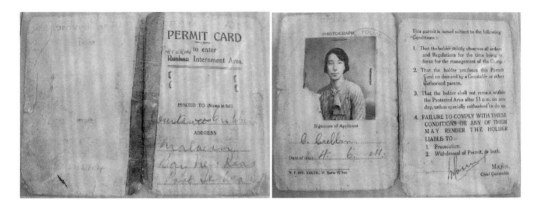

Many of the landladies who now housed the married internees found a different atmosphere within their homes. The couples who had been reunited were much more at ease, and friendships were forged that in some cases lasted for many years, corresponding by letters, regular Christmas cards and return visits to the Island. Many of the male internees were employed on the local farms or cutting back the brooghs (Manx for grass banks) above Chapel Beach.

Port Erin residents feel the strain

During the early months of 1941, a large number of residents within the district of Bradda made representation to the Port Erin Commissioners complaining about the problems experienced with boundaries and permits.

On 9th April 1941, Port Erin Commissioners met with the Chief Constable and the Camp Commandant to discuss a more equitable distribution of internees in the houses within the camp boundary as the number of internees declined and, if necessary, reduce the camp boundary, leaving a large portion of Port Erin open to house British refugees, as originally planned.

The Chief Constable stated that the first responsibility was security and this cause necessitated the reduction of the camp boundaries. It was proposed that

The district of Bradda,
Port Erin.
(Alison Graham)

Ballafesson Road be opened up for traffic and the creation of a 'no man's land' between Ballafesson Road and Port St Mary. It was accepted that some local residents would suffer hardship as the possibility of receiving visitors to boost their income would be remote.

The Commissioners requested that the Government Secretary make representations to the War Office to increase the 'billeting allowance' and also the 'reservation fee' for those with empty bedrooms as a result of the reduced camp boundary. Both towns were to experience difficulties as the camps changed and they were unable to fill their empty boarding houses.

Although representations were made by the Isle of Man Government to the Home Office, no further increases or allowances were introduced and the householders had to get by as best they could and rely on each other. Only when areas of the ports opened up, as the camp boundaries reduced, were they able to take in visitors, who continued to visit the Island throughout the war. Port Erin was not to receive further internees until the married camp was transferred there in 1942.

Christmas 1941 – mixed emotions for all

A reporter recorded in the *Isle of Man Times* of 27th December 1941 that regulations were relaxed a little to re-unite families and friends over Christmas[7].

The comfort of the internees in the camps was directly under the care of Commandant Cuthbert and his Deputy, Miss Wilson, and to afford an opportunity for internees to visit each other's billets the curfew for Christmas Eve and Christmas Day was extended to 9 p.m. Inter-camp visits took place when men from the Douglas, Ramsey and Peel camps, under military escort, met with their wives and children at Port Erin, with meetings usually taking place in Collinson's Café, Spaldrick. Coffee was provided, but no wines or spirits were allowed. Permission was given for food, cigarettes and presents to be exchanged within reasonable limits and under strict supervision.

Relaxation of rules at Christmas to re-unite families and friends (Courtesy of Alison Graham)

An arranged visit of the Port Erin internees to the married camp at Port St Mary took place and children's parties were held in both Port Erin and Port St Mary over the course of the Christmastide. Child Welfare Christmas Parties were held in Port St Mary as a treat for the local mothers and children. An old Austrian Nativity play was given by the internees at Dandy Hill Schoolroom in Port Erin during Christmas week and a Lutheran service was conducted by a German Pastor in the Wesleyan Church, Port Erin on Christmas Eve.

According to the article in the *Isle of Man Times* of December 1941, the number of women still in internment in Port Erin was about 1,125 and the married camp at Port St Mary consisted of about 400 men, women and children.

S.H. SA.   **TO BE FILLED UP IN DUPLICATE**

APPLICATION FOR A PERMIT TO VISIT.

.... at ....Camp

born on .... at ....

FULL NAME OF APPLICANT ....

ADDRESS OF APPLICANT ....

Write in

....

BLOCK

....

LETTERS

Date and place of birth ....

....

Profession or occupation ....

Relationship to internee ....

Reasons for visit ....

Proposed date of visit ....

Date of last visit ....

Nationality of applicant ....

Quote number of National Identity Card ....

If a member of His Majesty's Forces quote the Service Identity Number ....

If registered with the Police as an Alien, quote also number of Police Registration

Certificate .... issued by .... on ....

        I hereby certify that the above particulars relate to the undersigned and are

correct in every respect.

        Signature of applicant ....

        *Witnessed the above signature

        1 .... Address ....

                                         ....

                                         Occupation ....

        2 .... Address ....

                                         ....

                                         Occupation ....

Shock for newly-weds

In March 1942, *Mona's Herald* reported that a Port St Mary resident, who had returned to the Island with his new bride, on reaching the barrier at the Protected Area was informed that the Chief Constable, in the exercise of his powers under an 'Order under the Defence Regulations dealing with the Port St Mary Protected Area', had refused permission for his bride to enter the area in which his house was situated[8] His wife, it transpired, had been interned as a German in the women's camp in Rushen but had been released some considerable time ago under a Home Office Order and since then she had resided in the UK. The bridegroom, an elderly man, had lived retired in Port St Mary for some years and at the time of his marriage was a widower. The order gave the Chief Constable the power to refuse access to, or to remove, any person whom he considered would be undesirable to permit entry to, or remain within, the Protected Area. The husband was informed that he could proceed to his home, but not his wife. The couple at once returned to Douglas and stayed in a hotel there. At the time of the article, the reporter said, 'We understand that they are still living in Douglas.'

Staff changes

Miss M. R. J. Edwards, who had been Deputy Camp Commandant of the women's internment camp from April 1942, left the Island in January 1943 to take up duty as Private Secretary to one of the Under Secretaries of State at the Home Office. During her 10 months residence in Port Erin, the *Isle of Man Examiner* reported that Miss Edwards had been of immense assistance to Commandant Cuthbert and her diligence to duty and unfailing courtesy to residents and internees alike had earned the warm gratitude of all with whom she had come in contact.[9]

Woman Police Inspector Pike. (Reproduced by permission of the Metropolitan Police Authority (Heritage Centre))

Miss Edwards was a sister of Wing Commander H. R. A. Edwards, who saw combat during WWII while stationed at RAF Coastal Command as a squadron commander of a Liberator BZ 819, carrying out escort duties. Prior to the start of WWII, in May 1939, Squadron Leader Edwards won the Tynwald Air Race round the Island in an 'Avian' machine and Miss Edwards accompanied her brother on that memorable flight.

Miss Edwards' successor as Deputy Commandant at Port Erin was Woman Police Inspector Florence A. Pike of the Metropolitan Women's Police Force. WPI Pike was Sergeant-in-Charge of the Women Police at Port Erin whenever Miss Edwards had to return to London.

'Rushen' spies?

In 1996 a document found in files belonging to the Gestapo, by Dr Joachim Lerchenmuller of the University of Limerick, suggested that the Gestapo had an interest on the Island.[10] The document described the conditions afforded to the internees

THE
ISLE OF MAN AIR RACES
MAY 29TH & 31ST

THE LONDON
HANWORTH
ISLE OF MAN
AIR RACE

THE MANX
AIR
DERBY

THE TYNWALD
AIR RACE
FOR MACHINES
UNDER 80 H.P.

£500 IN CASH PRIZES & VALUABLE TROPHIES
ENTRIES CLOSE 14th MAY, 5 p.m.
LATE ENTRIES (BRITISH ONLY) CLOSE 22nd MAY MID-DAY, DOUBLE FEE.
FULL PARTICULARS AND ENTRY FORMS FROM YOUR CLUB SECRETARY
OR THE ORGANISING MANAGER— CAPT. R. H. STOCKEN, M.I.Ae.E.
3, ST. JAMES'S SQUARE, LONDON, S.W.1   WHITEHALL 6661.

Tynwald Air Race

No.	Pilot	Mach
2.	R. A. Winter	Gipsy Con
7.	S. Cummings ...	Blackburn Blue
13.	F. Dawson Paul	Chi
15.	Philip Avery	*V.E.F.
16.	Captain H. C. Latimer-Needhan	
		Luton-M
18.	R. A. Porteous	Chi
21.	Sq/L. H. R. A. Edwards	A
22.	E. D. Ward	Tipsy Tra
23.	Sq./L. E. Mole	Tipsy M
25.	W. H. Moss	Mossc

* Entered by Janis Vitols, a Latvi

Manx Air Derby

in Rushen Camp, showing they had access to reliable information. During a check through Isle of Man Police security files on WWII, for the summer of 1942, the archive (document) noted an attempt was made by two 'Austrian Jews' to be interned in the Rushen camp. All but the British Intelligence M15 agent on the Isle of Man at the time were convinced of the bona fide nature of the two concerned. They were sent back to England and were believed to have been Gestapo agents seeking entry to the Rushen family camp, to assess who would be of use to the German cause.

Miss Edwards accompanied her brother on his memorable flight in the Isle of Man Air Races. (*Mona's Herald*, Tuesday, 23rd May 1939, p.1)

Internment camp changes – Married Camp moved to Port Erin

In August 1942 busy scenes were witnessed during the transfer of over 300 internees from the married camp on Port St Mary promenade to Port Erin. Men and women internees assisted in the work of loading the lorries with baggage and unloading them at their new quarters. The much reduced camp for married couples and women was now the responsibility of Port Erin.

The Towers, Bay Cliffe and neighbouring houses in the Spaldrick area formed part of the married camp, enabling residents to pass between Bradda and Port Erin. The married and female camps were separated with a barbed-wire fence, which ran on the Bradda side of Collinson's Café: the Café remaining in the women's camp.[11]

By early 1943, as the married camp had now been removed to Port Erin, the landladies of Port St Mary promenade had to find other work to generate an income. Some obtained a few visitor bookings, others like Mona and Mary Quillin, landladies of Cronk Wyllin, went to work catering in the NAAFI in the Ballaqueeney Hydro, Port St Mary promenade, which had now been taken over by the Pay Corps Officer Cadet Training Unit (OCTU), working there until the OCTU returned to the UK.

Many of the camps' teachers and musicians had been repatriated or returned to the UK, which made it difficult to organise entertainment and many of these activities were abandoned. The International Red Cross made a camp visit in August 1943 and reported that, 'the majority of occupants arrived at the limit of their nervous and mental resistance and a block repatriation should be seriously taken into consideration by the Authorities responsible'.

On 25th October 1943, the nominal roll for Camp 'W' (women's camp) listed

Boarding houses, Spaldrick. (photo credit)

697 internees of which 37 were children, and 4 were Manx born. The nominal roll for Camp 'Y' (married camp) listed 295 male and female internees of which 54 were children, 11 born after May 1940 so were also possibly Manx, and seven were single (male and female).[12]

Collinson's Café. (Courtesy of Peter Fisher)

The women's and married camps remained in the Port Erin district and, following the repatriation of a large group of internees in 1944, there remained in 'the Camps' just a couple of hundred internees until the end of the war and the closure of the camp in September 1945.

Spaldrick, Port Erin – the site of the married camp from 1943. (Alison Graham)

PART 2:
THE
ILLUSTRATED
ROLL-CALL

A UNIQUE CREATIVE INITIATIVE BY TALENTED INTERNEES

After 75 years in a drawer, a unique creative initiative at the Golf Links Hotel was brought to light.

The *Illustrated Roll-Call* is a set of 48 unique Christmas greetings in poetry and art, by 70 German internees to their landlady, Mrs Majorie Crighton, in December 1940. The original belongs to Mrs Betty Kelly, daughter of Marjorie Crighton for whom the greetings were created, and it lay in a drawer in pristine condition for 75 years until first shown to the public in 2015. It was published as a book, *The Illustrated Roll-Call* by the Rushen Heritage Trust by kind permission of Betty Kelly. A selection of the greetings has been made for this Part 2 of 'Friend or Foe'.

The landladies – Marjorie Crighton and Alice Kellett

Marjorie Crighton (1902–1966) and Alice Latimer (1903–1998) were sisters, and their grandparents had started the Golf Links Hotel. The two sisters had been running the hotel for 10 years when the internees arrived, so were very experienced hoteliers, accustomed to working with a wide variety of British customers, mainly from Scotland and North West England. Marjorie Crighton was already married with children by 1940, but Alice's marriage to Mr Kellett came after the war, in 1948.

Landladies played an important part in the running of Rushen Women's Camp. If there was any trouble they had to report it to the Commandant, Dame Joanna Cruickshank. They followed a set of rules covering things like: summer and winter curfew times (9 p.m. and 5 p.m.); switching gas and electricity on and off at set times; blackout blinds; and meals and cleaning. They had to order supplies, organise rotas for management, waitressing, laundry and cooking by internees. The Golf Links was one of the few hotels with its own laundry, with

Alice Kellett (left) and Marjorie Crighton (right). (Courtesy of Betty Kelly)

a washing machine, ironing machine and large boiler. In 1940, after the internees arrived, 'the boiler had to be replaced by a coke furnace as it was doubtful whether we could maintain the oil-fired boiler'.[1]

Judging from the warmth of some of the greetings in *The Illustrated Roll-Call*, and her continuing contact with former internees after the war, Marjorie Crighton seemed to have been liked and respected by most.

But she stood no nonsense. Her daughter, Betty Kelly, recalls that when some of the internees gave her the Nazi salute, she retorted; 'Don't you ever do that again in my house!'[2]

Daily life at the Golf Links Hotel, 1940

Alice Kellett set the scene very well in her interview with Rosemary Walters:[3]

RW: Whatever did they do with themselves all the time?

AK: *Well, the government would find as much occupation as possible, and there were classes for secretarial work and typing, and lots of handiwork. Lots of knitting was done – beautiful cardigans they knitted – and embroidery and linen work with tatting and broderie anglaise. All sorts of needlework. They could also work on the farms with escorts. A policewoman would take them up to a farm, you see, and they would work there for the day, and also, if any of them were keen on gardening, they could have an allotment in Port Erin and work it themselves.*

RW: And how did you manage with the actual work of feeding that number of people then? Did you have to make a rota, and did everybody have a job?

AK: *For the internees? We had forms to fill in to give to the butcher to say how much meat we wanted and how many people, and also with other rationed food like butter and marmalade. Whatever was rationed – I have forgotten now. So we had to fill in these forms to make application for them.*

RW: And who did the actual cooking for that number of people?

AK: *Well, we had to organise all these women into a kind of rota for doing the housework and I asked for volunteers for cooking and kitchen work. So, we had half a dozen people on the list for cooks and they would work one week in three. They were paid five shillings. This was the sum allowed by the Home Office. And then the people who washed up the pots and pans were paid five shillings, and the woman who did the stoking for the hot water. The rest of the work of course was all ordinary household work which they used to look after themselves. They had to keep the lounges clean and light the fires in the winter, and they had to keep the bathrooms clean and their own bedrooms. And, of course, the dining room. They had to be fed, so we had so many girls each week on a rota as waitresses and these would look after all the others, you see, carrying their plates in and out. There were so many of them that when they first came, they only had to work one week in six because there were so many of them to go round, but as the numbers became reduced of course they had to work more often.*

Comments from *The Illustrated Roll-Call* indicating internee involvement in household tasks echo Alice Kellett's summary. Stephanie Schemel and Anna Schirmer appear to have been involved in cooking. Louise Pauly (G.36) viewed herself as 'the Head Stoker of the Golf Links'. Fini Haslinger (G.45) kept three coal fires burning.

Franziska Deinstler describes the activities of herself and two room-mates as: 'The one she sings, the other sews; the third one pushes pastry dough.'

Many women knitted, like Anna Neter and Helga Strauss ('knitting woolsocks for the King'), and the secret knitter, Gabriele Legath.

Like other internees in Port Erin, especially in the early days, those living at the Golf Links had complete freedom to move about the village and its surroundings within the barbed-wire perimeter. They could sit on the beach, swim, take rural walks, shop, attend concerts and entertainments organised by internees or go to the cinema.[4]

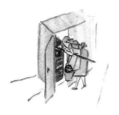

It gave me quite a shock,
When I heard of this book.
It is too late to do my bit.
I'll try to say a few words, fit
And suitable to season;
That is my few lines reason.
The Head-Stoker of GolfLinks here
Wishes „Merry Christmas and Good Cheer!"

Louise Pauly.

'The Head Stoker'.
(Courtesy of Betty
Kelly)

'The Fire Chief'.
(Courtesy of Betty
Kelly)

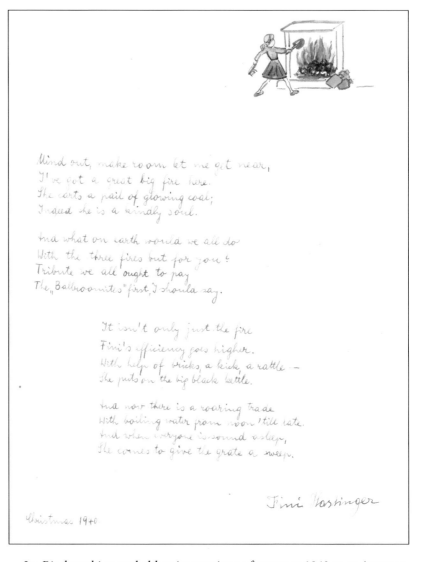

Mind out, make room let me get near,
I've got a great big fire here.
She carts a pail of glowing coal;
Indeed she is a kindly soul.

And what on earth would we all do
With the three fires but for you?
Tribute we all ought to pay
The "Ballroomites" first, I should say.

It isn't only just the fire
Fini's efficiency goes higher.
With help of bricks, a kick, a rattle —
She puts on the big black kettle.

And now there is a roaring trade
With boiling water from noon 'till late.
And when everyone is sound asleep,
She comes to give the grate a sweep.

Fini Hastinger

Christmas 1940

Ira Rischowski recorded her impressions of summer 1940 as an internee, and here is a summary of the key points:

The shops were nice, and shopkeepers were friendly. Some used internees as domestic servants. Ira wore her own clothes (some had been sent on) and the Service Exchange had a clothing department. Lots of internees had been domestic servants, and some would create or alter clothing. There were clothing coupons later. Ira did her own laundry, using wash boilers. There were laundry services. Medically there were three or four refugee doctors, and a sister in charge. The doctors were allowed to sign prescriptions, which were countersigned, but they were soon released. For dental work, internees had to journey to Castletown or Douglas.

However, there was always a shadow in the background because internees had been deprived of their freedom, separated from family, friends, and sometimes husbands and children.

The burning question with the vast majority of internees will still be, 'Why am I here?', and 'When shall I be released?'[5]

Profile of The Illustrated Roll-Call *contributors*

Our main sources of information are cards completed about internees at their registration in St Catherine's Church Hall, and Cary Ellis, who has been working as a volunteer at Manx National Heritage for over 20 years, specialising in card analysis. She has kindly provided relevant details about contributors to *The Illustrated Roll-Call*, where available. Cary's work has been invaluable to us.

Internee cards generally provide details of date of birth, nationality, occupation prior to internment, release date and place, together with any appearances before committees (e.g. for release), or disciplinary events, criminal or civil.

Alien registration cards still exist for many of the women interned at any time in the Isle of Man.[6] By contrast, little equivalent information is available for male internees – the records may have been destroyed.

From the 70 signatories of *The Illustrated Roll-Call*, we have 48 cards and have sometimes been able to supplement this with information from other sources. Based on this, here are some facts about the signatories:

Nationality	**Over 95% German or Austrian**
Average adult age	36 years
Age range	18–61
% Married	About 40%
Previous occupation	Over 70% were 'domestics'
Released before 31st March 1941	75%
Main place of release	London (42%), Manchester (16%)

Internee registration card. (Image courtesy of Manx National Heritage)

Nationality: Most of the signatories described themselves as German/Austrian or Austrian. Austria had been annexed by Germany in 1938 without a shot being fired, and by 1940 was, in practice, a state within Germany. We have no record of any Italian women at the Golf Links before Christmas 1940.

Average Age: The majority were aged between 25 and 40, but almost one-third were 40 or over – regarded as middle-aged in those days.

Married: With an average age of 36, one would have expected more than 40% to be married. However, in Germany as in Britain, WWI had taken a heavy toll of the number of men of marriageable age. In addition, some of the married people may have claimed to be single.

Accompanying Children: There were a few children under the age of 14 in the Golf Links Hotel, staying with their mothers, but the number is probably in single figures.

Previous Occupation: The vast majority claimed to have been 'domestics'. It has been argued that some of those categorised as such were in reality professional women who used the classification as an easy way to get a work permit.

However, there is other evidence that many of the women internees at Rushen Camp were former domestic workers:

Ira Rischowski (G.9) says in the interview with Lyn Smith that lots of the women internees were German domestic servants.[7]

Brigitte Davies notes: 'Largely they were Jewish refugees … and then these sort of ordinary German maids and nurses and so on.'[8]

The London Blitz.
(Imperial War Museum)

'The internees were mostly nurses, students and domestic servants.'[9]

Date of Release: The fact that the vast majority of internees were released before the end of March 1941 suggests that they should never have been interned in the first place.

Place of Release: The majority of Golf Links internees were released to London and Manchester, places which suffered heavy bombing. They had exchanged safe internment for dangerous freedom.

Was the Golf Links Hotel an 'Aryan' house? If so, when?

Ira Rischowski said about the Golf Links, probably referring to the period after spring 1941:

"I remember that some of the non-Jewish refugees declined very fervently to stay in this German house because they did not want to be identified with Nazis."

Aloisia Freissegger (G.46), a 26-year-old German, was aware she was seen as a Nazi (she wrote it with a small 'n'). Her well-illustrated greeting is plaintive:

> *Enemy number one they call me here*
> *And a dangerous nazi too I fear*
> *But all this I do not mind*
> *I know there's only gossip behind.*
> *A pity you couldn't choose the season's guest*
> *And glad you'll be if I leave with the rest.*
> *It's not my fault I was sent here by law*
> *And how long I'll stay depends on the war.*

She was in Rushen Camp until 25th October 1943.

Wanda Wehrhan, the leader of the German '*reichstreu*' – internees who acknowledged allegiance to Germany, but not the government. A fair number of National Socialists arrived at the Golf Links Hotel in spring 1941, and, according to Professor Charmian Brinson, Wanda 'was intent on turning (it) into an "Aryan house"'.[10] It is not clear whether she had much success in doing this, because she moved to Mona House, an 'Aryan' hotel, in early 1942.

Meanwhile, Windsor House and Ard Chreg were set aside 'for those of declared Nazi sympathies'.

What seems to be reasonably clear is that, at Christmas 1940, the Golf Links Hotel was not an Aryan house. It is inconceivable that the majority of those living there would have been released early, before end March 1941, if they had Nazi sympathies. From May 1941 the Golf Links Hotel housed internees classified as 'loyal to Germany.'

Wanda Wehrhan in evening dress. (Courtesy of Nina Miconi)

Were the* Roll-Call *authors trying to impress the authorities?

Release was naturally uppermost in the mind of internees. Did they paint a generally favourable view of life at the Golf Links Hotel in order to ingratiate themselves and so get an earlier release?

This seems unlikely since many of the greetings are relaxed, varied, humorous and quirky. Furthermore, some internees had already had their release recently approved, and others corresponded with Mrs Crighton after WWII.

***What was the origin of* The Illustrated Roll-Call?**

Bella Rothschild (G.4) recounts that, 'One day there was an announcement that rather worried me. We were to make a poem to our landlady.' The announcement was not apparently heard by Louise Pauly (G.36) since she wrote:

> *It gave me quite a shock,*
> *When I heard of this book.*
> *It is too late to do my bit.*
> *I'll try and say a few words, fit.*

Only 70 of the 121 occupants of the Golf Links participated, so involvement was not compulsory. And it sounds as if the announcement was fairly low key – perhaps a task to keep internees occupied and amused before Christmas.

***Main themes in* The Illustrated Roll-Call**

The most surprising and impressive thing about *The Illustrated Roll-Call* is the quality of the writing by women for whom English was largely a second language.

The main themes are humour, rooms and beds, thoughts about release, a desire to be remembered, and Port Erin weather, especially in winter.

Humour

Perhaps the *Roll-Call* will help dispel the misconception that Germans have little sense of humour. Here is an example (G.3) relating to Port Erin winter weather – a shock to many internees. The hotels and boarding houses were built for summer occupation by tourists, there was no central heating in those days, and the wooden window frames had gaps:

> *The winter storms are blowing*
> *You almost out of bed.*
> *The beautiful bay window*
> *Falls nearly on your head.*

There is only one remedy
If everything's in rain …
We will ask our landlady
To tie us to a chain.

And a poem (G.43) for Mrs Crighton with a topical twist in the last line:

I am writing in this book with reason
Of wishing you luck of the season
And that you soon get rid of us
And that there will be no more fuss
With this and that – one thing and another
And altogether all the bother
One thing – alas – that worries me.
Who'll bring you then your early tea?

Greeting 44, 'Bimbi, the famous Dressmuddler of Port Erin' is full of self-deprecating humour. Many of the illustrations, as in 'Nightmare of a Porridge Lover' (G.10), and 'The Most Besieged and Desirable Places …' enhance the verbal humour.

Rooms and Beds
The emphasis on these elements is not surprising. The room was home. Beds needed to be comfortable and were often shared. Rooms were mentioned by about one-third of contributors, and most of these specified their room number, almost as an indication of ownership. Greeting 6 is all about moving rooms, and eventually finding the right one. The room seemed to be a symbol of security in a difficult and rapidly changing world.

Beds featured almost as prominently in words and were often accompanied by humorous sketches.

Thoughts About Release
Almost one-quarter of the greetings contain thoughts about release, sometimes in a bittersweet combination, contrasting satisfaction about certain elements of life with a desire to leave. Here are some examples:

This hotel to all people who want to get away,
And have in Port Erin a fine holiday,
But however nice a time here, that we may have had,
To say good bye to this Island will not made us sad.

~~~~~~

About everything here I was very pleased
Though I hope badly to be released.

~~~~~~

'Bimbi the famous Dressmuddler of Port Erin.' (Courtesy of Betty Kelly)

'Nightmare of a Porridge Lover.' (Courtesy of Betty Kelly)

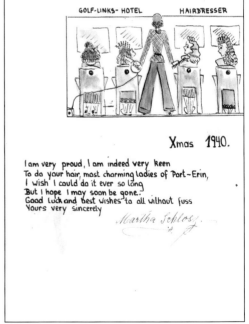

'Vision of an internee at 11 pm.' (Courtesy of Betty Kelly)

'I am very proud ....' (Courtesy of Betty Kelly)

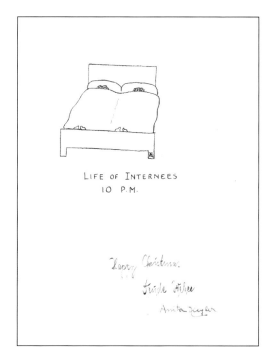

LIFE OF INTERNEES
10 P.M.

Happy Christmas.
Trude Weber
Anita Ziegler

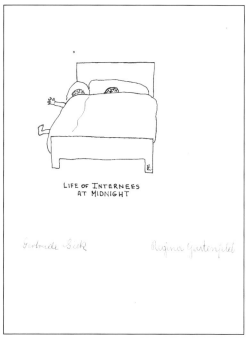

LIFE OF INTERNEES
AT MIDNIGHT

Gertrude Beck   *Regina Gartenfeld*

> *I am very proud, I am indeed very keen*
> *To do your hair, most charming ladies of Port Erin.*
> *I wish I could do it ever so long,*
> *But I hope I may soon be gone.*
> (Greeting 34)

Desire to be Remembered, or to Remember

This is often movingly expressed, as by Mrs Wally Ganowsky:

> *I live in peace and comfort*
> *Until my departure comes true.*
> *I will say farewell to the Hotel*
> *Good bye to the people I know*
> *For I will go back to London*
> *Will remember the little home.*

And Mrs Erika Guttentag:

> *I hope you will remember my name*
> *But if you do not, just the same*
> *I say to you when I leave here – Good Day.*
> *That is my name as in English you say.*

X mas 1940.

Roses whither
Ships disappear
But the remembrance
of Golf - Links
Will for ever be clear.

Cornelia Brandt

'Roses whither …..'
(Courtesy of Betty
Kelly)

Cornelia Brandt (G.28), for whom we have little information except that she has Dutch connections, is laconic:

> *Roses whither*
> *Ships disappear*
> *But the remembrance*
> *Of Golf Links*
> *Will for ever be clear.*

Finally, wistful thoughts back to Port Erin by Hermine Teizer:

> *And when one day I say good bye,*
> *I leave you, but my thoughts will fly*
> *Always back to Port Erin*
> *Where before I never had been.*

Port Erin Weather

Locally, we all know about the dramatic sunrises and sunsets, the beautiful days on the beach … and the wind and storms in the winter.

Summer 1940 was a good one – very warm, lots of bathing and time on the beach – so the Port Erin winter must have been a shock to the internees. Surprisingly though, only three internees mentioned the weather, influenced perhaps by the fact that many parts of Germany and Austria are much colder than Port Erin in winter.

Greta Wiedling and Josephine Boscowitz had decided views on Port Erin weather:

> *Only when summertime had gone*
> *Their happy time began to turn.*
> *They got to know the westerly gale,*
> *And woe betide those who are frail!*

Ilka Haase's evocative description of the sea in winter is included in full under 'Poetry' below, but the first verse is worth repeating:

> *Where the sea waves foaming break*
> *Against the sandy shore*
> *Where the mild north winds bleak,*
> *Here is our home.*

Rosel Koch acknowledged the positive side:

> *With my mother I live at number seven,*
> *And we stay up nearly 'till eleven*

For from our room we have a lovely view
The beautiful sunset, and the moon when it's new.

World War II did not affect the weather, and it was the same for both internees and locals.

What was not mentioned

Three issues – money, boredom and postal delays. We know that some internees had plenty of money, others none at all. But it was a very British, and perhaps German style, not to talk about money.

Boredom was a constant threat, but not something to write a poem about.

Postal delays, especially between husbands in Onchan Camp and wives in Rushen, were a major problem in the first months of internment, but by Christmas 1940 this may have been partly resolved.

The overall tone of the greetings to Mrs Crighton was reasonably upbeat, and at least three internees implied they would like to return to the Golf Links as a guest after the war was over.

The illustrations – who drew them?

The majority (79%) of the greetings contain illustrations. Did each page author paint or draw her own picture, or were there artists who did a number?

The evidence suggests that there was a combination of both. Our preliminary conclusions are that the same artist was possibly responsible for eight illustrations. On the supposition that the artist also painted her own greeting page, possible suspects are Lotte Salzberger, who was a student and responsible for the sets at 'The Golf Links Variety Show' in July 1940, and Ruth Borchard, who became a significant art collector after WWII.

It seems likely that Mrs Renate Garimbert (G.44), who was a dress designer, also painted the pictures in G.34 and possibly G.43.

Ira Rischowski signed the ink drawing for her own Greeting 9 with the initials 'IR' as well as Greetings 33, 40 and 41.

Most of the remaining illustrations were probably executed by the person or persons who wrote the copy for the greeting in which each picture appeared.

The poetry – two outstanding examples

The *Illustrated Roll-Call* contains a range of poetry in a variety of styles. Much of it is informative about internee lives and attitudes, as discussed earlier. Some poems are evocative and moving, and two in particular stand out – those by Susie Bock (G.25) and by Ilka Haase (G.12).

Susie Bock was married, but we know nothing about her husband. She was probably Jewish, and middle-aged, having turned 45 before internment on the Isle of Man.

It seems highly likely that Susie knew she was going to be released when she wrote this poem because on 11th November 1940 the committee exempted her

Llandudno in the
1950s. (Private
collection)

from further internment, and on 17th December 1940 she was released to Llandudno, another attractive seaside town. On a very clear day the Isle of Man can be seen from Llandudno, and for most of the first half of the twentieth century there was a daily boat service between Llandudno and Douglas.

In 'The Happy Prison' (our suggested title) Susie captures the tension between the fact of internment and happy memories associated with it. There is a tristesse in the poem. On the one hand, 'We did not hope it was for long', on the other, 'But now I often wish, my word, forever here to stay.'

The poem shows awareness of a longer poem written by Thomas Hood (1799–1845). Each verse begins with happy memories and ends in melancholy and regret. This is the first verse:

The Happy Prison
I remember, I remember the house near the beach,
That happy prison, I think you remember it each.
We did not hope it was for long,
Just for a holiday;
But now I often wish, my word,
For ever here to stay.

I remember, I remember, those months near the beach,
The life in Golf Links, you remember it each.
Where a home we had in this hotel,
Where all the time we felt so well;
So that I will forget it never
Remembering that time forever.

Susie Bock – Christmas 1940.

Susie's poem portrays the dilemma of two diametrically opposed desires – to be freed to go while yet wishing to stay. Once released, she seemed reluctant to leave. One wonders what happened to Susie. What life held for her in Llandudno, whether her husband and perhaps family were there or somewhere else.

Two other internees at the Golf Links, Mrs Clara Braun and daughter Lilo, were released a few weeks after Susie, also to Llandudno. Were they friends and did they stay in touch after release?

Ilka Haase (G.12), who wrote the poem we have entitled 'Waiting, Waiting', was German, aged 32, a 'domestic' by occupation, and released to London on 6th June 1941. She appears to have been unmarried. Ironically, in the months following the penning of her poem, she had a long wait between being approved for release (14th January 1941) and actual release date (6th June 1941). This gap was usually less than a month for internees, but we do not know why Ilka had to wait six months.

The poem is much darker than the slightly sad 'That Happy Prison'. It is definitely a winter poem and vividly captures the bleak, grey, rough texture of winter storms by the sea, when the crowded summer beaches are a distant memory. There is loneliness and almost desolation about the poem: 'Where the wild rough north winds bleak, there is our home', and 'No ships go passing by, no sunbeams from above'. There seems to be an implied analogy between the waiting for spring and the waiting for release: 'Waiting, waiting without moving'. For Ilka, release did come – with summer:

Waiting, Waiting

Where the sea waves foaming break
Against the sandy shore,
Where the wild rough north winds bleak
There is our home.
When the rough winds bleak
And the waves break high and rough.
On deserted sea and shore
And the sky's so grey above.
When the sea waves break
Against the sandy shore,
No ships go passing by.
No sunbeams from above.
Life is just a vegetation,
In this nature thunderbolt,
Waiting, waiting without moving,
Waiting for the spring to come.
When relax the nature forces
Warmth and sunshine to release,
Life will come forth, dwell, and mingle,
And the stormy wind will cease.

Ilka Haase, Christmas 1940

The Golf Links Private Hotel in 1940

The contributors to *The Illustrated Roll-Call* all lived at the Golf Links Hotel, an imposing Edwardian edifice, half way up Port Erin promenade, with a commanding position and magnificent sea and coastal views from its many bay windows.

The Golf Links Hotel was certainly one of the better hotels in Port Erin, and some of the 1940 Christmas Greetings to Mrs Crighton indicated a desire to visit the hotel as a guest when the war was over.

We do not know how many internees occupied the Golf Links Hotel at any one time. It may occasionally have exceeded the peacetime capacity of 130 people, especially in the first year of internment, from May 1940 to May 1941, when the number peaked. Based on the *Roll-Call*, some women appeared to have a single room, but most seemed to be doubles. Occupancy levels were probably similar to pre-war tourism norms, and internees were not stacked in rooms like sardines

However, during Christmas 1940, Mrs Schemel (G.23), who was one of the cooks, indicated that there were 121 occupants. She said: 'Feeding 121 is not a job too easy.'

In the 1920s the Golf Links was the first hotel in Port Erin to have hot and cold water in every room. But in the 1940s neither hotels nor private houses had en suite bathrooms, and there was often only one bathroom per eight or nine guests.

Alice Kellett was asked about this by Rosemary Walters in 1994, when Mrs Kellett was 93. Mrs Kellett responded: 'There was a shortage of bathrooms, always. I think people must have been expected to go into the sea! No, there never seemed to be a problem with a shortage of bathrooms really.'[11] It was all a matter of the level of expectation evidently. There was only one bathroom per eight or nine bedrooms in hotels in those days. People typically only had a bath about once each week and also bathed in the sea in the summer. They had washbasins in their rooms at the Golf Links Hotel, but not en suite toilets or bathrooms.

Lotte Salzberger's greeting (G.13) features a picture of people rushing to the bathroom which is described humorously as, 'The most besieged and desirable place.'

'The most besieged and desirable places… ….' (Courtesy of Betty Kelly)

The most besieged and desirable places ----

PART 3:
LIFE
IN THE
CAMPS

RUSHEN [...] CAMP

RULES (amended 9th Sept.1940)

HOUSEHOLD CONTROL   The Householder is under the Commandant, the responsible authority for the internal control of each household, and may appoint a representative from the internees - if he or she so desire - elected by the other internees, to assist in the arrangement of duties.   Representatives may, at the discretion of the householder, be changed at any time approved by the Commandant and Householder.

LIGHTS OUT.   Internees must be in their own rooms with lights out at 10 p.m. and silence thereafter.

HEALTH.   Internees requiring advice on health or dental treatment will attend at the Clinic, Chapel Hall, Victoria Square, between the hours of 2.30 p.m. and 3.30 p.m. each day except Saturday and Sunday.

DIFFICULTIES.   Any instance of difficulty will be reported to the Commandant and/or to her authorized representative.

BEDROOMS.   Internees are entirely responsible for the cleanliness and tidiness of their own bedrooms.   Articles of clothing must not be left lying about.

MEALS IN BEDROOM.   Meals in bedrooms are permitted only in cases of genuine indisposition and illness; no food may be stored in bedrooms.

BREAKAGES.   Breakages are to be reported in writing to the Commandant by the householders, giving the name of the person responsible who may be called upon to replace the damaged articles.

VALUABLES.   Householders will not be responsible for loss of money articles of value or clothing.   Money and jewellery must be deposited with the Commandant for safe custody.

NOTICES.   Notices may be displayed in the houses and on Notice board only with the approval of the Commandant and must be written in English.   A German translation may be permitted.

PROHIBITED

1. To hold meetings in bedrooms.
2. To smoke in bedrooms.
3. To lock bedroom doors at night: if bedroom doors are locked during the day, key must be left with the householder.
4. To have food in bedrooms.
X 5. Open flame candles, lamps or stoves and heaters of any kind in bedrooms.
6. To hang pictures and photographs on bedroom walls.
7. To visit other houses without the permission of the householder and a signed permit from the Commandant or her authorized representative.
8. To retire to bedrooms before evening Roll Call without the permission of the householder.
9. To throw anything out of windows or into handbasins or lavatories.   Rubbish for disposal must be put into the receptacles provided for the purpose.
10. To waste food by feeding gulls and other birds or in any other way.
11. To wash clothing in bedrooms.
    N.B. Washhouses are provided in garages for this purpose, water and the heating of irons is provided by means of slot-meters.
12. To visit Bars and to attend Dances in public halls or cafes, or to purchase any alcoholic drink.

JOANNA M.CRUIKSHANK,
Commandant.

X N.B. Nightlights may be used, where necessary, with the consent of the householder.

DAILY LIFE IN RUSHEN INTERNMENT CAMP

How Rushen Camp differed from all other internment camps

Rushen Camp differed from other camps on the Isle of Man and may have been unique among internment camps across the world:

The camp was initially for women only, but many brought children with them. There was a total of 3,025 women and 300 children. Later, a small married camp was setup with 162 males and 170 women, but women always comprised the majority of the overall camp.

Rushen boarding house owners remained in their boarding houses and ran them for internees. Elsewhere on the Isle of Man boarding houses were requisitioned and owners ordered to leave within days.

There were no soldiers at Rushen Camp. The Commandant reported to the Home Office, whereas the other camps reported to the War Office. A small number of civilians were responsible for administering Rushen Camp and police patrolled the perimeter wire. In practice, Manx landladies operated the camp following Home Office rules.

Individual Rushen boarding houses for internees were not surrounded by high barbed-wire fences, unlike the other Isle of Man camps. Instead barbed wire was erected around the camp perimeter and local residents needed permits to move in and out. While barbed wire was often a prominent feature in art from the men's camps, it was almost entirely absent from Rushen Camp art.

Rushen Camp had a distinctive form of gender government. At Christmas 1940, we estimate that over 80% of the Rushen population (inside and outside the camp) was female and the camp was run by women for women.

There was a relatively higher level of personal freedom in Rushen Camp than in the men's camps, especially in the earlier period when internees could shop, walk and bathe freely during daylight hours. Therefore, there was more interaction with local people than in the other camps.

We are not suggesting that Rushen Camp was a form of Utopia, since most internees were wrongly interned and lost their freedom. However, it had many distinctive characteristics. There were rules laid down by the Commandant, to ensure that the camp was run smoothly and the internees were treated equally (illustration opposite with transcription below)[1].

CHAPTER SEVEN

RUSHEN INTERNMENT CAMP

RULES (issued 9th Sept. 1940)

HOUSEHOLD CONTROL   The householder is, under the Commandant, the responsible authority for the internal control of each household, and may appoint a representative for the internees if he or she so desire – elected by the other internees, to assist in the arrangement of duties. Representatives may, at the discretion of the householder, be changed at any time approved by the Commandant and Householder.

LIGHTS OUT   Internees must be in their own rooms with lights out at

Opposite: Copies of House Rules were issued to all landladies to be put on the back of bedroom doors. (Courtesy of Nina Miconi)

10 p.m. and silence thereafter.

HEALTH   Internees requiring advice on health or dental treatment will attend at the Clinic, Chapel Hall, Victoria Square between the hours of 2.30 p.m. and 3.30 p.m. each day except Saturday and Sunday.

DIFFICULTIES   Any instance of difficulty will be reported to the Commandant and/or to her authorised representative.

BEDROOMS   Internees are entirely responsible for the cleanliness and tidiness of their own bedrooms. Articles of clothing must not be left lying about.

MEALS IN BEDROOMS   Meals in bedrooms are permitted only in cases of genuine disposition and illness: no food may be stored in bedrooms.

BREAKAGES   Breakages are to be reported in writing to the Commandant by the householders, giving the name of the person responsible who may be called upon to replace the damaged articles.

VALUABLES   Householders will not be responsible for loss of money, articles of value or clothing. Money and jewellery must be deposited with the Commandant for safe custody.

NOTICES   Notices may be displayed in the houses and on Notice Board only with the approval of the Commandant and must be written in English. A German translation may be permitted.

PROHIBITED

1. To hold meetings in bedrooms.
2. To smoke in bedrooms.
3. To lock bedroom doors at night: if bedroom doors are locked during the day key must be left with the householder.
4. To have food in bedrooms.
X 5. Open flame candles, lamps or stoves and heaters of any kind in bedrooms.
6. To hang pictures and photographs on bedroom walls.
7. To visit other houses without the permission of the householder and a signed permit from the Commandant or her authorised representative.
8. To retire to bedrooms before evening Roll Call without the permission of the householder.
9. To throw anything out of the windows or into handbasins or lavatories. Rubbish for disposal must be put into the receptacles provided for the purpose.
10. To waste food by feeding gulls or other birds or in any other way.
11. To wash clothing in bedrooms.
    N.B. Washhouses are provided in garages for this purpose.
    Water and the heating of irons is provided by the means of slot-meters.
12. To visit Bars and to attend Dances in public halls or cafés or to purchases any alcoholic drink.

JOANNA M. CRUICKSHANK

X   N.B.   Nightlights may be used, where necessary, with the consent of the householder.

Restricted items

There were a number of items that internees were not allowed to have in their possession or to use:

- Torches and candles were prohibited in case the internees should be tempted to signal to passing ships or enemy aircraft.
- Maps of the whole or part of the UK or Isle of Man were also prohibited and sale of these in shops required a licence.
- Any 'high frequency' equipment which generated or used more than 10 watts was prohibited.
- Telephone, telegram or wireless apparatus were not to be used by internees. Telegrams could be sent on their behalf by authorised operators with permission from the Camp Commandant.

Early days

The total recorded number of refugees who were housed in the Rushen camp varies from 3,000 to 5,000. However, in an article dated February 2008, Alan Franklin (who was then the librarian at Manx National Heritage) concluded that there may be a number of duplicated entries. From a handwritten table within their records, a total is given for those in camp, plus those already released or transferred, of 4,150 in October 1941.

Residents were issued with permit cards to gain access to and from the camp, but, as previously mentioned, the main difference between the Rushen internment camp and the other camps in the Island, was that Rushen Camp was operated by the Home Office and not the military authorities. Apart from restrictions going in and out of the camp boundary, the camp was effectively run by the landladies and the owners of the properties where the internees were housed.

Landladies would order and arrange delivery of the required food rations as directed in the 'Regulations Governing the Rushen Detention Camp'. In many cases the internees would prepare their own meals and take care of the cleaning and laundry.

Boarding house owners would be responsible for restrictions such as 'lights out'. This would vary from summer to winter, depending on the daylight hours, and the electricity would be switched off at the mains.

Initially there was urgency to accommodate the sudden large influx of internees, but the mix of Nazis and those fleeing from Nazi oppression was later to be an issue for some people. Some re-organisation took place to address any difficulties. Brenda Watterson remembers that:

"On Hitler's birthday, sometime in April, each year they gathered gorse and made it into a huge swastika and placed it in the centre of our large round oak dining table and stood round it and said, 'Heil Hitler', me joining in until I was pulled out and told I didn't do that, they were Germans and we were at war with them."[2]

'We all just rubbed along together'

June 1940. The beautiful beach in Port Erin, the promenade and the shops were packed with people, but these were not the normal tourists of past seasons. In late May, approximately 3,500 women and children classed as 'enemy aliens' descended on a combined population of the two villages of under 2,000.

No one, least of all the volunteer Commandant, was expecting such an influx on 29th May 1940, but by nightfall all had been billeted. Such was the shortage of beds that many had to share a bed with a complete stranger. It is ironic that, a year later, the Commandant faced a similar lack of double beds when the married camp was set up.

As the long hot summer gave way to cooler days, some of the well-educated internees realised that boredom was going to be the worst enemy with such a mix of women. The Commandant had already approved the establishment of schools for the children. Two such schools, a kindergarten and a 6–16 school, were set up by Minna Specht, a famous educationalist, in Port St Mary, almost opposite what is now Schoill Purt le Moirrey. Talented internees initiated classes in painting, sculpture and tailoring for the adults (see Chapter 10.) A professional singer, Jeanette Simon, established a choir so well-rehearsed it could have performed professionally. There were musical evenings and amateur dramatics (see Chapter 15.).

Greatly encouraged by the Commandant, Ruth Borchard set up the 'Service Exchange' (see Chapter 8). This was to provide services bartered for other services in exchange. Anna Hornik took over the running of the Service Exchange when Ruth Borchard was released in 1941 and, when it closed, she reported that 17,000 hours had been bartered. During this period many internees made various items of clothing for local residents. Food rationing was in place, but the refugees received food parcels and tins of salmon were bartered as the local residents were pleased to barter for such a wartime luxury.

There was little to show that there was an internment camp, except for the barbed wire and barricades at control points. The latter proved to be more of a nuisance to local residents with a constant need for permit cards whenever they left or returned to their homes. When the International Red Cross and the Home Office came to inspect the camp, after visiting camps all over Europe, they were so impressed with the high standard of living in Rushen Camp that they wrote letters of appreciation to the Commandant, Dame Joanna Cruikshank, who had been so highly decorated for her work in WWI, and also to the local Commissioners.

After the war, many of the internees kept in touch with their hosts and, some years ago at a reunion of residents and internees, a group was asked what it was really like. Their smiling reply was, 'We all just rubbed along together.'

THE SERVICE EXCHANGE: EXPERIMENT IN ECONOMICS

CHAPTER EIGHT

Ruth Borchard (1910–2000)

Ruth Borchard was born in 1910 in a fishing village near Hamburg. She was the eldest of four children born to assimilated Jewish businessman Robert Berendsohn and his wife Alma, and was brought up as a socialist and free thinker. She studied at the University of Hamburg, spending a year as an exchange student at the University of Wisconsin and gaining her doctorate in economics and social psychology.

In 1937 she married Kurt Borchard, who ran a family shipping business in Hamburg and later in London. She and her husband fled to England in 1938 to escape Nazism and settled in Reigate, Surrey. They had three daughters and a son. Later, Ruth Borchard and her husband lived for many years in Switzerland.

Interned in May 1940, first in Holloway Prison, Ruth was transferred to the Isle of Man together with her eldest daughter, Katherine (Hallgarten), who was just one year old. By Christmas 1940 they were living in the Golf Links Hotel where she contributed, together with Karola Kohlberg, to *The Illustrated Roll-Call* as follows:

> *7 Nice Ladies sitting near a wall*
> *As 5 Nice Ladies received the*
> *Release – Call*
> *There were Two Nice Ladies left*
> *Lonely near a wall*
> *And We 2 Ladies are waiting*
> *For that call*
> *So that we'll be released, after all.*

The Service Exchange

In September 1940 with no real prospect of gainful employment Ruth developed the idea of the 'Service Exchange'. This was a simple mechanism based on socialist principles through which goods made by each of the internees could be exchanged within the camp through a system of tokens (as the internees were not allowed money in the camp), arguing that 'morale could be kept up only if the women were kept busy'.[1] The virtue of this idea was recognised by both Quaker volunteer, Margaret Collyer, and Camp Commandant, Dame Joanna Cruickshank.

In 1942, following her release, Ruth wrote at length in *The Manchester Guardian* about the internment camp experience of creating an artificial micro-economy. In 1943 her article 'The Service Exchange in an internment camp', published by the Society of Friends, was awarded a prize by

Ruth Borchard and her daughter, Katherine. (Katherine Hallgarten)

Ruth and daughter Katherine

the Joseph Rowntree Trust. Ruth's article from *The Manchester Guardian* is set out below.[2]

EXPERIMENT IN PLANNED ECONOMY
The 'Service Exchange' By Ruth Borchardt
(as published in *The Manchester Guardian* 29th August 1942).

There we were, 4,500 women in the alien women's internment camp at Port Erin with nothing whatever to do. Since May (I speak of 1940) we had been clamouring for the chance of earning 1s 7d a day like the interned men. Now, in September, there was still no prospect of work for us. Many had come to the end of their savings. So between us we dug up reminiscences of schemes for 'productive unemployment relief' (like those of the late Professor Lederer and of Professor Heimann, now of New York).

The idea of the 'Service Exchange' was simple enough on the surface. Instead of everybody doing everything for herself, let each do what she knows how to do best and exchange it for what the others know how to do better. In other words, let us raise the standard of living by the differentiation of labour. As a means of exchange we proposed work receipts, 'service tokens'. Thus, we set out boldly to create what was no less than an artificial market economy.

In September 1940, we put up a notice asking for experts in sewing, cutting, dress and hat making, laundry work, gardening and hairdressing. All we offered was payment in service tokens, of which one of us was busy producing some thousands by cutting up corn-flake boxes and using a rubber stamp on the bits – our mint. To our surprise, during the first two weeks 1,200 women volunteered.

INITIAL CAPITAL
We started from scratch. The Commandant granted a small, empty room for an office, some unstable chairs, and four discarded dressing tables for desks. Procuring filing cards, ink and coal for our one fire took us well into October. The Commandant contributed about £20 worth of tools. Between us we raised £2 for material. This and the credit our workers were unwittingly granting us by accepting our tokens for payment constituted our starting capital.

Within six weeks the 'exchange of services' could begin. We had a busy laundry going. A hairdresser's and beauty parlour were set up. Gardeners extended the allotments which had been started by the Quakers before. In a small workshop, cutters were working; here the work was given out to be finished at home and inspected again, here also some milliners were busy and the brassiere and corset sewers competed for the use of our one sewing-machine by the hour. Work was dealt out to the knitters. We secured a shop of a sort fitted with old boxes. Handicraft articles were to become our main form of employment, as they involved least cash expenditure per head for material.

It was interesting to notice how individual ingenuity was stimulated by the prospect of payment, though it was only in bits of cardboard. Even though board and lodging may be provided, with the average person income earned appears to be the yard-stick for achievement, for time not being wasted. The absolute buying power seems surprisingly unimportant; people adapt themselves fairly easily to new standards once these hold true for the whole community. We paid two tokens for a half-day of work, no matter how skilled or unskilled. This caused some difficulties with our more skilled workers, but any differentiation would have led to endless arguments. Eight tokens could be exchanged for 2s 3d once a fortnight. This cash from a Home Office employment fund greatly increased the trust in our tokens. By drawing back about a quarter of the tokens from circulation it helped to balance our strained currency system.

As there was never enough work to go round, employment was limited to six half-days a week, but we always aimed at having every precious tool employed full time. This meant running a laundry, a shop, field work, and a hairdresser's in two shifts, which is enough to make one's hair stand on end. The sharing of tools definitely lowered the standard of responsibility. Cash from 'moneyed' internees availing themselves of our services began trickling in – export bringing foreign currency into the system. We always made just enough to keep our various departments going.

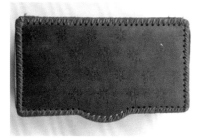

Inside and outside of a leather box made by internees. (Courtesy of Pam Costain)

INFLATION DANGER

By the middle of December angry women stormed our office. What were they to buy for their tokens? We had about 6,000 tokens in circulation. Inflation was imminent. They did not want their hair done or their things washed or any of the thousand odds and ends from our shop; they needed stockings and sewing material and food. We were making money they knew. We explained that we simply had to put every penny we made into material for further employment – but the argument never got across.

But during Christmas week all our bric-a-brac sold like hot cakes. We earned pounds and shovelled in tokens. In a lively black market owners of cash bought tokens from our workers at a rate gradually becoming stabilised at 3d before entering our establishments. At last we could buy wool for socks, hoods, gloves; material for blouses, aprons, assortments of sewing materials; we even got to supplying tasty bread-spread. We cleaned and remade the least good of the second-hand clothes sent for needy internees by overseas Quakers. At last we had more practical things to offer for tokens, but never enough. From January 1941 on the system was established.

At its height, the Service Exchange employed over a thousand women from occasional jobs to 'full time'. From October onwards, however, we were building on shifting sand. Every week some old helper was released and new ones had to be trained. In a population dwindling to less than a thousand the exchange functioned but was shrinking gradually. It was formally wound up a short time ago and the institutions were taken over by the camp.

During the 15 months of its existence the turnover was nearly £1,500, of which £480 was in cash. On the average, it took 1s 8d to supply six half-days of employment. There were about 8,000 tokens in circulation which came back ten times. The expense to Government funds (initial equipment and 2s 3d pocket money) was £340, which provided 120,000 hours of employment.

MANAGEMENT PROBLEMS
Running this small, centrally planned economy brought home some of the problems inherent in a system where the decisions on the direction of capital and labour, on prices and wages, on employment and welfare are necessarily arbitrary.

How to spend the money we earned (direction of capital) was a continuous problem. From the consumer's point of view spending meant high expense for material in relation to the labour involved. Or were we to stretch the money so as to provide most employment even if it meant turning out less desirable goods? Was it more important to buy more wool or tools for setting up shoe repairing? Were clips for the hairdresser's, another iron for the laundry, or repair of the axe most pressing? There is no way of making sure.

The heads of our departments pressed for the employment of the best workers; the camp authorities pressed for the engagement of the 'destitute', even at the expense of efficiency. We tried to balance the two. Every decision was attributed to favouritism – and, indeed, the manner of representation often enough tipped the balance.

We had a weekly staff meeting for the allocation of money. Our shop staff had to provide the 'function of the price'; what could it be people wanted most? The answer depended largely on whether the shop-girl happened to be of a practical or an aesthetic turn. Prices were fixed according to the labour and expense involved. But there was a curious tendency to raise the prices of goods much in demand – capitalism seems ingrained more than skin-deep in most of us.

As always where there is scarcity, the staff, those in the know, were accused of snatching up the best bits before the general public had a chance at them. Actually, it required continual appeals to morale to keep this from happening.

Compared with a straightforward job and a real wage what the Service Exchange had to offer was mere child's play. Compared with enforced idleness it was a great deal. It was surely one of the most inexpensive schemes for productive unemployment relief that could be devised, and well worth remembering as such. As an experiment in a centrally planned economy it showed that it can work, owing to the virtually unlimited adaptability of human nature, but mainly it was a lesson in the difficulties involved.

Subsequent Life

The economist: After her release Ruth worked at the London School of Economics as assistant to Professor Friedrich Hayek, helping him with his research and writing on John Stuart Mill.

The author: Ruth became a successful author whose writings ranged from children's books, to biography, poetry, historical and crime novels and mysticism. Her unfinished novel, *We are Strangers Here, An 'Enemy Alien' in Prison in 1940*, was written, but not completed, in 1943 and only came to light after the author's death. First published in 2008, it is a mixture of fiction and autobiography and tells the story of a young German refugee, Anna Silver, arrested as an 'enemy alien' in Britain in 1939 and her subsequent detention in Holloway Prison and eventual transfer to Port St Mary in the Isle of Man. The story, in some of its broad details, mirrors Ruth's own experiences.

The art collector: Ruth Borchard started collecting British self-portraits in the late 1950s, her interest spurred by viewing art school shows, the 'Young Contemporaries' exhibitions of student art and by Jack Bebbington's book: *Young Artists of Promise*. With astonishing bravado, she set herself a ceiling of 20 guineas (£21) for any one picture, irrespective of the artist's fame, and usually succeeded. In all, between 1958 and 1971, she collected some 100 self-portraits by British and British-based artists dated between 1921 and 1971. Towards the end of her life Ruth realised that her collection would be of broader interest. Her son, Richard, engaged assistance from art dealer Robert Travers (Piano-Nobile Gallery, London), who arranged for publication of the collection in a monograph written by Phillip Vann. Following her death, the collection found a permanent home at Kings Place Gallery, London, where it was first exhibited in 2009. The pictures are now displayed annually and in 2011 a Bi-annual 'Ruth Borchard Self Portrait Prize and Exhibition' was inaugurated. Ruth Borchard died on 6th November 2000 in Jerusalem, aged 90.

Portrait of Ruth Borchard (1958) by Michael Noakes. (Ruth Borchard Collection, courtesy PIANO NOBILE, Robert Travers (Works of Art) Ltd.)

HEALTH AND WELFARE OF THE INTERNEES

CHAPTER NINE

On arrival

The welfare of the internees began as soon as they stepped off the boat at Douglas Pier on the 29th May 1940. A small group of volunteer nurses were at hand to attend to any minor medical needs.

A basic clinic was set up under the Villa Marina, Douglas and immediate care was given when an internee had fallen and injured herself during the rough boat crossing. Others had arrived with existing chronic conditions or were heavily pregnant.

From the early days of the camp, internees both male and female who were qualified in the medical profession, be it doctors, nurses or dentists, were required to assist with the medical needs of the internees.[1]

Medical Practitioners

Dr Anselm Horowitz, whose daughter visited both our exhibitions, was an internee given permission to practise in Castletown. Female internee, Mrs Eva Horowitz was also a qualified doctor and the wife of Dr Anselm Horowitz. After the war they stayed on the Island.

Existing local practitioners such as Dr Lewthwaite whose surgery was in Port St Mary and Dr Brennan in Port Erin would attend to both locals and internees, as would dentists Mr Trustrum and Mr McArd, whose practices were located in Port Erin.

Some of the principal causes of illness were boredom, depression and anxiety, and within a few weeks of setting up Rushen Camp two internees, a 67-year-old lady and a 52-year-old lady, had to be certified and taken to Ballamona Hospital (the Island's only mental hospital).

There were many internees in the camp with medical training and one of the many trained Deaconesses, Sister Anna Jochmann, who was Matron of the

Far left: Youth and Age – A human incident during the disembarkation of women internees at Douglas on Wednesday. (Courtesy of Manx National Heritage (*Isle of Man Examiner*, Friday 31st May, 1940, p.4)
Left: A First-Aid Nurse on the Pier helps a German woman who has sprained an ankle. (Courtesy of Manx National Heritage (*Isle of Man Times*, Saturday, 1st June, 1940, p.12)

Publication: IOM Examiner: Date: 27 Dec 1940

AUSTRIAN DOCTOR TO PRACTICE

Official sanction has been given to Dr. Anselm Horowitz to practice in the Isle of Man. The Government notice which gives this information contains the following by way of explaining a decision which may not be popular among all classes of the community:-
"Dr. Horowitz was born in that part of Austria which subsequently was included in Poland, and came to the Isle of Man before the war as a refugee at the time when a limited number of refugee doctors were being admitted into the United Kingdom.
"Dr. Horowitz, having been admitted to the Register of the British Medical Association to practice in the United Kingdom, has now been authorised to practice in the Isle of Man, on the understanding that on the conclusion of hostilities he will revert to his original proposal to practice as a specialist in rheumatism."

Dr. Anselm Horowitz, an internee, was given permission to practice in Castletown.
(Courtesy of Manx National Heritage (*Isle of Man Examiner*, Friday, 27th December 1940, p.1)

Dalston Hospital, London, was appointed by the internees as Camp Leader.

The Rushen camps had a very good medical back-up. The Hydro Hotel (name later changed to Ocean Castle Hotel) in Port Erin was the Commandant's office and the hospital with maternity unit. It was also used as a sick bay for both Port Erin and Port St Mary camps and latterly, was the medical centre for the married camp.

A Home Office doctor from London, Margaret Colls, was put in charge of medical needs and she stayed until the end of the war. Local and internee doctors and dentists visited the camps daily and there were four State Registered Nurse (SRN) camp district nursing officers. A separate Sister and staff were responsible for the hospital in the Hydro Hotel.

Medical treatment

When directed by a GP, or for surgical and ongoing medical cases, patients would be taken for treatment to Noble's Hospital, in Douglas, the Island's main hospital, 14 miles from the camp. Female internee patients from Rushen would have their beds screened off when admitted to a general female ward and Nobles would also receive maternity cases.

The local Commissioners of Port Erin and Port St Mary would be under strict instructions regarding any reported cases of infectious diseases, notified to them by either a district nurse, local GP or first-aid post, on how each case would be dealt with: isolation, transport to the White Hoe Fever Hospital (staff at the entrance of the White Hoe pictured left) and payment of the cost of any treatment received by the patient.

Staff at the entrance to White Hoe Fever Hospital, Douglas. (Courtesy of Manx National Heritage)

The White Hoe near Douglas, was the Island's isolation hospital and any suspected fever cases or those suffering from polio would receive treatment there. Any suspected cases of tuberculosis would be taken by escort to Cronk Ruagh Sanatorium in Ramsey for investigation.

Ballamona Hospital, Braddan, came under pressure from internee cases and in the early years of the camp figures of 107 admittances per year, including internees, were noted. This figure increased to over 300 by the end of 1941 and only the upsurge of releases saw the figure rapidly decreasing; the main causes being depression. When the last of the camps closed in late 1945, eight internees were left behind in Ballamona.

In Rushen Camp 10 deaths were noted in the first two years, but on further analysis it was on a par with the civilian population's natural death rate.

Clinics were set up in the local villages and many internees suffered greatly from the problem of body and head lice, possibly owing to the close proximity and

Matron, Sisters and nursing staff at Noble's Hospital, Douglas, Isle of Man. (Courtesy of Manx Museum)

overcrowding of their living conditions when they initially arrived, having to sleep two to a bed. At these clinics they would be treated with lotions and lice powder.

It followed that the landladies and their children, and any occupants of the boarding house, would also become infested and they too had to attend for treatment at the clinics! The bed linen and clothing also had to be treated and it is probable that the property also had to be decontaminated (de-loused).

Dame Joanna's opinion

The Camp Commandant for the first year of Rushen Camp, Dame Joanna Cruickshank, reported:[2]

"The Camps had a wonderful health record. Many women had arrived as chronic cases, but had a great improvement in general health. Children had been poorly when they arrived, suffering from malnutrition and were now bursting with health and happiness. One would not see bonnier children anywhere."

Each camp had a 'Health Superintendent' assisted by internee doctors and nurses and there were separate clinics for adults and children. In six months there had only been one death – the internee suffering from a bad heart condition. Dame Joanna commented: 'Our own people would have to pay a high price for the treatment the camp's maternity cases were receiving.'

As a health professional, Dame Joanna established that she had 300 pregnant ladies in her care, but she made no distinction in terms of religion or political persuasion: her role was to keep those in her care healthy and this she achieved. The local doctors were highly praised by her for their outstanding devotion to their oath, as were the local dentists, and in the press the medical services, including the maternity care, were seen as better than could be paid for in England. In this respect, she was grateful to the interned Matron of the Dalston Hospital, London, Sister Anna Jochman, and her 44 nurses, all Lutheran Deaconesses, who provided a willing auxiliary nursing and kindergarten service.

Dame Joanna was criticised for utilising the skills of the Lutheran nurses and in particular Sister Anna, the camp leader, because they were so-called Nazis; a misnomer for many of the women who simply wished to return to

Ballamona Hospital, Braddan for patients with mental illnesses. (isle-of-man.com)

Germany and, in the case of the Sisters, to their mother house at Sarepta. In 1940, over 2,000 Deaconess nurses trained at Sarepta and were deployed on their humanitarian mission to minister to those in need throughout the world.

In the first weeks, letters of complaint made their way to the UK such as a pregnant woman sharing a bed with a tuberculosis (TB) patient. Almost all internees had to share a double bed because the hotels had few single rooms, but these problems were addressed speedily.

What was not addressed was the opposition from the authorities to the idea of a woman in charge. From the Chief Constable to the locally elected Commissioners this was a new concept, and one that was not welcome. However, the Town Clerk of Port Erin Commissioners, Alec Clague, was an exception to this and, in modern terms, a feminist.

Food, diet, health and effects of rationing

Internees, both male and female, were employed by local farmers to assist with crops, growing vegetables and tending livestock. In 1944 ration books were issued to residents of each district so that the local shops would be used, helping to keep the shopkeepers and grocers in business.

The internees in Port Erin were given permission by the Commandant to start their own small piggery and they also kept hens and were very good gardeners, so dependent on the weather, there would always be a ready supply of fresh food stuffs.

With the availability of their own grown food, internees would barter these with locals in exchange for confectionary, toiletries, and clothing, in fact any items that were hard to come by. But this was occasionally discovered and the locals would, along with the internees, be up in front of the courts.

There were some difficult times, but being an Island with the ability to provide for their needs, in general the dietary intake was good. Traditional recipes such as broths and soups would be prepared by the landladies, which

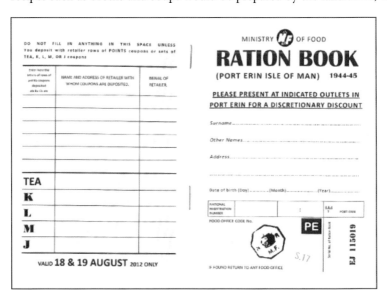

Ration Book.
(Courtesy of Manx
National Heritage)

helped rations go further, but with the availability of fresh foods the general health of the community of Rushen, which would include the internment camps, was good and the reports from the various welfare groups that visited the camps would corroborate this.

'Internees Underfed'

Many of the landladies and their families were introduced to new tastes as the internees would prepare their own meals and, when certain ingredients were plentiful, they would prepare cakes such as stöllen and their own soups and meat dishes. All householders who were billeting internees would have received the directive from the government advising the minimum rations to be given to each internee.

Internees Weekly Food Rations to be provided by the Boarding House and Hotels from a Government Directive IoM:

12oz Bread
2 oz Flour
3½ oz Meat
10 oz Fish
1 oz Margarine
¾ oz Tea/Coffee
1½ oz Sugar
½ Pint milk
1 oz Cheese (2 days per week)
½ oz Oatmeal
1 oz Jam
½ oz Beans/Peas
14 oz Potatoes
1½ oz Rice
¼ oz Nut oil
3 oz Fresh vegetables
1/100oz Mustard
Salt/pepper

Internees weekly food ration taken from an IOM Government Directive. (Courtesy of Manx National Heritage)

An article which appeared in the UK *News Chronicle* dated 15th October 1941 headed, 'Women Aliens in Isle of Man Underfed'[3], did not give this impression. The group responsible for the article was called 'The Free German League', whose patrons included the Bishop of Chichester, David Grenfell MP, Professor Gilbert Murray, J. B. Priestley and Dame Sybil Thorndike.

The article reported a number of false accusations. These included that there was only one doctor assisted by one nurse for the 4,000 refugee and alien internees; many of the women were invalids. Most of those who received treatment, the nurse reported, were suffering from hysteria.

Further, a pregnant woman was forced for three months to share her bed with a tubercular case, a child suffering from chickenpox had to share his mother's bed and a 10-year-old child lived in the same room and so on. Some of the reports that applied to the initial set up of the camp were true: Nazi women and refugees were compelled to share a room and a bed, and the refugees were being threatened and terrorised by the Nazi inmates. These circumstances were known to the camp officials and were changed as soon as they were able to alter the living arrangements.

They also reported that:

The boarding houses had no heating arrangements (true) and it would be felt during the winter months, and that most of the landladies were charging for washing, some a penny for hot water for tea or hot water bottles, and some charging a penny for ironing.

Food was insufficient, daily meals had been reduced from four to three and vegetables were hardly ever served.

Only one boarding house gave milk to pregnant women and although there were a few hundred children nothing was done by the authorities about their education. There was one kindergarten which charged fees too high for the majority of interned mothers, and receipt of mail was delayed.

Again, some of the accusations were true. Initially the mail took many weeks to be read and censored in the early months, but so many internees were being released on a regular basis throughout the first 12 months of the camp that sorting out what would be required must have been a nightmare.

The article prompted a rebuttal from an Italian internee in the Rushen camp, stating that everyone in charge of the camp had done their utmost to house and feed the internees. Port Erin's population had trebled overnight with the arrival of the 3,500 internees in May 1940 and thankfully, the situation settled rapidly within a few weeks.

Everyone had to pull together

When needed, locals supported each other, but found that in many cases the health and welfare services available to the internees were better than their own as they had to pay for their healthcare – doctors, dentists and hospitalisation costs. Camp staff, through the Isle of Man government, would claim back any costs from the Home Office to provide all essential healthcare and welfare needs for the internees.

Rationing, although not initially causing any hardship for the people of the Island, was introduced in the latter part of the war, particularly in the towns such as Douglas, and lasted in the Island until 1952. An example of rations is shown below:

What you would have been entitled to per week during WWII. (information sourced from Historic UK: Rationing in World War Two by Stephen Wilson, historic-uk.com)

Government Directive - UK

The ration for one adult per week:

BACON AND HAM 4oz
MEAT .... to the value of 1s.2d
Sausages were not rationed but difficult to obtain
Offal was originally un-rationed but sometimes formed part of the meat ration.
BUTTER.............. 2ozs
CHEESE .... 2ozs sometimes it rose to 4ozs and even up to 6ozs
MARGARINE 4ozs
COOKING FAT....... 4ozs often dropping to 2ozs
MILK .... 3 pints sometimes dropping to 2 pints Household (skimmed, dried) milk was available. This was 1 packet each for 4 weeks.
SUGAR 5ozs
PRESERVES .... 1lb every 2 months
TEA 2ozs
EGGS .... 1 shell egg a week if available but at times dropping to 1 every 2 weeks.
Dried eggs - 1 packet each 4 weeks
SWEETS .... 12ozs each 4 weeks. In addition, there was a monthly points system

An example of how these could be spent. With the 16 point that you were allocated you were allowed to buy one can of fish or meat or 2lb of dried fruit or 8lb of split peas

Babies and younger children, expectant and nursing mothers had concentrated orange juice and cod liver oil from Welfare Clinics together with priority milk.

The internees in most cases had no complaints with the food provided and their landladies took charge in regard to well-being and health and dietary needs. Some said they fared much better than many of the local population.

A complete contradiction of the article placed in the *News Chronicle* in October 1940 was an article which appeared in a newspaper called the *Daily Dispatch*, the author being a Mr Ernest Lewis, he wrote:

"I talked with some of them as they boarded the boat for the mainland. They all praised the quantity and quality of the food and nearly all said they had never met kinder folk than the Manx landladies."[4]

Farmers and butchers would call on the boarding houses in horse-drawn carts and wheelbarrows and sell any spare rations available, such as bacon, butter, turnips and potatoes. The internees were very resourceful and could produce nutritious meals from basic ingredients, which the whole household would enjoy.

During WWII, diet in the south of the Island would contain plenty of fresh produce: fresh meat and vegetables including some fruits, crab and lobster, delicious stews and pies, roasted vegetables, plenty of eggs, kippers, mackerel, preserves and 'keep fit pills' or vitamins. However, in Douglas,

Foods available in the South of the Island and war time advice on diet. (Source: War time advertising)

rationing was quite strict with one egg per family of four, long queues and many shortages.

The landladies and hotel owners were recompensed for 'looking after' the internees and they would receive a claim form, which was to be returned every fortnight to the Camp Commandant's office. They would receive £1.1s.0d for each adult internee per seven day week, 10s.6d for 14–17 year olds and 8s.6d for children under 14.

Information courtesy of Alan Franklin, *AJR Journal* March 2008, and Manx National Heritage (*Isle of Man Examiner*, 10th September 1943, p.8)

As the internees were released, and there was no possibility of receiving visitors, the landladies would receive a retainer payment, otherwise it would have been extremely hard for the them to survive. Many were missing the revenue they were used to receiving during the summer months, which would have exceeded the payments received for housing the internees.

An article prepared by Alan Franklin in the *AJR Journal* in March 2008 noted the death of a female internee in October 1941.[5]

Mortuaries were located in both Port Erin and Port St Mary, (J. J. McArd and Cringle & Cooil in Port Erin and T. S. Keggin & Son in Port St Mary), but as

Surname	Christian Names	IOM Card No.	Date Arrival in IoM	Previous Address or Camp	Reg. Cert No/Identity Book	Nat
Schiendler	Margarete (on list) Margaretha	2934	18.7.40	31, Leopold Street, Loughborough	757396 issued 28.8.39 at	Ger

Rushen Camp - Date of Birth 25.5.1892 in Ratibor. - Occupation Domestic. - Address of last residence outside U.K. Berlin, Ludwigskirchplatz 12. - Single. - German passport No. N5171/39/2 14.8.39 Berlin. - 26.8.39 Con. landing at Harwich. - 6.12.39 Metro. Tri. No. 27. Exempted internment & special restrictions. - Refugee from Nazi oppression. - 27.6.40 Reg. Adv. Com. No. 3. To be interned until further order. - Refugee from Nazi oppression. - 9.10.41 Deceased. - Letters attached to R.C. - First dated 10 October 1941 from ?Wilson Deputy Commandant to Chief Constable, Douglas. Ref. DJW/BM, "Dear Sir, I have to report that Margarete Schindler, born 25.5.92 at Ratibor, Silesia, die here on 9th October, 1941, and to request that you would kindly send her police registration book immediately to the Police at the last place of Registration". - Second dated 11th October, 1941 from Major Chief Constable (Douglas) to The Chief Inspector, Aliens Registration Office, Piccadilly Place, London, W1. Ref. WEC/ACU, "Dear Sir, Margarethe Schinlder, R.C. 757396, Bow Street, 28.8.39. Enclosed please find Registration Certificate for the above named alien who died at the Women's Internment Camp, Port Erin, Isle of Man, on the 9th October, 1941". - Third card No. 139 acknowledging the receipt of the letter dated 11th October from the Aliens Registration Office. No. 1214/10/41. Your Ref. WEC/ACU. - Buried in Jewish section of Douglas Cemetery. Headstone reads Margarete Schindler 9 October 1941.

Isle   of   Man   Examiner
September 10th, 1943

Marie Kwapil (50), a German subject born in Warbenthal, Austria, and interned in the Island, died in Noble's Hospital last week, whilst under an anaesthetic   before   the operation could be performed. At the inquest the verdict returned was "death from natural causes". A tribute to the health of the internees in the south of the Island is the fact that out of the total number who have passed through   the   camp,   the percentage of deaths is only equal to 2.66 per 1,000 since the camp opened.

Death of Marie Kwapil recorded in the *Isle of Man Examiner*, September 10th, 1943.

with all sudden deaths, the Coroner's Office would be informed and would take over the arrangements for the burial.

A further death was recorded in the *Isle of Man Examiner,* September 10th, 1943.[6]

The nursing care received by the internees during their time in Rushen Camp was documented by members of various refugee organisations who would visit the camps and report their findings back to the United Kingdom and European authorities via neutral Sweden.

By the 25th May 1945, the Rushen camps housed around 200 internees. The last group left on the 5th September, 1945, including 60 women and 25 children, of which 11 were Manx born. There were two internees taken to the boat on stretchers, one with rheumatoid arthritis and the other with back problems, and an internee recovering from an operation for a duodenal ulcer.

Many internees agreed that their health and welfare needs were adequately catered for as their health was generally good, they received a well-balanced diet and were able to exercise regularly. They had suitable clothing and their accommodation and living conditions were more than adequate under the circumstances. All in all, their medical treatment was thorough, of a high standard and well organised.

EDUCATION – SCHOOLS AND TEACHERS

Soon after the camp opened, it became clear that the children needed some structure to their lives. A number of the internees approached the Commandant about setting up a school and, on issues concerning children, Dame Joanna was always helpful.

Schools

Initially, two kindergarten classes were set up. Although the kindergartens were open all day demand was high, so children either attended in the mornings or the afternoons.

There were several teachers interned, including Minna Specht (see Chapter 12) who set up a kindergarten class for under sixes at Cowley's Café, the former boys' and infants' school, and a school for 6–16 year olds at the Cornaa Boarding House, both in Port St Mary.

In Port Erin, a kindergarten was set up in the clubhouse at Rowany Golf Club. As numbers increased at Rowany the kindergarten moved to one of the hotels on The Promenade, until the landladies became unhappy with the arrangement.

The group then moved to Dandy Hill Schoolroom, where there were already nine classes for 6–14 year olds. These older children moved to rooms at the rear of the Strand Café in October 1940. The headmistress there was Dr Ingeborg Gurland, a former lecturer at Durham University. Some classes were also held at the Bradda Private Hotel.

Below: Cornaa Boarding House, Port St Mary. (Doreen Moule)

Right: Cowley's Café, former infants' and boys' school, Port St Mary. (Doreen Moule)

Below: The Strand Café, Port Erin. (Private collection)

CHAPTER TEN

Children's welfare

Many of the children had been 'severely disturbed as a result of their past experiences, others were running wild'[1] and the need for structure was deemed necessary for their progress.

In January 1941, a report by Theo Naftel, a member of the International Co-operative Women's Guild Committee, after her official visit to the camp, stated that:

"Everyone agreed that regular schooling has had a very beneficial effect on the children, they love school and are much brighter and less nervy since they have not been in such constant contact with the adult life in the hotels."[2]

Erna Nelki, an interned teacher, psychologist and socialist, also approved of the provision made for the children. In an article in the Independent Labour Party's *New Leader* in 1941, she said:

The outlook of the majority of the refugees on the Isle of Man was anti-German. The children often refused to speak German. Most of them wanted an English school, with an English curriculum and English ideals. We tried to give them that. But for those who were willing to play their part in building up a new free Germany, we tried to give the knowledge which will help them in that task.[3]

The children were being prepared for their future, whether that would be in England or in Germany, which suggests that they were taught in both languages.

Below: Collinson's Café. (Private collection)

Bottom left: Dandy Hill Schoolroom. (Courtesy of Ashton Lewis)

Bottom right: Marine Biological Station. (Private collection)

Adult education

The biggest threat to morale among the internees was boredom, but many of them were well-educated and had considerable skills, so the women set up a wide range of activities and courses.

In Port St Mary, there were 30 different courses including: Greek, German Literature, British History, Reading Shakespeare, Problems of Life & Mathematical Training, plus practical skills such as glove making and shorthand.

In Port Erin, there were 17 different, more practical, courses including: weaving, dressmaking, spinning, music appreciation and a small orchestra. Many of these courses

took place in Collinson's Café, which was also a meeting place for the women to socialise.

A third venue at Dandy Hill Sunday schoolroom, also in Port Erin, offered a further 13 courses on English, Swedish, Philosophy, European History, Shorthand, Faust, Russian, French, Latin, Psychology, Phonetics, Spanish and Italian.

In addition to the courses, 40 of the internees were registered at the Marine Biological Station, where they carried out research and gave lectures to other women who were suitably qualified. All these women were permitted to use the Quiet Room and the library and, in return, they re-organised and catalogued several thousand papers on marine biological and hydrographical topics. Bridget Jacobs, a zoology student prior to internment, was in charge of six women collecting seaweed for making agar jelly used in the research work.

The library

Many books were supplied by both individuals and charitable organisations. Ruth Michaelis-Jena, who had been a bookseller in Scotland, was asked to organise the books into a proper library at Collinson's Café in Port Erin and she enjoyed the opportunity to do so. The library was a huge success, with hundreds of readers and a constant supply of books.

The teachers

As Rosemarie Dalheim says in her book, *The Sunny Hours*:

'There were plenty of intelligent, educated women to draw on, who were glad to share their expertise and knowledge and teach any subjects required.'[4]

This was just as well, as there were both children and adults for whom to provide educational courses.

Many of the internees were qualified teachers and others had expertise in academic and/or practical subjects, so a wide and varied programme of courses was made available.

The following are just 20 of the people who would have been able to make a valuable contribution to the ongoing welfare of the internees and their children. The vast majority were born in either Germany or Austria, all were teachers or governesses, and many would have been practising as teachers in the UK prior to arrest.

Qualified Teachers/Governesses

Sister Mary Gisela (born Berta Waffler) was born in Ratisbon (Regensburg), Germany, in 1900. She was teaching at a convent in Faversham when arrested. She was billeted at Collinson's in Port Erin and released in August 1940 to a convent in Lingfield.

(Images this page courtesy of Manx National Heritage)

Ruth Bischoff was born in Stuttgart, Germany, in 1918. She was a teacher and she was living in London in 1940 when arrested. She was billeted at the Eagle Hotel in Port Erin and released to Lightwater in Surrey in October 1942.

Inga Rosa Kramer was born in Baden, Austria, in 1894. She was a governess and living in Wimborne in Dorset when arrested. She was billeted at 'Mallmore' in Port St Mary and released to Wolverhampton in January 1941.

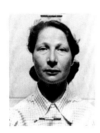

Hertha Feder was born in Berlin, Germany, in 1906. She was a teacher and living in Oxford when arrested. She was billeted at the Strand Café in Port Erin and released to Grayshott, then in Surrey, in February 1941.

Hedwig Baruch was born in Hanover, Germany, in 1890. She was a teacher and living in Liverpool when arrested. She was billeted at the Towers Hotel, Port Erin and released to Hampstead, London in November 1940.

Elisabeth Bremer was born in Berlin, Germany, in 1902. She was a teacher and living in Liverpool when arrested. She was billeted at the Imperial Hotel, Port Erin and released to Manchester in July 1941.

Anna Rathmann was born in Pohldorf, Germany, in 1892. She was a nurse-governess and living in London when arrested. She was billeted at 'Lincluden', Port Erin. She was unwell in autumn 1940 and admitted to hospital, but released back to the camp after a month, apparently well and happy. Sadly, in January 1941, she was found drowned near the Lifeboat Station in Port Erin. The inquest found no evidence as to how she came to be in the water. She was buried at Rushen Church in 1941, but her body was moved to the German Military Cemetery at Cannock Chase in 1962.

Hildegard Hachenburg was born in Osnabruck, Germany, in 1899. She studied at the Universities of Marberg, Heidelberg and Hamburg and had a Doctorate in Philosophy from Heidelberg. She was married and living in Nottinghamshire when arrested. Billeted at 'Wavecrest', Port St Mary, she lectured to the women internees on

English history and the history of the Middle Ages and taught History in the camp school. In December 1940, after preparation, she was confirmed into full membership of the Church of England at St Catherine's Church, Port Erin, by the Lord Bishop, Dr W. Stanton Jones and released to Oswestry, Shropshire in March 1941.

Gertrude Kolisko was born in Ymunden (Gmunden), Austria, in 1910. She was a teacher and living in Cheshire when arrested. She was billeted at Purt-y-Shee, Port Erin and released to Manchester in November 1941.

Margarethe Schmid was born in Vienna, Austria, in 1910. She was a music teacher, married and living in Nottinghamshire when arrested. She was billeted at 'Beach House', Port Erin and was released to London in November 1940.

Luise Dub was born in Steyr, Austria, in 1903. She was an assistant teacher and living in Littlehampton when arrested. She was billeted at 'Clifton', Port St Mary and was released to Rugby in February 1941.

Dr Ingeborg Gurland (mentioned earlier in this chapter) was born in Latvia in 1913. She had been a lecturer at Durham University and held a teaching certificate from the National Froebel Foundation. She was living in Durham when arrested. She was billeted at the Towers Hotel in Port Erin and was Head Teacher at the camp school in Port Erin. She was released to Hoddesden in Hertfordshire in May 1941.

Teachers/Students of Languages

Annie May Döhring was born in Berlin, Germany, in 1908. She was a teacher of languages and living in Bearsted, Kent when arrested. She was billeted in Port Erin, but it is not clear where. She was released back to Bearsted in October 1944.

Erna Nelki (mentioned earlier in this chapter) was born in Berlin, Germany, in 1914. She was married, a socialist and a teacher of languages and living in Crowborough, then in Buckinghamshire, when arrested. She was billeted at the Strand Café in Port Erin. She taught in the camp schools and was released to London in June 1941.

(Images this page courtesy of Manx National Heritage)

(Images this page courtesy of Manx National Heritage)

Tilly Frank was born in South Africa of British parents in 1888. She was divorced from her German husband and was a teacher of languages, living in Surrey, when arrested. She was billeted at the Snaefell Hotel in Port Erin and released to Leicester in December 1940.

Luise Josephine Freitagsmuller was born in Castrop Rauxel in Germany in 1914. She was a student of languages and living at a convent in Hendon when arrested. She was billeted at Bradda Glen in Port Erin and released back to the convent in August 1940.

Erika Goldschmidt was born in Lubeck in 1902. She had lived in Hamburg before coming to England. She was a teacher of German. She was billeted at 'Breakwater' in Port Erin and released in February 1941 to Oxford.

Else Jönsson was born in 1885 in Vienna, Austria. She was married, a teacher of languages and living in Scotland when arrested. She was billeted at the Peveril Hotel in Port Erin and released in September 1942 to Glasgow.

Isabella Zlatkes was born in 1919 in Vienna, Austria, but had taken German nationality. She was a teacher of languages and lived in London when arrested. She was billeted in the Falcon's Nest Hotel in Port Erin and released in April 1941 to return to London.

Josefine Franz was born in 1912 in Hohr Grenshausen in Germany. She was a student of languages and living at the same convent in Hendon as Luise Josephine Freitagsmuller when arrested. She, too, was billeted at Bradda Glen and returned to the convent in August 1940.

(Courtesy of Manx National Heritage (*Isle of Man Examiner*, 22nd November 1940, p.6)

Mr Charles A. Kidd has been appointed teacher-in-charge of adolescents (boys ranging from 11 to 15 years) at the internment camp at Port Erin. About thirty boys—the children of internees—are in attendance. The classes are being held in St. Catherine's Hall, and the subjects taught include English, reading, writing, arithmetic, history, science, drawing, etc. Mr Kidd was for several years before the war teacher-in-charge of unemployed youths at Douglas, where his services were much appreciated.

The older boys were proving to be something of a challenge in the classroom, so it was decided to bring in a teacher from outside the camp, who could address their particular needs both academically and as a male role model in the absence of their fathers.

It will be noted that the teachers were very experienced – half were over 35 years old – and some had outstanding qualifications. Most (80%) were released by mid 1941.

ROLE OF THE CONSTABULARY

Volunteers required

Port Erin police station, a local police Constable writes up in the police book after returning from his rounds: '3rd September 1939: Carried out routine patrol and returned to station, nothing to report. War broke out.'[1]

During a War Cabinet meeting held on the 24th May 1940 in Downing Street, the War Office requested:

"The internment of all enemy aliens and the imposition of severe restrictions upon neutral aliens. The Home Secretary represented that an attempt to intern all aliens forthwith would cause a breakdown of the machinery and would not be effective, since the danger to be apprehended from neutral aliens was not quite as serious as the danger from enemy aliens."[2]

As war with Germany loomed for Britain, the Home Secretary considered that the alien refugees now reaching Britain fell within the category of causing a danger to the safety of the country, thus approval was given to intern all German and Austrian women in Category B between the ages of 16 and 60 and detain them in the Isle of Man. The majority of the female internee registration cards held within the Manx Museum show the arrival date of the internees as 30th May 1940; the actual arrival date commenced on the 29th May 1940 with further internees arriving up to a week later.

Rushen Internment Camp it was decided, would be managed by the Home Department (Home Office) with security undertaken by the Metropolitan Police Force, assisted by the local Isle of Man Constabulary. Scotland Yard sent out a request to the Met for volunteers from the Women Police Officers, for duty in the Isle of Man. WP Inspector Pike and four WPCs, travelled from London to the Island escorted by (Superintendent) Miss Peto in July 1940.

Miss Peto accompanied 'her girls' to the Island and stayed for a couple of days, with two ladies who were doctors in the camp in Port Erin, to see them settled in. Miss Peto OBE., wrote an account of her experiences during the time of the 'Detention Centre' in her unpublished memoirs:

Miss Peto (second row, first left) and WPCs on Board HMS *Wolfhound* sailing to the Island. Accompanying the ladies was a contingent of Special Branch officers. (Reproduced by permission of the Metropolitan Police Authority (Heritage Centre))

CHAPTER ELEVEN

Disembarkation of Metropolitan Police and other passengers or internees from HMS *Wolfhound* – port not known. The first ship to arrive in the Island carrying women and children internees was a Belgian cross-channel ferry called *Princess Josephine Charlotte* on the 29th May 1940 and berthed in Douglas. (Reproduced by permission of the Metropolitan Police Authority (Heritage Centre))

"*The Isle of Man was chosen as a detention centre, partly on account of its distance from the probable area of attack and partly because it afforded suitable accommodation for a large numbers of detainees in the hotels and lodging-houses normally occupied by holiday visitors.*"[3]

Miss Peto recalled that Miss Hall, who was a senior civil servant in the Isle of Man government, had asked that the Metropolitan Police Commissioner might lend a Woman Police Sergeant and four Women Constables for the duties of custody and escort of enemy aliens in the proposed Port Erin and Port St Mary Internment Camp. WP Inspector Pike was selected to take charge of the detachment of four WPCs and the first escort of women and children internees, first to Fulham and then to Fleetwood via a special train from Paddington. The final leg was the steamer to the Island.

Duties of the WPCs

The duties of the WPCs consisted mainly of seeing that no detainee crossed the barbed wire, which stretched between posts marking the camp boundary, and escorting those who had permission to go from Port Erin into Port St Mary, and vice versa, or who had to go to Douglas or Liverpool for hospital treatment. Occasionally an escort would be required to travel from the Island to London when an appeal against a detention order was being heard in court. On arrival, the WPCs would search the internee's luggage and escort them to their allocated billets

A number of local PCs were involved in these duties including William Brown and Edgar Qualtrough, who lived in Port Erin police station around 1940. The local PCs assisted with manning the road barriers and checking national identity cards and permits of local residents and visitors entering and leaving the camps.

Local male residents who weren't eligible for war duties also manned the

Local, Constable Edgar Qualtrough on the left with WPC Hillary. Constable, right unknown. (Courtesy of The Mayor's Office for Policing and Crime. (Heritage Centre))

Back row L-R: Locals PC Arthur P. Cowin; PC R. S. Bannan; WPC Ivy Baxter; WP Inspector Florrie Pike; WPC Pole; PC William H. Brown and PC Charles Faragher. Front row L-R: WPC Joyce Ball; WPC E. Hynd; WPC E. Layram and WPC Eleanor Cottle. WPCs each had between 2 and 4 years service, Inspector Pike had served for 8 years, mainly in the East End of London. (Reproduced by permission of the Metropolitan Police Authority (Heritage Centre))

road barriers and some were rather officious. Many a local was up in arms if they had forgotten their ID cards and the 'guard', whom many knew well or even lived alongside, would refuse permission to enter or leave the camp until they returned with them.

Other duties for the WPCs were to escort the internees between the two villages of Port Erin and Port St Mary, where they could meet up with friends and visit the local shops on the two allocated days each week. Escorts were also required for trips to the cinema and other recreational adult activities, such as

walking trips up what Ivy Baxter described as 'Colby Mountain', which may have been South Barrule, for those who were fit enough.

Miss Peto's memories

One occasion seemed to touch Miss Peto prior to the forming of the married camp, in her words:

"One of the real hardships of the alien camps during their first years of existence was the segregation of husbands and wives in different parts of the Island. I have a vivid recollection of the great day when a meeting was arranged for them in Port St. Mary, the women being brought over from Port Erin to a large hotel at the farther end of the sea front, [this was The Balqueeney Hydro] there to await the arrival of their men folk, who were to come by train from their Camp in a more northerly part of the Island. At last a large body of men came into view at the farther end of the Promenade, escorted by their guards.

It was a moving sight, in both senses of the word; as they advanced, the orderly procession quickened pace until the whole party were racing along the sea front with arms outstretched to greet their wives and families. In particular, I recall an elderly couple of German detainees, caretakers at a German Consulate in some English seaport town, wandering about in blissful reunion arm in arm, until the time came for the men's return to their own camp. Happily, however, not for long; married quarters were arranged shortly afterwards at Port St. Mary for alien families and these and other couples were united once more. When this took place, a male commandant CID Chief Inspector Cuthbert was appointed for Port Erin and Port St. Mary, with WP Inspector Pike as Deputy Commandant in charge of Women Aliens until the end of the War".[4]

Miss Peto's final comment on the camp was:

"One further and rather delightful instance of considerate treatment of interned aliens was that of an archaeologist [she almost certainly would be referring to Dr Gerhard Bersu at the married camp] who was provided with a shepherd's hut on wheels and a special guard, so that he could occupy himself with excavating a pre-historic tomb on a hillside in the Island. One might, perhaps, couple with this instance, two delightful German women who set up a little factory for making garden manure out of seaweed, dead rabbit bone and a variety of other ingredients. Dead rabbits were plentiful, because Manxmen looked on rabbits as vermin and unfit for human consumption – even in war-time!"[5]

Dr Gerhard Bersu.
(Image Wikipedia)

Commandant Dame Joanna Cruickshank and the local constabulary

Conflicts

No initial segregation of the internees was possible and this would later be used as a reason to direct criticism towards Dame Joanna, obviously not taking into account the lack of information and urgency of the situation that she faced. There

Back Row L-R: WPCs Bunn, Baxter, Pole; Front Row L-R: WPS Hill, WPC Chesney. Photograph appears to have been taken at the entrance of Castletown police station. (Courtesy of The Mayor's Office for Policing and Crime. (Heritage Centre))

were no fewer than 300 expectant mothers along with some serious cases of infectious diseases such as TB. The authorities in the UK had intended not to intern chronically sick or infirm aliens, but unfortunately that is exactly what happened.

Dame Joanna did not have the best relations with the local Constabulary. When attending a meeting with the Chief Constable Major J. W. Young OBE, Inspector J. T. Kneale (Police Officer, Castletown) and HM Attorney General, Mr R. B. Moore at her headquarters in the Hydro Hotel (later renamed the Ocean Castle Hotel), Port Erin in June 1940, she informed those present that: 'The internees are under her authority for all matters of discipline and general behaviour, but if they (internees) commit an offence against the Civil Law, they (internees) are liable to be dealt with by the Civil Authorities.'[6]

Inspector Kneale wrote to the Chief Constable regarding criminal offences carried out by the internees. Dame Joanna had requested that 'when an internee

Dame Joanna, left. (©National Portrait Gallery, London) with Major Young, centre and Inspector Kneale, right (Private collection)

committed an offence inside the camp, the person to deal with them was herself and that she had a strong objection to the matter being taken before the civil court without her consent'. She stated that 'she had full authority over the internees from the Home Office, to deal with the internee as she thought fit'[7]. The question arose when Dame Joanna was informed that an internee had been arrested by a Constable of Port Erin and would be brought before the High Bailiff in Douglas charged with larceny. Dame Joanna maintained that during the time that the women were interned, they were not subject to Civil Law and should be dealt with by her only. Inspector Kneale added 'if this is the case, then an impossible position arises'.[8]

Incidents within the Camp

One incident initiated some strong words from the Chief Constable Major Young. An internee was due for release the following day, when her luggage was searched by a WPC. One of her cases was found to contain a large quantity of correspondence in German, concluding with the words 'Heil Hitler'. There were also debts owing to local shopkeepers and her release was suspended. The papers were handed to the Camp Registrar Miss Broome by Dame Joanna and the internee was duly reprimanded. Inspector Kneale interviewed Dame Joanna and requested the confiscated papers.

Dame Joanna replied, '*No, not on any account and what is done with them is no concern of the Police as there was nothing in them which called for Police action.*'[9]

The Chief Constable was informed of this by Inspector Kneale and within his reply he stated that the Commandant does not appear to regard the police as other than her agents and that the Law of the Isle of Man still prevails in the Rushen Area.

The letters must have eventually been handed over to the local police as the internee was charged with attempting to smuggle these out of the Island and went to prison for two months. When she was released, she did not return to Rushen Camp, but instead was taken to the boat under guard back to England and placed in an internment camp there.

Dame Joanna wrote to Major Young in July 1940:

> "*While I quite appreciate that action in cases of crimes such as theft would come under the Civil Law and enforced in the normal way, I do feel that in cases in which internees are involved, they should come under me for due disciplinary action, and I would like the matter taken up by the Government in order that they may extend my powers in this direction.*"[10]

Incidents occurring within the camp appeared mostly to be confined to petty theft. These cases would

Sergeant Ivy Baxter with three WPCs searching luggage and parcels at Port Erin Railway Station. (Courtesy of The Mayor's Office for Policing and Crime. (Heritage Centre))

appear in the local newspapers, as the internee responsible would be taken before the civil courts. One internee stole items of clothing from another internee who had been released, while helping her pack and who was also billeted with her in the Snaefell Hotel in Port Erin. In court, a further internee who was billeted in the Snaefell Hotel received a letter from the released internee, who was now in Surrey, advising of the missing clothing and she was therefore able to identify the articles produced in court. The theft was admitted and the internee was bound over for 12 months in her own bond of £5.

Another young internee was bound over for 12 months at the Castletown High Bailiff's court charged with stealing a silver ring valued at 15s from another internee. The owner stated that she had missed the ring from her bedroom and saw it on the other internee's finger at the Port St Mary clinic.

WPC Rose Nial said that the defendant first denied having the ring, but later admitted she had taken it. The defendant admitted that she had no money and when she got out she would need every penny. The assistant superintendent at the time, Miss M. C. Shone, appeared to try to help mitigate the internee's situation by saying 'the defendant had put up a hard fight; had a three month old baby, no money and felt she was against everyone, but now it was possible for her to earn a little money by knitting.[11] The High Bailiff added that it was fortunate for her that the assistant superintendent had spoken for her. The sad situation was that some of the internees were destitute and these were extraordinary times forcing them to obtain the means, however they could, to assist them once they had been released.

Dame Joanna relinquished her position as Camp Commandant 12 months after the opening of Rushen Women's Internment Camp. The new arrangement for the camps had been introduced in April 1941 with the provision of a mixed camp on Port St Mary promenade. A number of married internees and their children in the various camps around the Island were reunited and the single female internees were moved to Port Erin Camp. Newly promoted Chief Inspector Cyril Cuthbert was appointed to take charge of the internment camps

Sergeant Baxter, three WPCs, Port Erin Station Master Mr Nelson, his assistant Mr Maddrell and a young internee sorting luggage at Port Erin Railway Station.

Letter from Constable
E J Qualtrough, Port
Erin police station to
Inspector Kneale at
Castletown police
station advising of the
placing of an internee
in a cell in Port Erin for
breaching 'camp rules'.

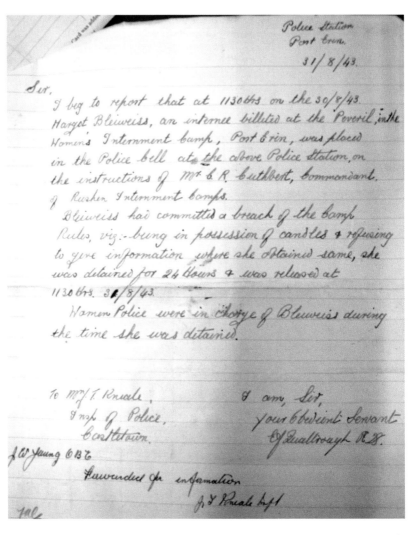

and his Deputy was Miss D. J. Wilson who was formerly at Strangeways Gaol.

Sergeant Ivy Baxter recalled many young internees were a bit unruly and the one cell at Port Erin police station, which was manned by the local Constable and his wife, and which at that time may have been Constable Qualtrough, always had an internee doing seven days 'jail'.

The WPCs would supervise internees who were given permission to work on the nearby farms and in a fish smokehouse in Port Erin.

Ivy Baxter received her promotion to sergeant while on duty in the Island and when Commandant Cuthbert travelled to the Home and Foreign Offices in London she was left in charge of the camps, along with seven WPCs and the Port Erin Police Constable. After a number of weeks, some of the WPCs asked to return to London as they felt the Island was too quiet. Returning to London and the bombing raids, they would soon learn it was in stark contrast to the peace of the Island. Replacements WPCs were sent and they stayed until the end of the war.

The internees were very good at growing vegetables and very clever when it came to handicrafts such as knitting and dressmaking. The local newspapers reported a number of local residents being brought up before the courts for dealing directly with the internees.

Fairy Bridge, Ballalona, Isle of Man. (Courtesy Valentine's Postcards)

One local resident of Port St Mary promenade, Miss Mona Quillin, had a number of internees in her boarding house. She recalled that one married internee went missing and did not return to the house by curfew. Mona contacted the police and advised that she was missing – the police then sent out a search party, firstly in and around Port St Mary. Later in the evening she was located hiding on Port St Mary breakwater where she was awaiting an Irish fishing boat in an attempt to escape. She was brought back to Port Erin police station for the night and the following day was escorted to the boat and back to Holloway Prison. Mona did not see her again.

A new replacement WPC arrived in the Island in June 1941 and was collected by Commandant Cuthbert, who took his hat off at the Fairy Bridge explaining that 'one had to salute the fairies or else they would be upset and that wasn't wise'.[12]

Her duties included searching the luggage of internees who had been released and were travelling back to England, and escorting internees to London Holloway Prison. One internee that she was collecting from Holloway Prison to escort to Rushen Camp was the daughter of the famous piano manufacturer, Bechstein. Waiting for the train at Euston there was a severe air raid and they both wondered if they would survive.

Police duties included manning Port Erin police station and barrier manning with 'guards' who were mostly local fishermen. One other memorable escort duty was to take an internee to Douglas to see the bone specialist at the hospital, Sir Herbert Barker, who greeted her with 'are you well, Officer?' She replied that she was well, but that she had a bit of a bad back, which he asked her to explain. He then said, 'Get yourself on the Sunday a.m. list at Noble's Hospital and I will see you.'

WPCs Hillary, Hancox and Round on guard duties. (Reproduced by permission of the Metropolitan Police Authority (Heritage Centre))

On the Sunday she delivered the internee to see the specialist and then it was her turn. The specialist was at her head and his assistant at her feet and they twisted her like a rope, she sweated with pain and fright as she was quite sure he had broken her back, then her legs were lifted up over her head. Afterwards she was exhausted and she and the internee returned to Port Erin, where she went to her bed for the rest of the day.[13]

Repatriation

During October of 1941, there were a number of internee exchanges; the *Sunday Express*, London 5th Oct 1941 reported that:

"*Forty-eight German women, who are to be exchanged for*

50 *British women now held by the Germans, arrived at a north-west port from the Isle of Man. They later joined a train for London. All of them are believed to be confirmed Nazis, who are being sent to Germany as soon as possible. They were removed at dawn yesterday from the women's internment camp at Port Erin, Isle of Man and shepherded into specially blacked-out railway carriages by an escort of London Metropolitan policewomen. At Douglas they were transferred to a double-decker bus, the windows of which were obscured with green canvas blinds. In the train which met them at the north-west port they were again cut off from the outside world by strong blinds over the windows. The women varied in age from 20 to 60. Two German Nuns were among the party and one child. Other women wore fur coats and smart clothes. They were mostly sunburned and looked anxious rather than happy at the prospect of rejoining their relatives in Germany.*"[14]

WHAT HAPPENS TO THEM DEPENDS ON GERMANY

The *Daily Mail*, 6th Oct 1941, included a picture of German internees waiting to be repatriated, their comment:

"*Some of the 43 German women internees who were to be repatriated. They arrived in London on Saturday night and spent yesterday behind barbed wire, guarded by women police. You can see a policewoman giving directions on the right of the picture. The women had an anxious Sunday, but the answer which had to be given to their questions was always the same: {What happens depends on your Government}.*"[15]

An extract taken from the *Daily Herald*, Manchester, 7th Aug 1941, made interesting reading:

"Women police 'snooping'?
Women police are providing a controversial topic in the Isle of Man. In some quarters resentment is being expressed that they are taking over general police duties when there is not enough work for the male police. These women, it is pointed out, were appointed originally for duty at the women's internment camps. Now, according to some critics, they are acting as 'snoopers on shopkeepers'. We have not turned up any mention of this 'resentment' from the shopkeepers in the south of the Island, so the said critics are unknown?"[16]

A cutting from *The Star*, London, 8th Oct 1941 stated that: "German women internees from the Isle of Man

Above right: Women internees waiting for repatriation (Courtesy of *The Daily Mail*, 6 Oct 1941)

Below: Women internees continue to wait for repatriation (Courtesy of *The Star*, London, 8 Oct 1941)

Guarded German Women Wait In London Garden

were still waiting today at a house in South London before starting their journey home under the exchange of prisoners' scheme. They are in the garden of the house, which was formerly a home for Jewish children."[17]

The *Sheffield Telegraph*, 8th Oct 1941, illustrated 'German nurses from the Isle of Man internment camp on their way to be exchanged for British nurses in German hands.'[18]

Closure of the camp

NURSES ON THEIR WAY BACK TO GERMANY

German nurses from Rushen Internment Camp exchanged for British nurses being held by the Germans. (Courtesy of *The Sheffield Telegraph*, 8 Oct 1941)

The WPCs were involved in the preparation, in September 1944, of the repatriation of a large number of internees as part of the Gothenburg Exchange of prisoners with Germany. A large quantity of luggage had to be searched and they filled the Port Erin bus station to the roof with the luggage. Sergeant Pike was in charge of the escort. The internees came from various camps around the Island, around 600 men, women and children, and left the Island for Liverpool. They left Liverpool on the Swedish liner *Drottningholm*, arriving in Gothenburg on the 9th September 1944.

The Rushen camp was now closing. On 5th September 1945 the WPCs collected the remaining married couples, women and children (around 200 from Port Erin and Port St Mary), and they travelled to Douglas by train, leaving Port Erin for the last time. The steamer left the Island around noon and sailed to Fleetwood, where the internee duties for the WPCs ended.

The Constabulary of the Isle of Man would not have coped with the manning of the male and female camps set up during WWII without the assistance of the volunteers from the Metropolitan and other UK police forces. Unlike the women's camps, the male camps in the Isle of Man were run by the military and guarded with armed personnel. It was considered appropriate that the women's camps would be sufficiently controlled by the local Constabulary with the assistance of WPCs from the UK and this proved to be the right decision.

Swedish liner *Drottningholm* which took internees to Gothenburg. (Private collection)

PART 4:
THE PEOPLE
IN THE
CAMPS –
INTERNEES
AND LOCALS

INTERNEE PERSONALITIES AND STORIES

The Wehrhan Family – Nazi … or … nice?

Described in many publications as a 'notorious Nazi', Wanda Wehrhan was one of the characters I researched for this book. I read that this Pastor's wife was a trouble-maker, bribing young internees to return to Germany and agitating for segregation. I was intrigued.

The redoubtable Wanda Werhran, née Goeppert, was born in Lodz, Poland, in August 1891. Her Lutheran family owned a large hat-making factory employing over 500 people. She helped her mother and inherited her mother's skills in organisation. With orders from Russia, England, Germany and the large Jewish community in Poland, Wanda became fluent in these languages by the time she was 15 years old.

She met and fell in love with Theobald Immanuel Fritz Wehrhan, a Lutheran Pastor from Poznan, and despite a 20-year age gap, in May 1916, her parents agreed to their marriage. They had five children: Dietrich, Gunter, Isolde, Helmut and Gisela.

Sons Dietrich and Gunter were born in Poland in 1917 and 1919, while Fritz was on active service as a Field Chaplain. He had been visiting his mother, who had moved to Berlin to be close to her sister, when WWI was declared, and had served as a provincial Pastor in Flanders before being discharged and returning to his appointment as Pastor of the German Evangelical Christ Church in Westminster in 1920. The German Embassy was in the parish of this church and the Pastor had a duty to officiate at all the official services. Wanda was delighted to join him and settled in their new home in Barnes with their young sons.

Wanda relished the role of Pastor's wife. While Fritz fulfilled various honorary roles (President of the German Seamen's Mission; Vice President of the German Protestant Churches of Great Britain; Director of the Society of Friends of Foreigners in Distress [the Quakers]), Wanda was organising a

Frtiz and Wanda Wehrhan. (Courtesy of Nina Miconi)

CHAPTER TWELVE

Where Isolde learned her acting skills - the children entertaining Gisela (with the suitcase). (Courtesy of Nina Miconi)

women's retreat for 'fallen women', women's clubs at the church, and every month an open house gathering for members of the congregation. She prepared huge buffets for this and planned musical entertainment.

Isolde was born in January 1921 in London, followed by Gisela in 1925, and both were schooled at home, before passing examinations to attend Richmond Girls' School.

While Wanda played the lovely Bechstein piano, Fritz's favourite instrument was the French horn. When the family was together, Gunter, Isolde and Gisela were expected to entertain the guests; Fritz had made a stage at the end of the garden for the performances.

Gisela. (Courtesy of Nina Miconi)

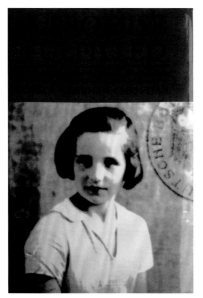

To provide some extra income Wanda ran a small finishing school, coaching young ladies in social graces, taking them to the theatre, improving their language skills, and it was one of these wealthy young ladies that her son Dietrich later married.

Arrest

Wanda was horrified when her husband was arrested in 1939, despite having a letter from the Home Secretary giving him permission to stay in London and continue his pastoral work with German refugees. However, a member of the congregation, Major General Ashmore, secured his early release.

Major General Ashmore had become a friend of Fritz while attending services, initially to improve his German language skills. The General continued to find the sermons uplifting and one day went to Fritz to confess his part in shooting down a dirigible and killing 20 German airmen in WWI when he was in charge of London's air defences. They visited the site where the airmen had been buried in Potters Bar and found it derelict – Fritz called for volunteers from the congregation and the site was restored to a respectable resting place. Major General Ashmore and Fritz organised a rededication service with a procession led by WWI veterans and a military band. Ashmore went on to establish the Royal Observer Corps

Ashmore's intervention in Fritz's internment was short-lived. Fritz was re-arrested in January 1940, and despite numerous letters vouching for his good character he was to remain interned. (Years after Fritz's death, Wanda's constant appeals to the British authorities and Members of Parliament finally secured permission for the copies of the letters to be delivered to her.)

Organised as usual, Wanda realised that with anti-German feeling running high all aliens were facing arrest. She prepared for the removal of their treasured possessions, the Bechstein piano and musical instruments. All the china and crystal had been packed and collection had been arranged for the very day that the police arrived to arrest Wanda. Gisela was just leaving for school and had already been told that in the event of Wanda's arrest Hilly (Hildegard Hyneman), Wanda's closest friend, would take care of her and Isolde. Gisela remembers being unable to see her diminutive mother because of the packing cases as she waved goodbye to her. She cried all the way to school.

Wanda was sent to Holloway. She was surprised to find the Sisters from the Dalston Hospital had been arrested too. They told her that Isolde was now one

Tele: Battersea 6109.
Organist der deutschen
BOTSCHAFTS-KIRCHE,

LONDON.

101, TRINITY ROAD
LONDON.S.W.17.
9th October 1939.

As I have been Organist of the German Christ Church at Montpelier Place, S.W.7. for nearly 30 years, I have, of course, known Pastor Wehrhan intimately during the whole of his Pastorate there, and I wish hereby to state that during the whole of that period, I have never heard him make any reference to or speak about either German or English politics whatsoever.   It is with profound reg: that I learn of his removal by the authorities from his Ministry, especially as the congregation consists of elderly people who have been resident in England for very many years, and I sincerely hope the Authorities will see their way to reconsider their decision and allow Pastor Wehrhan to come back and resume his ministry to a desolate congregation

Signed Wm F. Hall
Englishman

Letter of support for Fritz from the organist at the German Christ Church in Montpelier, London. (Courtesy of Nina Miconi)

of just a handful of nurses caring for people injured in local bombing raids. Wanda was leaving her children to endure nightly bombing raids. She still had no knowledge of where Fritz had been taken. What she saw as the unfairness of the situation prompted her determination to help those around her and gather her family together. Hilly telephoned the Matron at the Dalston Hospital, where Isolde was a Deaconess nurse in training, and asked her to inform Isolde of the situation.

Internment

The Deaconess nurses had led a sheltered life caring for the sick and disadvantaged. Many had joined the convent-like community at Sarepta Bethel as teenagers and had little or no knowledge of the political troubles in Germany. Wanda, as far as I can see, had never been to Germany, and there was an

Extracts from a letter from Wanda to the Swiss Delegation detailing problems that some of the internees were experiencing. (Courtesy of Nina Miconi)

increasing feeling of injustice among both Wanda and the nurses as, along with refugees fleeing oppression, they were herded into trains and spent the night in appalling conditions, in what had been described as a football stadium with an inadequate provision of sanitation. The following morning they endured being jeered and spat at as they walked to the ship that was to transport them to an unknown destination. Canada? Australia?

The final destination was much closer to home – a lovely holiday Island in the Irish Sea – the Isle of Man. Two seaside villages in an area at the southern tip of the Island had been set aside as Rushen Internment Camp, with some grand holiday accommodation on the promenades. For the next five years, for some, home was to be Port Erin and Port St Mary. (The sheading of Rushen is one of the six administrative divisions of the Island originally from Viking times. Each sheading would have sufficient men –25 to 60 – to crew a longboat.)

Wanda travelled with the Deaconesses and was billeted with them at Ard Chreg, a large guest house overlooking the beautiful Port Erin bay. Restrictions were few, newspapers were available, and there was freedom to move around the villages within the barrier area. However, everyone required a permit – not just the internees. The residents were effectively interned alongside the internees.

The Letter Campaigns

Wanda's first acquisition was an old typewriter, invaluable in her quest to find out Fritz's whereabouts and to get her daughters to the safety of the Isle of Man. Wanda wrote to the Commandant on an almost daily basis: requests for shoe leather and a small remuneration for the Deaconesses; cod liver oil, and milk for the pregnant women; changes of billets. There was an endless flood of letters to the Swiss Legation, the newspapers, the Lutheran Church – and the Commandant.

It was Wanda's desire to protect the 214 internees that she had listed as wishing to return to Germany. This list was compiled when there were nearly 4,000 persons in the camp. One letter mentioned a young girl who wished to return to her parents and was suffering 'pin pricks' living in a house with Jewish refugees who saw her as a Nazi.

She was successful in procuring religious text books for the Sunday schools run by the Deaconesses. She also sourced funds which the Commandant and Sister Anna Jochman distributed to those who wanted to be repatriated but would otherwise have had no help from refugee organisations because of their desire to return to their homeland.

Camp Leader?

There was an election for Camp Leader and Wanda was upset to lose out to Sister Anna by two votes. Wanda felt Sister Anna Jochman was far too unworldly to deal with the realities facing the internees. Despite not being elected, she continued to campaign for the internees who had complaints, with an unceasing flood of letters.

Further extract from Wanda's letter from to the Swiss Delegation. (Courtesy of Nina Miconi)

Finding Fritz

Wanda was instrumental in: arranging a Christmas communion in German for those who spoke little English; putting pressure on the Commandant for a meeting with husbands interned in the Island; and at last getting Gisela to the Island. But news that Fritz was on a ship to Canada caused most distress, especially when so many lives had been lost on the *Arandora Star* (see page 21). Wanda's anxiety increased as the weeks went by. Finally, a telegram to the camp from Hilly: FRITZ-NOT-ON-ARANDORA-STAR. Such relief, Wanda was determined to have Fritz returned not only to England but transferred to the Island. Wanda could not understand how a rather frail man of over 70 could be sent to a Canadian labour camp, but it was later learned that many men had swapped identities, which is why identification had taken so long. We do not know whether Fritz had tried to help someone in this way.

Gisela and Isolde united

After successfully getting Gisela across to the Island (see Teenager's Tale page 122), next came Isolde. Isolde's natural talents in acting were to see her starring in the dramatic productions that entertained the internees and residents. Willie Blasé from the Lilliput Troupe (a group of dwarf actors), detained while in a show in London, was a skilled playwright. He would borrow a book from the library and within days the internees were rehearsing another play that he had written.

Wanda's joy at having her daughters close to her is shown in the photograph of them all strolling arm in arm on Port Erin promenade in suits knitted by Wanda. And there was further good news. After the three of them sharing one room, two bedrooms had become vacant at Mona House, so the girls had a room and Wanda finally had a bed to herself. When they left the Golf Links Hotel for the comfort of Mona House, some of the residents wrote a moving poem to her, describing her as 'Mrs Pastor'. I feel certain she saw herself in that role in the camp.

In Parting

Your courageous persuasions and ceaseless urging,
Selfless devotion brought about that everyone's wish became reality

And collected us Germans together.
A life of camaraderie soon developed,
Sorrow and joy shared with cheerful song.
It's apparent we had happier times
Mrs Pastor alone brought this about.

Hotel Bellevue I.O.M.

Fritz's Arrival

Now all Wanda's energy could be channelled into efforts to have Fritz returned to her. Against all the odds, in 1943, she succeeded. Fritz arrived at the men's camp in Ramsey but he was so ill that Wanda appealed to Inspector Cuthbert who arranged for Fritz to be transferred to a home he had found for the family above a shoe shop.

Fritz had to be carried upstairs by the ambulance men who brought him to Rushen Camp. Wanda and Isolde nursed him day and night, and after many weeks he began to recover and asked to be repatriated. The request was denied. Fritz then wrote to the authorities saying that in that case they would all stay in the Island because he would never be separated from his family again.

Closure of the Camp and the Wehrhan's Return to Germany

By this time the camp was being readied for closure so the permission to leave was finally granted. The local newspaper reported on the frail old man following the women from Rushen onto the boat leaving the Island.

The always organised Wanda seemed to have slim awareness of the circumstances they would face in Germany after repatriation. She was totally unprepared – no home, no money. She sold her hand-knitted clothes to provide some food for the family. The girls were told they had to join anti-aircraft units, but after protestations Gisela was allowed to work on a farm and Isolde rejoined the Deaconess nursing order at Potsdam hospital.

Berlin was home until the Church could find a place for them in the countryside away from the nightly bombings – this was in Icking, Bavaria, but it was very basic and they had to share with another family. They did not, as suggested choose to live in an area where the infamous Goebbels' family lived, nor was it a Nazi enclave.[1]

It was not a satisfactory situation, but then a local couple befriended them and offered an annex in their home. Paul was an architect and Else Wenz a famous book illustrator. They became lifelong friends and were a great comfort when Fritz and Wanda were informed that their beloved Isolde had been killed by a British bomb in April 1945. It had taken 10 months before the news reached them that Isolde had died protecting a child from the bomb that killed her. By a miracle the child was pulled alive from the rubble.

The Sons

As for Wanda's sons, Dietrich was working for Bayer in Germany when war was declared and was immediately called for mandatory service in the army. He was killed in Tunis in 1942.

Gunter believed he was part of a conspiracy to oust Hitler and was discovered. Gunter was on holiday in Holland when war was declared, and having worked for Leitz GmbH in London, he went to the company headquarters in Wetzlar. Mr Leitz gave him a job as a photographer and he became part of the family. However, with the help of his uncles in the Dutch underground movement, he escaped to the USA in November 1939.

Helmut, born in October 1923, had begun his preparation for the ministry in the Bethel Seminary, Bielefeld. He could not face the prospect of killing anyone and it must have tested his faith to be at war. The last that Wanda heard from him was in May 1943. His remains were never found and Wanda kept a suit in the wardrobe for him hoping that one day he would return.

Post-War and a Promise Fulfilled

Heartbroken and frail, Fritz died on 17th May 1951. Wanda continued visiting the sick and was an active member of the Church until her death on 29th June 1971. She kept copies of all the letters she had written in the camp hoping that Gisela would one day write their story. Gisela promised her mother she would, and in 2003 *A Promise Fulfilled: Memories of World War II and its Aftermath*, was published to acclaim by Gisela Wehrhan Christian and Martha A. Malamud [Professor in Classics Department, Buffalo University].

The Enigma

Still eager to find out more, I traced Gisela's daughter, Nina, to the USA. She generously gave me a shoebox full of Wanda's letters written in Rushen Camp. It was plain that Wanda Wehrhan was a woman fiercely devoted to her husband and family. Her determination throughout the difficulties in her life was sustained by her undying religious faith. Reading Wanda's love letters to her husband (translated opposite), however, brought me to tears. They showed an unexpected aspect of this woman who had been the bane of Rushen Camp.

12 year old Gisela. (Courtesy of Nina Miconi)

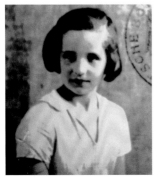

Gisela's story – a Teenager's Tale of Troubled times.

My name is Gisela Wehrhan. I was born in London in 1925. I have an older sister Isolde born in 1923 and three brothers, Dietrich and Gunter were born in Poland in 1917 and 1919 Helmut was born in London in 1923.

We lived in a large house in Barnes, Papa was the senior Lutheran cleric in London, he had two large congregations and he was a Director of the British Society of Friends for Foreigners in Distress. He was honorary chaplain to the German Embassy that was in his

Translation of a love
letter from Fritz to
Wanda. (Courtesy of
Nina Miconi)

Translation by Gisela W. Christian of Father's letter to my Mother for their Silver Anniversary,
he being detained in a Canadian camp and she in Port Erin on the Isle of Man

Internment Camp R
Army Base Post Office
Ottawa, Canada

May 9, 1941

My beloved Wanduschel!

As a sign that on this day I am thinking of you with abiding love and faithful gratitude, I am writing this
little letter to you today. Here it is now 11:00 PM, i.e., 7:00 PM in Lodz (Poland), and that is the time in
which we were united with each other for time and eternity under the word of Isaiah Ch. 54, v. 10. And if
we let the past 25 years glide through our memories in our current solitude, then we must gratefully
acknowledge that our Heavenly Father has, despite much care and despite this horrible separation, richly
blessed our union, especially through our dear children, who gave us much anxiety, but also provided us
the greatest joys. I wonder if they too might be remembering this day? (Translator's Note: Before the
war we children always pampered our parents on their anniversary, preparing breakfast trays decorated
with flowers and cards, each of us expressing our gratitude to them for their love and perpetual care for
our well-being). I can clearly sense that you too are thinking of me and that you carry me, as always, but
especially today, in your loving and interceding prayerful heart. I sent a telegram to you specifically
for this day. I hope you received it on time. With letters it will become increasingly more difficult,
timewise, so I will therefor send you a telegram more frequently.

Thank you so much for your letter of April 5. I am so glad that you are well and that Gisela is keeping
busy learning in order that, hopefully, time isn't totally lost for her. You don't mention Isolde and I am
deeply worried for her. If only she could join you there. Should I too submit a petition to this effect? If
only she would send me a note. I haven't heard from her since October.

And this is my deepest and greatest wish; that our dear Lord may soon grant us a couple of quiet and
peaceful years together with all our dear ones. I am therefore doing everything I can for my health, so
that I may survive. You need not be anxious for me as our provisions here are quite adequate. But I am
worried about you, especially our lanky Gisela. I wonder if you received the money, 4 Pounds, 7 Shillings
and 10 Pence, from the Springer Bank? Would you be able to buy some extras? Through Prior
Marczinski of Buenos Aires (of the Lutheran Relief Organization in Argentina) I am financially cared for.
Much, much love and God's blessings. Greetings to Gisela, the "Sisters", and to our lonely Lolle in
London, from your old and faithful

Fridolin

parish and Pastor to the Dalton Hospital. Mama was a great help to him, she
spoke five languages fluently including Yiddish, which was useful with so many
German Jewish refugees arriving in the area.

Each month she organised an open house, with the help of the church ladies.
Tables of food were laid out and Papa and Mama, both skilled pianists, would
entertain. We were also encouraged to entertain and a stage was built in the
garden for our performances. Isolde was a natural actress, Helmut was a
wonderful mimic, and I sang – but without much skill.

We were all schooled at home. Hildegard Hyneman taught us mathematics,
even after Isolde and I passed the scholarship to Richmond Grammar School,
and the boys were sent to boarding school in Germany, a decision that led to
them being conscripted into the German army. Hilly came every Friday to help
with the church administration and join us for dinner.

When war was declared Papa was expected, as the senior Lutheran Cleric in
London, to stay in post and help with the growing influx of refugees, and he
had a letter from Herbert Morrison the Labour MP to this effect. Mama was
shocked when in September 1939 he was arrested. She appealed to Major
General Ashmore. Lord Ashmore had originally gone to Christ Church to learn
German but he enjoyed Fritz's sermons and became a member of the

congregation. He secured Papa's release.

In March 1940 Papa was re-arrested and, despite numerous letters from members of the congregation, he was not released. Mama, ever the organiser, made a photograph album of memories for each of us in case we were separated by war. In May 1940 early in the morning the police arrived to arrest her.

Isolde was at work, she was in training at the Dalston Hospital as a Deaconess nurse. Mama had been fearing that all German nationals would be arrested and had organised professional packers to pack all the china and crystal. The packing cases were stacked high in the hall and I remember Mama kissing me and waving me off to school, but she was so small I could not see her above the crates. She told me I had to be brave and that Hilly would collect me that evening from school. I cried all the way to school.

Hilly was a wonderful friend and she kept me busy. The Beckstein piano, Papa's musical instruments, including his beloved French horn, and linen were all to be packed and sent into storage with the packing cases. The car was on the drive and one day we saw the man next door and his friend start the car and drive it away.

The house now emptied, Isolde and I moved in with Hilly. Isolde spent what little time off she had trying to find out where Mama had been taken, but with nightly bombings in London the Dalston Hospital was inundated with casualties. All the senior nurses who were Deaconesses from Germany had been arrested and interned. Isolde was worn out with work and worry. I concentrated on my schoolwork, many times reading by torchlight under the blankets to block out the noise of the bombings.

At school during the second week of September 1940, the door of our classroom flew open and two policewomen walked in. 'Stand up Gisela Wehrhan,' said one of them. 'You are to be arrested and interned.' I was terrified, my classmates all started crying, I was crying and begging them to let me speak to Isolde or Hilly, but to no avail. They held my arms and marched me to a waiting car which took us to a hotel in Charing Cross where more children were gathered. Most were younger than me. Everyone was crying.

We were given a bag of jam sandwiches and a label was fastened to everyone's coat. We were marched to the train station and onto a waiting train. The journey took hours. Most fell asleep exhausted from crying, and asking where we were going. No one would tell us.

Once off the train we were lined up in pairs, I counted about eighty, and with our labels flapping in the breeze and passers by jeering at us we walked to the waterfront. Most had never been on a boat and we were hurried up the wooden ramp to a large room. The noise was dreadful. We were all screaming and crying, terrified of what was going to happen to us.

The policewoman stood on a chair and shouted above the noise: 'We are taking you to your mothers – but only if you stop making this noise!' There was instant silence, soon followed by retching as the boat tossed from side to side.

When we arrived we were put on a little train. It rattled through the green fields, and after a short ride we were once again assembled in pairs and marched past the shops to a small hall. The doors opened and our mothers were lining the walls. Everyone hugged and cried. After some paperwork we walked hand in hand along the lovely promenade to our billet.

I had to share a bed with Mama but I did not mind. I slept like a baby. The next morning, we had porridge and bread and jam for breakfast. The Sisters from the Dalston Hospital were also in our house, but the lady who ran the house was not very nice to us, she thought we were the enemy.

Mama had bought a second-hand typewriter and set up a little office in our bedroom. I can still hear the noise of the tapping of the keys on that old typewriter and when she had finished the tap tapping, sending letters for the day, the click, clicking of her knitting needles took over as background noise.

Daily life in Port Erin after the dark days of the Blitz in London was wonderful. The shops and cafés were all open, there were very few restrictions, we could not move outside the village as there were guards at a barrier and we had to be in our houses by 9 p.m., but apart from that we played every day on the beautiful beach, we went swimming, caught shrimps and clams, and cooked them in an old can, the shops had plenty of food and I grew taller and taller.

Wanda and her two daughters in their knitted suits. (Courtesy of Nina Miconi)

I made new friends, some were local girls but they knew the rock climbs better than Eleanor and I. One day I slipped on the rocks and badly damaged my ankle. Later on, when I twisted it again, Dr Frieberg suggested that I was old enough at 15 years to look after her baby daughter, rather than risk another bad sprain and end up crippled.

The days of sunshine were fading into the mists of autumn and after Mama's numerous letters of complaint to the Commandant we were moved to a nicer hotel and life settled into a pattern: morning prayers, school work, and in the evening, helping to serve the dinner, with my friend Eleanor. More people came to ask for help. The Commandant must have received daily letters from Mama, as did any organisation worldwide that she felt could help our situation. The Jewish people received parcels with tinned salmon, cigarettes and other goodies as did the refugees, but any of the Germans that wanted to return to Germany, like Dr Frieberg with elderly parents living in Germany, and the Deaconesses and Lutheran Pastors who were attached to the village of Bethel where they had been trained, received no such luxuries.

The Pastors' wives and children were soon all billeted together after numerous requests that women who wished to return to Germany after the war wished to be billeted together. To avoid the 'pin pricks' from others, Dr Frieberg and many others who wanted to return to their elderly parents or, as was the case with the Lutherans to their mother house at Bethel, were moved to the Belle View, a lovely hotel with a large fireplace in the hall around which we all gathered for evening prayer, accompanied by the clicking of knitting needles. Mama knitted lovely suits for us. One had a pretty pleated skirt. She knitted a jumper in a few days and these provided a little extra money for food, but the constant click click and the tap tap of the old typewriter would drive me from our room. Even when it was cold I would go and sit on the rocks. Sometimes my friend Dagmar would join me and we would dream of our future. Dagmar wanted to fly aeroplanes which seemed like a pipe dream to me, but after the war we kept in touch and she became a commercial pilot.

Isolde was a British citizen over 18 and could not be interned, but Mama's persistence in writing to the Home Office paid off and Isolde finally joined us. Such joy. The clicking needles had produced three beautiful knitted suits and we strolled down the Promenade delighted to be together.

Isolde became the star of many of the amateur dramatic productions in the camp. We went to watch the shows and I remember one time she played a cockney girl, her accent so perfect one would have thought she was born within the sound of Bow bells. We were all sharing a room at the Belle View when mother heard that two rooms had become available at Mona House, and, after more tap tapping, secured the adjoining rooms, so Mama had a bed to herself. She was no longer waking in agony as my long legs kicked her varicose veins.

The two ladies that ran the house were so nice. They had a little girl, Brenda, living with them. Mama knitted suits, swimming costumes, and made dresses for Brenda from discarded curtain fabric. When I met with Brenda Watterson she said I was the best dressed girl in Port Erin, and she still has a book that Wanda gave her for her birthday,

One morning at prayers Mama told us that Papa was joining us but that he was very ill, we were once again to move, to a flat above a shoe repairers in the next village of Port St Mary. I felt guilty as I carried the typewriter to our new home, having complained about its noisy keys, when the avalanche of letters it produced had brought Papa back to us.

Isolde and I were horrified when we saw Papa. He arrived in an ambulance too weak to walk, hardly able to speak. We did what we could to help but Mama nursed him day and night and finally he was able to walk again and we would help him to a seat by the harbour to benefit from the sea air.

Our next move was to be to Germany. All our possessions in storage in London had been destroyed in the bombing, so we had little to organise. Having packed all our clothes, a letter arrived to say that Isolde and I could not go with our parents. Papa said we would never be separated again and filled in the official form to say we would stay on the Island.

Did we go or did we stay?

We left the Island. We were met on arrival in Germany by the Lutheran Bishop and went to stay with Dietrich's wife and the baby that was born after Dietrich's death.

Dietrich's family had a little house in the country and they let us have it as a home, but we had not known how destroyed Germany was, and I worked on a farm to provide food, Mama sold knitted items to buy meat, and Isolde returned to her training as a nurse in Potsdam. We did not know until Papa died two years after our arrival that dearest Isolde had been killed by a British bomb only six weeks after we arrived in Germany.

Mama continued her work with the church, committed to helping others by visiting the sick and elderly, work that continued until her death.

Isolde, Gisela and Dietriche's daughter, Heidi (whom he never saw) in 1944 a few weeks after moving to Bavaria. (Courtesy of Nina Miconi)

Dietrich Killed
Helmut Killed
Isolde Killed
Papa Died
Mama Died
Gunter in Dutch underground escaped to USA
I inherited Mama's gift for languages and worked for the American Army.

Gerhard and Maria Bersu (26th September 1889 – 19th November 1964)

As a teenager, Gerhard worked on the excavation of the Romerschanze stronghold near Potsdam, Brandenburg in Germany. He became fascinated by archaeology and went on to live his dream, becoming one of the leading excavators of his day. Even before his studies in geology and archaeology were completed he was appointed as assistant in the Office of Monuments in Stuttgart.

Renowned archaeologist Gerhard Bersu. (Wikipedia)

Bersu volunteered to fight for Germany during WWII and he was seconded by the German High Command to be in charge of monument protection in the occupied countries, and at the end of the war he worked in the Ceasefire and Peace Delegation to arrange the return of cultural property.

By 1924 he was working at the German Archaeological Institute completing his studies, which began in 1911, and his excavations were seen as a milestone in the study of systemic settlement, which led to the Institute becoming one of the world's leading archaeological organisations.

With the rise of National Socialism, Bersu's Jewish parentage became an issue and he was forced to retire in 1937. He left Germany and emigrated to Britain with his wife, Maria, and was able to continue his work. In England he directed a series of excavations and won many accolades worldwide, with further acclaim for his excavation at Little Woodbury in Wiltshire.

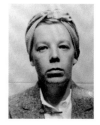

Maria Bersu. (Courtesy of Manx National Heritage)

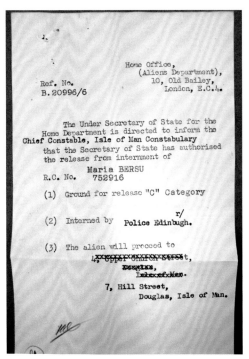

Letter detailing release of Maria Bersu. (Courtesy of Manx National Heritage)

Below: Aerial view of the Viking Ship burial – Balladoole. (Courtesy of Manx National Heritage)

Bottom right: Looking out over Scarlett from the Viking Ship burial. (iomguide.com)

At the outbreak of the Second World War, Bersu and his wife Maria, both German nationals, were arrested and interned, Gerhard in Douglas and his wife in Camp W, Rushen, although for some time, like many others, they were unaware that they were both in the Isle of Man.

In Douglas, most evenings he visited his fellow archaeologist Paul Jacobsthal (1880–1957) at Hutchinson Camp who, until interned, had been working in Dublin. This was strictly against the rules, but seemed to have been openly discussed among other internees.

His reputation as an archaeologist did not escape the notice of Eleanor Megaw, the Temporary Director of the Manx Museum, who decided to utilise these considerable skills with sponsorship from the Society of Antiquities. Gerhard and Maria were now living in Primrose Cottage in the married camp, in Port St Mary.

They carried out a sustained programme of research at the highest level, with Maria surveying and documenting the sites and Gerhard directing the digs. The digs were coordinated by the Manx Museum using parties of internees working under armed guard.

As a token of appreciation for the work 'of this great archaeologist', when Miss Megaw visited the sites she would drop a little box of Gerhard's beloved snuff into his wellington boot.

The Bersus discovered the Viking ship burial at Balladoole, and the Celtic discoveries at Ronaldsway, Ballanorris and Ballacagan. They stayed in the Island to finish the digs after peace had been declared.

After the war, in 1947, Bersu was invited to be the Professor of the Royal Irish Academy by the controversial Eamon de Valera, who trod a fine line between Nazi Germany and Britain in WWII. Bersu stayed there until 1950 when he took up his former position as Director of the Romano Germanic Commission (the German Archaeological Institute).

His challenge was to position the Institute in the new political system and rebuild the war-ravaged Institute building and, before his retirement in 1956, the building was reopened.

Christa Citron (1920–2014) – a promising career forfeited

Christa Citron had trained as a ballet dancer and was due to make her London stage debut on the day she was arrested. She never did make her debut and later said, 'Every time I see ballet, I feel half sad not to have been able to fulfil what I could have done.'

After a month in Holloway Prison, she arrived in the Island and was interned in Port St Mary. She recalled: 'Karin Berkler and I came to Miss Gorry on The Promenade. We were in the attic, together in an old bed, surrounded by all the chamber pots. I wished I had stayed in Holloway.'[2] Christa was involved in some dancing at the Ballaqueeney Hydro while she was in Port St Mary.

Christa Citron.
(Courtesy of Mrs Iris Burton)

One year later, she and Karin moved to the Towers Hotel in Port Erin. She described Port Erin as a 'cultural centre' with German scientists, artists and doctors, who tried to do things for other internees. She danced: there was an English entertainments manager who arranged plays and dances in Collinson's Café and St Catherine's Church Hall.

Later, she met Iris's mother, Mrs Henrietta McGlashen, who had seen her dance and invited her to stay at her house, 'Chatsworth', where she was very happy.

Christa worked in kippering with Karin – she stacked them and Karin put them into boxes. They also made things like cardigans, with diamond patterns, from Loaghtan wool, leather slippers, gloves and jewellery and these were sold at 'bazaars' (craft fairs).

Christa in training.
(source unknown)

Christa was repatriated on 31st August 1944 as part of the German exchange organised by the Red Cross. The ship to Germany passed close to Port Erin and everyone was waving. Landladies were in tears. Christa returned to Berlin, looked after her mother and never married

Christa Citron became a close friend of Manxwoman Iris Burton (see page 162), she exchanged letters with Iris for 50 years and they remained in close touch until Christa died in January 2014, aged 94. Christa returned to the Island in 1987 and 2005, staying with Iris, as part of the 'Wire & Wool' Event – a re-enactment about the internment camp. In an interview with Culture Vannin, she said that her return in 1987 brought back happy memories because her time with Iris and her parents was like a home.

Memories of Port Erin – Bradda Head.
(Sandra Davidson)

Jochanan Frank's journey

Jochanan Frank was six years old when he first arrived in Port Erin. His parents, Emil and Eva Frank, were both eventually internees in Rushen. Many years later, when he was an adult living in Israel, a friend brought him a visitor's guide to the Isle of Man. Amazingly,

Jochanan still had his childhood drawing of Milner Tower with Loaghtan sheep, and the comparison triggered an urge to visit the Isle of Man again to see if what lay buried in his memory was really true.

The Journey

Aged six, he had travelled from London by train to Fleetwood, via Crewe and Liverpool. Then there was a rough four-hour sea crossing to Douglas, followed by another train journey from Douglas to Port Erin. In 2000, by contrast, he hopped on a plane at City Airport and was at Ronaldsway around an hour later.

His Worst Memory

He recalled that Collinson's Café was where the internee families were able to meet together before the Rushen married camp opened. It held a traumatic memory for Jochanan. It was there he discovered that his father wouldn't be coming: it was three years before Jochanan's family was reunited. His father had been sent to Australia on the infamous HMT *Dunera* – the refugee internees were badly treated during the voyage and had their belongings pilfered. The Captain was court-martialled.

The Schoolboy

In 2000, Jochanan looked for the school on Dandy Hill that he had attended, but it had been demolished. He was in Form 11B at the Port Erin Camp School in 1941. His school report said:

> **English:** *Excellent pupil. Keen and intelligent. Inquisitive.*
> **Handicrafts**: *Quite good.*
> **Gymnastics**: *Good.*
> Signed by
> **Form Master**: J Wolff
> **Head Master**: Chas. A Kidd

Presents from Family Afar

Jochanan's little sister longed for a doll's pram from their father, 'a red one', like other girls whose fathers were interned in the Island, but three years was a long time to wait.

Jochanan's uncle, a tailor in Israel, sent him a red suit with leggings and a cap, which when outgrown was passed to his little sister. An auntie sent plasticine and a cut out aeroplane.

Jochanan collected all the stamps from the family letters, from Germany, Australia and the Middle East. Stamp collecting was popular then.

Jochanan Frank's father had been transported to Australia on the notorious HMT *Dunera*. (Private collection)

Johanna Metzger-Lichtenstern (1916–2012) – opera star to internee

Johanna (Hanni) Metzger was born on 8th April 1916, the youngest of three girls. Her father ran a tobacco shop in Berlin and her mother was a seamstress. The family was Orthodox.

Johanna Metzger-Lichtenstern. (Jewish Chronicle, 8th June, 2012)

Hanni left school in 1933 and spent a year living in Denmark in preparation for kibbutz life, but, as this did not appeal to her, she returned to Berlin. She went back to education and studied a course under pioneering educator, Nelly Wolffheim, which included music. Hanni had an incredible voice and Wilhelm Guttman, a celebrated Jewish baritone, taught her for free.

Hanni made her stage debut, at a concert for the Jewish Winterhilfe relief campaign, as a mezzo-soprano, but switched to soprano, taking her first major part in the title role in von Suppe's operetta, *The Beautiful Galatea*. Her future husband, Paul Lichtenstern, was the accompanying pianist and they were engaged in 1938. Hanni and her family left Germany and came to England on a domestic permit in July 1939, with Paul following soon after. They were married in March 1940, only to be interned in the Isle of Man within a few months.

While in the Rushen Women's Internment Camp, she became friendly with Dora Diamant, the last lover of Franz Kafka, who taught her Yiddish songs. Paul and Hanni were released in 1941 and went to London, where they were bombed out. They lived briefly in Bangor with Hanni's grandparents before moving to Manchester, where Paul made army buckets in a factory. Eventually they moved back to London, where their son was born. Hanni again took singing lessons, this time from top Jewish singer Sabine Kalter, who had also been forced out of Germany.

Paul began playing again as organist in Progressive synagogues and accompanied Hanni at concerts. In 1951 she sang at the Whitehall Theatre, the Rudolf Steiner Hall and the West End Great Synagogue. She sang at many events around the country and abroad, including the Ben Uri Arts Society and the Wigmore Hall. When the war ended, Hanni taught at the faith school of the New Liberal Jewish Congregation, Belsize Square. She created and founded both children's and adult choirs, performing Yiddish songs at the 1977 memorial service commemorating the Warsaw Ghetto uprising.

She stopped giving concerts in the 1980s when Paul retired, but kept her mind active with teaching, studying and entertaining at old folk's homes. Her husband, Paul, died in 1990, while Hanni stayed independent in her own home until she died on 22nd March 2012.

William Kaczynski – a life's work

William Kaczynski (aged four) and his brother Edward (a baby) accompanied their mother Edith into the women's internment camp in Port Erin. His mother's story is told in Chapter 15, but this is his story.

Like Jochanan Frank, William collected stamps. Postal communication was a vital lifeline in those times. By William's retirement, in 1989, he had amassed

William Kaczynski with
his book – *Fleeing from
the Führer – a Postal
History of Refugees from
Nazis.* (Courtesy of
William Kaczynski)

a large collection of WWII postal artefacts. From these he was shocked to learn that internees were scattered in camps all over the world:

"I found that those deemed aliens by the British state were sent as far away as Uganda, Mauritius, Jamaica and Cyprus. Some of them would never return."

In April 2015, William Kaczynski spoke on YouTube of his parents' experiences and their internment in the Isle of Man. Somewhat surprisingly, he was in sympathy with Churchill's 'collar the lot' move because he said there definitely were spies among those held in the Island.

He has made it his life's work to spread knowledge and understanding to ensure that the refugee experience in WWII is not forgotten. He has given talks, interviews and made school visits. And his experience is all the more relevant with the current influx of desperate refugees to Europe from Syria and other places.

In collaboration with Charmian Brinson, Professor of German Studies at Imperial College, London, he wrote *Fleeing from the Führer – a Postal History of Refugees from Nazis,* (2011). It was a monumental task which took four years and contains some very moving stories.

The main sadness for William and his brother, Edward, was that there were no tangible traces of their mother's singing career. She had been forced to stop performing in 1934 simply for being a Jew. All she had left to show for her career was her scrapbook of programmes where she had performed.

Once, when William was in New York (promoting his book – *Fleeing the Führer*), he was called by CBS Radio in Canada to ask if he would give a talk on the envelopes he collected. He agreed, not realising that he was actually 'on air' there and then!

A Canadian listener to that broadcast contacted him and asked if William would like to have the envelope of the last letter he had received from his parents. It was from a concentration camp.

When this Canadian next came to London he asked William if he had any recordings of his mother Edith singing, but the family had been looking for years with no success. The Canadian then suggested contacting Munich International Sound Archives. And there a 1928 Parlophone recording was found of Edith singing – *Der Rote Sarafan.* It was the most wonderful result and must have been quite overwhelming, after all that time, for the brothers to hear their mother's voice at the height of her fame.

William's son-in-law, Oliver Bloom, made it into a DVD, with cuttings from the scrapbook Edith had made of her career.

William and Edward kindly offered this to the Rushen Heritage Trust who played it at their 'Friend or Foe' exhibition in St Catherine's Church Hall, Port Erin, in the summer of 2016. That church hall is where Edith would have been registered for internment, along with over 3,000 plus other weary women and children, in May 1940.

Although William was not well enough to visit the exhibition his brother

Edward came and brought some of his family. We all had a meal together with some of our team, at Bradda Glen café.

The Munzer family – from persecution to peeress

Kurt Munzer, a 30-year-old businessman, could see the increasing difficulties for Jewish people in the small German town of Munster and planned his escape to Holland. Jews were allowed to travel, but not allowed to take any money out of the country, so he taped all his money to the underside of his car and drove over the Dutch border. He immediately claimed political asylum in the minor town of Enschede and because he had sufficient funds he was allowed to stay – though denied a work permit. The Dutch were welcoming and he made a living trading.

Frieda and Kurt were married in Holland. (Courtesy of Baroness Henig)

The young 17-year-old, Elfrieda Goetz, visited Kurt's shop on the first day she arrived in Enschede and they formed a friendship; Frieda came from a very wealthy family that, like Kurt, had fled from Germany. Frieda had enjoyed a good life before fleeing Germany and in Enshede that continued as she found a love of photography and became apprenticed to a local firm. After learning Dutch in three months she opened her own business.

The relationship between Frieda and Kurt blossomed, and then Kurt asked Frieda to marry him. Frieda felt she was too young, but her mother was convinced that in such unsettled times Frieda should have a secure future so there was a wedding.

The newly-weds were living too close for comfort to the German border and so moved to The Hague, but the news that the Dutch had surrendered on 14th May was devastating. Young Frieda, now five months pregnant, became completely hysterical, insisting they drove to the coast which Kurt knew was the only escape route.

In the harbour at Scheveningen, they came across a group of students who had 'liberated' a lifeboat. Frieda begged to go with them and they piled on board the little boat, which was made for perhaps 12 but now held 46 people. A fisherman helped them start the engine and the heavily overloaded *Zeemanshoop* ['Seaman's Hope'] slid out into the approaching night. Fortunately, the sea was calm and at first, they made good progress on one cylinder.

The *Zeemanshoop* ('Seaman's Hope'). (Moore/Rodguard published Holywell House publishing)

As night drew on, however, the boat broke down and they were helplessly adrift. The following day, by chance, they were spotted by a British destroyer. The crew aboard this ship included Manxman Chief Petty Officer (CPO) Leslie Collister. The ship had come off the West African Patrols and was heading to the Arctic convoys through the English Channel.

The group was taken aboard and revived with cups of hot tea. Their relief at this almost miraculous rescue must have been overwhelming. By contrast, on arrival in the UK port of Dover, they were horrified to be taken prisoner.

Frieda was put into London's Holloway Prison. She was terrified. Her friends told the Warden that she was pregnant and she was taken to the hospital wing

Refugees from the Dutch lifeboat, the *Zeemanshoop* safely aboard *HMS Venomous*. (Lt Peter Kershaw RNVR)

to be given some bromide to calm her nerves. This made Frieda even more hysterical: she thought they were trying to abort her baby and refused to take any medication.

It was not long, however, before Frieda was on the move again, by train and then boat, heading she knew not where. She was just one of 3,000 women internees and their children bound for the Isle of Man. She was particularly terrified now because for the first time in her life she had no support and no idea how she could manage.

A few days after her arrival in Rushen Camp, Frieda's spirits lifted. She was billeted in a grand hotel in Port Erin, and then learned that Kurt was also in the Island, in the men's camp in Douglas.

Frieda received wonderful maternity care. The Camp Commandant was a highly qualified nurse and midwife, and the health services established by her for the camp were said to be better than in England and for the general public in the Island. The other internees in the house all looked after her and there was no shortage of food. She said later, 'I could wander freely, clamber around from morning until night, I really enjoyed it'. Her joy was complete with the safe delivery of her baby, Grace Evelyn, in a 'wonderful maternity home' in Douglas.

Family letters exchanged. (Courtesy of Baroness Henig)

Kurt was allowed to visit and the men in his billet made a card and had a collection for the baby. When Frieda returned from hospital to Port Erin there was a gift from every one of her 70 friends in the hotel, even an electric fire for her room. Kurt wrote to Queen Wilhelmina of Holland telling of their daring escape, and she sent a superb layette for the baby.

When the married camp was established, Kurt joined Frieda and baby Eva in Port Erin. After two years in the Isle of Man they were finally allowed to return to England.

In 1943 Frieda had another baby, Ruth, who grew up to become an eminent Professor in European History, was awarded the CBE for her services to policing, and in June 2004 she was raised to the peerage. Ruth Munzer now Ruth Henig, is Baroness Henig of Lancaster and Deputy Speaker in the House of Lords. Of course none of this would have happened if her parents had not been rescued by HMS *Venomous*.

We invited Baroness Henig to open our second internment exhibition and she graciously accepted. It was a wonderful occasion. Then came a surprise.

One of the Directors of the Rushen Heritage Trust, Steve George, mentioned that his aunt was the widow of seaman, Leslie Collister, who was on the HMS *Venomous* at the time Ruth's family were rescued. Immediately, Ruth wanted to meet her and this was arranged. It was a memorable meeting for both women, seen here holding hands.

Mrs Collister and Baroness Henig meet for the first time. (Courtesy of Pamela Crowe)

Ira Rischowski (1899–1989) – a trailblazer for women in engineering

Ira was born in Germany to Jewish parents. Her father owned a shipyard. Aged five, she saw the compressed-air riveting process being used and immediately decided to become an engineer when she grew up. In 1919 she began her degree studies at Darmstadt University and was the only woman among 3,000 engineering students.

While at university she became a member of an anti-Nazi group and in 1936 moved, with her husband, to England. She worked initially as a domestic servant, since that was the only type of work the Home Office would allow her to do, but later joined an engineering business established by her ex-husband and his friends. Ira's children were living with her mother in Germany: in 1938 her mother brought them to England to live with Ira and this was the last time Ira was to see her mother.

Ira Rischowski. (Courtesy of Manx National Heritage)

As an alien, Ira was classified as Category C. She was arrested at the end of May 1940 and taken to the East End police station. Ira and others were given lunch and taken to a collecting station in Fulham where they spent the night. The next day they were accompanied by the Women's Voluntary Service on a train to Liverpool and, in the evening, were taken to the Isle of Man boat where there were cabins for some women, while others used lifebelts as pillows. They sailed to Douglas the following morning.

She initially stayed at the Golf Links Hotel in Port Erin,

but later moved to the smaller Baycliffe Hotel (Rushen Heritage Trust's registered office is now at Baycliffe).

Ira sent a questionnaire to internees at all the hotels and boarding houses, to check their attitudes and concerns, and brought the results to the attention of the Commandant, Dame Joanna Cruickshank.

Standards varied widely – some hotels treated the internees well, like summer guests, others were abominable, would not even supply towels and did not allow mothers to wash nappies. The Golf Links Hotel was of middling standard. Dame Joanna, who demanded a minimum standard, reacted positively to Ira's recommendations and things improved in the worst houses.

Thereafter Ira had monthly meetings with Dame Joanna, discussed grievances and said Dame Joanna was quite reasonable. One major issue in the early days was internee mail. There were delays of up to six weeks for letters, because initially there was no censorship office in Liverpool so letters were held. Having letters neither forwarded or received was very harrowing for internees.

At first there was no visiting of other houses, but this was later relaxed. In the summer of 1940 there was lots of freedom. Ira said the weather was lovely, the beach was crowded and the sands golden. Many people went swimming and you were allowed to visit shops: Ira liked the Manx wool – dirty but marvellous. The shopkeepers were friendly since the internees were year-round customers. Ira walked the hills and the golf course, had some clothes sent on and got some from the Service Exchange. Lots of the internees had been domestic servants and were good at creating or altering clothes.

Ira had to assist with general household duties, which included washing-up accompanied by her singing and this led to the formation of the Golf Links Choir. Some of the internees were well off while others had almost nothing. The older, richer women did not want to do their own washing and the Service Exchange was much used for laundry and hairdressing. Some internees made necklaces from seashells and sold them to Manx people for real money. They were very popular.

The internees were mainly Jewish or recent refugees who had not been able

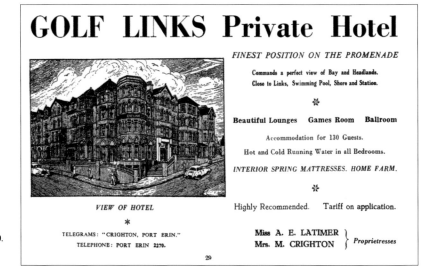

Golf Links Hotel c1960. (Courtesy of Isle of Man Tourism)

to establish connections and were therefore not considered reliable by tribunals.

Ira assisted with adult education classes and taught French, Spanish and technical drawing. She felt standards of education for children were fairly high, although some of the children had been disturbed by their experiences. When Minna Specht, the distinguished educationalist, was released, Ira, on her recommendation, ran her school until a new appointment could be made.

After the war, Ira resumed her career as an engineer, joined the Society of Women Engineers and gave speeches at international conferences.

Minna Specht (1879–1961) – education for the future

Born in Germany in 1879, Minna Specht was her parents' seventh child. The family lived at Reinbeck Castle, Schleswig-Holstein, acquired in 1874 and converted into a hotel. As the result of an accident, her father died in 1882, leaving the family in financial difficulty.

From 1884 to 1894, Minna was educated at a small private school and a girls' school in Bergedorf. Then from 1896 until 1899 she worked at a convent school in Hamburg, where she trained as a teacher in order to help support the family. She worked as a governess and, in 1902, was invited by a former teacher at the convent school to teach at a new girls' school in Hamburg, where she discovered a love for teaching.

Starting in 1906, she attended university for three years, studying geography, history, geology and philosophy. When she completed her course she returned to the school in Hamburg, but in 1919, aged 40, she returned to university to study mathematics, gaining a qualification which allowed her to teach higher grades and become a head teacher.

Minna Specht.
(Courtesy of AdsD /
Friedrich-Ebert-
Foundation)

Until 1931 she taught at a number of progressive boarding schools then, in 1933, she returned to the Walkenmuhle school, near Kassel. The school was closed early in 1933, because Minna, as Head Teacher, 'would not conform to the Hitlerian principle of military education'[3]. She fled with some of the pupils to Denmark, where she established a school for German émigrés. In 1938, when the situation in Denmark changed, she left for Wales and later Bristol, where she was arrested. She was interned in May 1940, but her public opposition to the Nazis led to her release after one year.

She was interned in Port St Mary, where it soon became obvious that the internee children needed direction and purpose. She established a kindergarten for children up to the age of six years in Cowley's Café, which was a former boys' and infants' school. Across the road, at the Cornaa Boarding House, she established a school for 6–16 year olds.

Educational opportunities for adults were also provided.

Minna, along with many of the other teachers in the camp, had been affected by their experiences. As a result, efforts were made to educate the children in such a way that they would be prepared for the future, whether that should be in England or in Germany.

After she was released, Minna worked in London with young people who

Top right: Former infants' and boys' school in Port St Mary which, during the war was Cowley's Café. (Courtesy of Doreen Moule)

Above: Port St Mary – Cornaa Boarding House, a school for 6 – 16 year olds. (Courtesy of Doreen Moule)

had been brought up with Nazism, whose lives had been shattered by the war. In autumn 1945, she was the only German to be invited to Zurich for a conference about these children. There she was asked by Edith and Paul Geheeb to be head of the progressive boarding school, Odenwaldschule, which they had founded but had to leave in 1934. She ran the school from 1946 until 1951.

She became a member of the German commission for UNESCO and Associate of the Educational Institute of UNESCO in Hamburg. In this position, she worked to progress the methods of experiential learning established by Maria Montessori. As an Inspector of Schools, in 1955, she received the Goethe Plaque for Training and Education for her service in educational science, theory and practice. Her focus was self-determination and self-discipline. She died in 1964 in Bremen, Germany.

After her death, a primary school bearing her name was established in 1964 in the Schwanheim district of Frankfurt am Main. It is a community school with 950 pupils and 85 staff (2018).

Eva and Chris Rieger – An unexpected discovery

Johanna Rieger, mother of Eva & Chris. (Courtesy of Manx National Heritage)

While researching in the Manx National Heritage Library I came across a little brown box containing some papers and a bible.

The inscription read: *With best wishes from: From the German Deaconesses, The Three Salvationists.*

I knew from papers in the box that the bible was presented to Eva, the youngest daughter of Johanna Rieger, a Lutheran Pastor's wife (see Chapter 14). Eva was born in Port Erin on 21st November 1940. While I am sure the baby brought new joy, Mrs Rieger was struggling to cope with three other young children in an unheated hotel room with just a cold water washbasin. The Lutheran Deaconess midwives, who provided maternity care in Rushen Camp, helped as much as they could, but mother and baby ended up in the camp hospital.

There is no record of husband, Julius, being allowed to visit: he was interned in the Douglas camp. He had been a curate in Berlin then the family moved to London in 1930, attached to the historic St George's Lutheran Church.

Letters between husband and wife relate to the difficulties of feeding 'little

From the German Deaconesses, the three Salvationists, Sister Emmeline and Rev. J. B. Harrison. (Courtesy of Manx National Heritage)

Eva' and worrying about their finances. Money worries dominated much of their correspondence. After a time, Johanna and her family moved to the Belle Vue Hotel with the other Pastors' wives, which made life a little easier.

I searched the internet for 'Eva Rieger' and finally, in Liechtenstein, I found one who had been born in November 1941.

Professor Eva Rieger is a German musicologist and a worldwide specialist in the social and cultural history of women in music.

We corresponded and found that she had written a biography of Friedelind Wagner, granddaughter of Richard Wagner, who coincidentally was also in the Rushen camp. Friedelind had had a fascinating time in Port Erin that we had documented and we were able to give this information to Eva.

I invited her to come to Port Erin to see the internment exhibition. We had a musical weekend with recitals by some wonderful local artists (re-enacting a concert once performed by the internees), and talks from the Rieger family and their friend, Dagny Beidler (Wagner's granddaughter, whose father was anti-Nazi, unlike the other branch of the family). Dagny gave an illuminating talk on the Wagner family, the feuding over the Bayreuth Festival and the courageous and dignified behaviour of her father, who was also a close friend of Thomas Mann, the Nobel prize-winning author.

Eva Rieger. (Courtesy of Eva Rieger)

Eva's brother, Dr Chris Rieger, had a lively and amusing interactive session with local people who remembered the internment period.

He has since sent to Sandra Davidson the notes he made for his talk, which follow[4]:

Hugh Davidson, Dagny Beidler, Pamela Crowe, Chris & Eva Rieger at the Wagner Weekend held at the Erin Art Centre, Port Erin. (Courtesy of Rushen Heritage Trust)

The story begins with the revelation that I was never personally interned [because children under sixteen were never classified as internees]. Having been born in London in 1934 and living there since then, I was, according to British law, a citizen of the United Kingdom and Colonies. But, because my father and mother were German, I was also German according to German law. I was never actually interned on the Isle of Man, but my mother was, and she was permitted to take her non-adult children with her. What else could she do?

The German army under Hitler's rule had conquered France, had just occupied Norway and was ready to invade Britain. The occupation of Norway had been achieved with great ease because there were many sympathisers in the Norwegian population who assisted the invaders with crucial information.

I think the term 'enemy alien' is a misnomer since it suggests that aliens are enemies per se, which of course they are not. Aliens are foreigners, but whether they feel enmity or fraternity with the local population is a different matter. Many aliens – particularly those of Jewish descent – had fled the Nazi regime and were refugees in Britain. Many of them were in positions that were important for the British war effort. But when asked, which of the enemy aliens should be interned, Winston Churchill, being aware of the potential danger of such a 'Fifth Column' in Britain, is said to have answered promptly: 'Collar the lot'. The idea was to arrest all enemy aliens first and then to bring them before a tribunal that would examine their credentials and could recommend or refuse their release as seen fit.

My father, Julius Rieger, a minister of religion at one of the German churches in London, came to Britain in 1930, at the age of 29, to stand in for the deceased pastor of St George's German Lutheran Church in London. Shortly after arrival he was asked by the journal GOOD WILL, A Review of International Friendship, *to comment on the current economic and political situation in Germany. His short paper entitled 'Germany's Despair' appeared in January 1932, exactly a year before Hitler's ascent to power [see Appendix 2].*

Barely 12 months after the publication of this paper, the implied prediction came true with Hitler's march to power. My father might have been elated by the fact that his analysis had proved to be sound, but not by the way in which the system developed into a totalitarian state.

In 1934, together with almost all the other German pastors in Great Britain, he refused to accept the subordination of his Lutheran congregation under the State Church and joined the so-called Confessional Church, which stood in opposition to the prescribed subordination of the Church and adoption of the 'Führer'-principle of the Nazi system. The decision was not so easy to take, because the German pastors were paid by the Church foreign office in Berlin, and were now forced to make do with a weekly payment provided by their respective congregations. Needless to say, this led to quite a few problems that they and their families had to cope with.

At the outbreak of war in 1939 my father decided to stay put in England and to serve his congregation of German-speaking Christians in London. In addition, he acted as an intermediary between the Christian resistance of Dietrich Bonhoeffer in Germany and the Bishop of Chichester, George Bell, with whom he developed a close friendship.

In mid May 1940, when an invasion of Britain seemed imminent, my parents were interned. My mother, who at the time was pregnant and expecting her fourth child, was permitted to take her three children with her into the women's camp in Port Erin. I was six years old.

Although my reminiscences of internment are mainly positive, one of the biggest problems was the lack of communication between husbands and wives in the early days of internment. I have found a number of letters that were written during this period and will quote from them here. The letters written by our father were kept by our mother, whereas the replies written by our mother have been mostly irretrievably lost, (I am told that this is quite normal with married couples!) The language used was mostly English in order to facilitate and speed up the censorship that had been imposed. Parts translated by me are indicated by [trans CR].

18th June 1940. Mother in Belle Vue Hotel, Port Erin to Father in Internment Camp Douglas:

How glad I was yesterday when your letter arrived! It was the first sign I got of you since we were separated, because I never received your letter of the 27th [May]. // To facilitate the censors work I will only shortly tell you what happened. The voyage from London to here took 2 ½ days and you may imagine that it was not an easy task for me with the three children. The boys behaved very bravely*, little Renate tried to do so too, but she was greatly disturbed on seeing so many new faces. Since about a week she is no more so shy as she was. On a whole we may be very glad to be at such a lovely place, the children play most of their time at the beach or go sea-bathing. The boys get a bit wild, having only very short lessons during the day, but I hope we will get them straight later on.

*Comment: translation error from 'brav' in German meaning 'well behaved'.

18th June 1940. Father in Douglas to Mother in Port Erin:

Since the day of my arrest I have received no news from you. That's five weeks now. … I don't understand it and, together with many other comrades who are in a similar position, find it incomprehensible that we are being burdened with this totally superfluous uncertainty in our present predicament.
… Signed 'Your worried and a little embittered Väti' [trans CR]

25th June 1940. Father in Douglas to Mother in Port Erin:

It's now nearly six weeks that have passed since our farewell … although only a small distance of less than 12 miles separates us. [trans CR]

1st July 1940. Mother in Port Erin to Father in Douglas:

I hope you got at least one of the two letters I wrote to you. I am so glad that you are so near to us and I am quite sure that it will be now much quicker to communicate with each other. I am writing to you today by special permission of the Commandant, because financial matters have by now become so muddled owing to the delay of letters.
    [Lengthy financial details follow regarding bills to be paid, savings and current accounts not or only partly available etc.]

7th July. Father in Douglas to Mother in Port Erin:

It's now fully seven weeks after internment that I remain without a personal word from you, although our camps are well connected by bus transport or separated by a brisk walk. [trans CR]

11th July 1940. Mother in Port Erin to Father in Douglas:

We were promised that this letter will reach you in the shortest time and that we will get an early reply from you, let us hope so! Mrs Diehl and I sent just a letter to the Bishop of Chichester, because we thought, we must try everything to prevent the pastors with congregations here in England to be sent to Australia. We are quite sure you will have tried hard to do the same. But probably you may be forced to go, what shall we do then? I am prepared to go with you wherever it may be, but we heard, if wives follow their husbands, it means then complete emigration and we may all have to pay our fare back for ourselves. Who will do and can do that for us after the war, because we, I mean especially pastors, will not have any chance of getting these means by work over there? Probably Mr. Heckel will do it for us [reference to the Head of the foreign affairs department of the official State Church in Berlin]. On the other hand, it would be extremely difficult for me as expectant mother to stay here alone with 4 children. Please, try to answer these questions. I wrote several times but got no answer.

12th July. Father in Douglas to Mother in Port Erin:

My darling, I have – at last – received your letters of 18/6, 27/6 and 4/7. I have up to now not received your registered letter containing the Post Saving Book, but hope that it will reach me very soon so that I am able to send you the money you were asking for. Please keep the receipt!

27th July. Family Reunion in Collinson's Café, Port Erin:

The meeting was arranged to permit couples to decide whether to accept a transfer to Canada or Australia, both Commonwealth countries having agreed to assist Britain by taking in a number of enemy aliens. Our mother together with another internee from Port Erin Camp wrote to the Bishop of Chichester that a passage to Canada or Australia would put the pastors into a very difficult position after the end of hostilities, since there would be no one to pay for their repatriation to their congregations in Britain.

28th July 1940. Father in Douglas to Mother in Port Erin:

What a respite these 30 minutes were in your midst!

My father later told us that while most couples enjoyed their reunion, the members of the Jewish congregation used the time available to hold a service with their members.

21st November 1940. Eva born in Port Erin. Father permitted to visit wife and newborn child in Port Erin.

2nd December 1940. Father from Liverpool to Mother in Port Erin:

On Monday (25th November) I came back to Douglas from Port Erin in high spirits and had to report your condition and the baby to many friends. Oh, so many friends and strangers congratulated us and wished us happiness and luck, so that, at least from here, Eva Maria should have a good life. Without further expectations I went to bed, on Tuesday I cleared up my room, when an acquaintance from the next house confided and subsequently a message from the camp office informed me officially that I was on the release list for Wednesday. I was perplexed, thought of you and of the possible excitement in the hospital bed on receiving such news, and tried to extend my stay in Douglas for two or three further days. Nothing helped. I had just been in Port Erin, so that a second visit was not required. The christening could be postponed. The Camp Speaker tried his best, and I went to the officer. No use. I learned that, as suddenly as one is interned, so suddenly one is released. You can imagine what my farewell day was like. Packing my suitcase, police checks, bank account closure, farewell visits in our house, an air raid alarm during the night, then to sleep in this excitement – that's what the last hour in Pompeii must have been like. Wednesday early morning at 7 o'clock: With 18 others, the historic last walk through the barbed wire gate, and I was free!

2nd January 1941. Mother and four children were released from internment and reunited with father in Buckhurst Hill, Essex [evacuation address].

One of the main reasons for the improvement of communication among married couples was the intervention of the Bishop of Chichester, George Bell, when he visited the Isle of Man. After talking with some of the internees he visited the office of censorship in Liverpool and insisted on seeing the letters that had not yet been processed. It has been reported, that when the key to the respective cupboard could be found and the cupboard was opened, piles of letters stacked there fell out onto the floor. George Bell was instrumental in seeing to it that the letters were immediately distributed to the addressees without further processing.

Now let me turn to a few anecdotes that I can remember from my stay in Port Erin from May 1940 to January 1941.

On the evening of our arrival on the Isle of Man we were assigned two bedrooms in Belle Vue Hotel in Port Erin. Our mother took one room together with sweet little Renate (two years old). Gottfried (my elder brother) and I slept in the other. We went down to the general hall, where a fire was burning cheerfully and where many internees were gathered together. Quite a few of the latter were trying to toast bread on forks in front of the fire.

On our first run down to the beach Gottfried and I saw a group of lads digging a deep hole in the sand. We were informed that the goal of the project was to reach Australia, and so we helped as well as we could. Unfortunately, the project could not be completed before the tide came in and next day, nothing could be seen of the previous day's work.

There was boy who fascinated me with a report that a sweet had been developed that did not shrink with time but which remained a sweet forever. In fact, whenever I saw him he was chewing. When we were together next day he brought one of these marvellous sweets and offered it to me. As an alternative he also offered to give me the one he was chewing, and because I thought this was the real thing, that is what I selected. What a disappointment when I realised that chewing gum, although not shrinking, unfortunately loses its taste in time. I could have kicked myself for the wrong selection!

The ladies of the camp were quite friendly, but they literally went too far at times. Again and again we were invited to accompany someone on a walk, invariably to Bradda Head. There is no doubt that that is a beautiful spot and even that the walk there can be pleasant. But daily repetition can be boring and exhausting too. So we declined, again and again.

And when the weather turned cold and windy, we preferred to stay inside. We devised a sport in our 'boy's room' which excluded Renate. The idea was to take a run-up to the bed set near the wall, to take a headlong jump followed by a somersault on the bed and then to roll off at the other end. This we did repetitively with enthusiasm for quite some time. A friend named Jochen Spanier joined us, but he was rather ungainly because of his stature and weight, and when he misjudged the run-up he hit the wall soundly with his rear end and a large slab of plaster fell from the wall revealing the bamboo-split structuring [lath and plaster?] that had held it up to now. Of course, we had to report to our mother who scolded us thoroughly. How she managed to get the hotel management to repair the wall we don't know to this day. But we all felt bad about it.

When our mother went to hospital, helpful ladies suggested we could prepare for our next brother or sister by 'knitting' a washing line from a ball of string. One of them took us to the loft, where she spent much of our time trying to find the middle of a ball of string, walking to and fro and creating large and confusing loops of string. In the end, we did produce a washing line sufficiently long to accommodate maybe two or three diapers. We were proud of this although most of the line had been produced by the willing lady's hands.

The Manx Cat made by Chris Rieger. (Courtesy of Manx National Heritage)

One of my remarks became a standing joke throughout the Island. Having heard that men of 16 years or older were interned in the men's camps in Douglas, I said that I looked forward to becoming 16 in order to be transferred there. This was at a time when everybody was hoping for a quick release from internment and nobody except me wanted to stay for another 10 years!

Unfortunately, the camp ladies also organized a school for the camp children. I remember the 'arts' class in which we were asked what we wanted to produce. An option was a paper place mat, requiring the weaving of coloured strips of paper through the slits in a prepared sheet, and due to the absence of alternatives, this was chosen by almost everyone. Before it was my turn to propose a project, my brother Gottfried informed me that other proposals would surely be in order, so when my turn came to answer, 'Christoph, what would you like to make?', I answered 'A Manx cat'. The teacher seemed enthusiastic and helped me cut out the cloth and showed me how to stitch the pieces together. The body was filled with cotton wool, and I reported that stitching the tummy was the most difficult part. The result of this project can now be seen in the museum in Douglas, I am told.

Talking of Manx cats, I found a poem by one of the male internees in Douglas, which I would like to quote here[5]:

THE MANX CAT
by F. O.

Around a Camp of Internees
They make – don't ask me why –
A fence or two of wire and
Of poles, quite straight and high.

On one of these, some time ago
't was in the early dawn,
A seagull sat while down below
A cat stood on the lawn.

The cat looked at the bird and said
'How do you do my dear!

Why will you not come down to me?
't is so much nicer here!'

The seagull turned her head around
And beat her wings – flop, flop.
'You think I dare not, silly cat!
But why don't you come up?'

The cat got quite annoyed and then
With vehemence she said:
'And you, old fool, you think I can't
I'll show you! Will you bet?'

The seagull was a wise old bird
And knew, not e'en a cat
Could overcome the wire's points
And climb to where she sat.

'I'll take you at your word, my friend!
My wings against your tail!
Do you agree? Then try your luck,
I hope you will not fail!'

The cat gave just an angry howl
And jumped, but half way up
The pointed wire held her fast –
She fell back with a flop!

She tried again and yet again
But all was quite in vain.
The wire's points they scratched and hurt
And made her cry of pain.

At last she gave it up and said:
'I'm sorry, friend, you've won!
I'll pay my debt, but tell me pray,
How is this to be done?!'

The seagull merely said: 'You'll see'
And with a speedy dive
She snapped the tail and flew away –
The clock struck half past five!

And this is how it comes that on
This island far and wide
The cats are without what with us
Is known to be their pride!

Believe it or believe it not –
What counts for us is that
We can compare our lot with both
The seagull and the cat.

For though we're up the pole we know –
We cannot climb it, yet
If we were in the seagull's place-
We'd also lose the bet.

How else can you explain that when
To Douglas we were shipped
All cats had still their lovely tails –
While our wings were clipped?

The Camp, No 3, October 1940
Published in Hutchinson Camp, Douglas,
(courtesy of the Leo Baeck Institute, New York)

Friedelind Wagner (1918–1991)

Granddaughter of Richard Wagner, Friedelind was born in Bayreuth. As with all members of the family, she was a close friend of Adolf Hitler, but she began to be an outspoken critic of the policies of the Third Reich.
She left Germany in 1939 and emigrated to England, where she began to write articles, highly critical of Hitler, for the *Daily Sketch* newspaper.

Along with 64,000 Germans in Britain, she was interned and came to the Isle of Man, where she met Jeanette Simon, an opera singer from Berlin (see Chapter 15). This was to become a lifelong friendship. The musical entertainment in the camp provided much relief from boredom. The summer weather provided ample opportunity for swimming in the sea and walking, but music was at the heart of their friendship.

Eva Rieger's book about Friedelind Wagner. (Image courtesy of Eva Rieger)

In Germany, Goebbels was furious and felt that the articles in the *Daily Sketch* written by Friedelind – whom he described as 'the fat Wagner girl' – were written to incite Italy to rise against Germany. While in the camp, Friedelind was punished for trying to smuggle letters past the censor. Was she friend, or was she foe?

MI5, the UK security section, was watching her activities very closely. They thought 'Mausi', her nickname from childhood, was her secret agent's name and, after three months, she was taken to Wandsworth Prison annexe.

The UK authorities thought that she would be better out of England and her visa to Argentina was granted, after the famous conductor, Toscanini, agreed to pay for her passage.

More of her fascinating story can be read in *Friedelind Wagner* by Professor Eva Rieger.[6]

Irma Lange. (Courtesy of Manx National Heritage)

Irma Lange – 'my loss of freedom did not trouble me'

Irma, née Miskolczy, came from a wealthy Viennese Jewish family. In July 1914 she married Walter Johannes Lange, who ran a successful furrier business in Berlin. According to Irma's records, the business enjoyed the protection of Hermann Goring, who was a customer of long standing.

Irma and Walter had a son, Hanns Lange, who was born in July 1915. Irma was not religious so it was easy for her to convert to Christianity at the wish of her mother-in-law and Hanns was baptised in January 1916.

At the end of 1938, after the annexation of Austria, the November pogrom, and the increasing persecution of the Jews, Irma concluded: 'In these circumstances, it was now clear to us that we could not stay in Germany for much longer.'

In March 1939, her son Hanns, now 23 years old, received a permit to work in England, leaving Germany on the 15th March. Irma followed in July of the same year with husband Walter on the ship *Bremen,* arriving in the UK on the 5th August 1939. They rented a house in Purley, near London, Irma not suspecting then that she would spend the rest of her life there. She wrote, in her unpublished autobiography[7]:

"Now came the day when our household goods were packed into two large containers. Now I became really conscious that I had to say goodbye to everything that was dear to me. Above all to my mother, who was very close to me, and about whom I worried as she had no opportunity to emigrate at that time."

Her husband Walter returned to Germany a month later, just before the declaration of war, and remained there until 1947.

After the start of WWII, Irma and Hanns, as aliens, were initially allocated to Category C, where there were no doubts about reliability. However, from May 1940, Category C aliens were also interned.

Hanns recalled[8]:

"On Monday 8th July about 5 p.m., as I was just digging over a new bed in our small vegetable garden to plant vegetables for the winter, dressed in shorts in the pleasant sunshine, mother suddenly came up to me, accompanied by a man. This man turned out to be a detective and he requested me to be at home on the following day, as the detective sergeant at our local police station wanted to talk to me... Next morning, we got up at 6.30 a.m. in order to be ready, should the policeman arrive early. The uncertainty of the waiting time was terrible. Eventually I heard the steps. With the customarily polite formulation, 'I'm sorry but we have to intern you,' they destroyed all the hopes and fears of two unfortunate people."

From July 1940, Hanns was interned in Central Camp, Douglas, then moved to Onchan Camp, and finally to Camp Mooragh in Ramsey. He kept a diary for the entire period of his internment and one of his articles is recorded in 1941 in a book called *The Onchan Pioneer* with the title 'Onchan Camp Youth', which is held in the Manx Museum archives[9].

Irma received notice of internment in September 1940 and was first detained in Holloway Women's Prison in London for six weeks, then transferred to Rushen Women's Camp, arriving on the 1st November 1940.

In December 1940, she received permission to visit Hanns in Douglas[10]:

"We met in a large ballroom in Douglas, and our joy was so great, after six months of separation, that we forgot everything that lay behind us. The two hours together went all too quickly, and we parted for me to return to Port Erin by train, which was a nice change. Now I would have to wait another 4 weeks for the next meeting."

Irma remained in internment for almost two years until July 1942. In retrospect, she judged her time in the camp as positive:[11]

"As I always felt myself to be mentally very free, my loss of freedom did not trouble me. I am also not at all despondent on very many things that most women cannot manage without, and I am so well catered for on this delightful Island and it did not cost me a single penny."

Her son, Hanns, was released in October 1942, through the support of Ernest. W. Halberstadt, a grandson of Sigmund Freud, whom he had met during internment in the Isle of Man.

Contact with Walter was limited to Red Cross letters and then broke off entirely until the end of the war. Walter did not get permission to visit his family in England until autumn 1947. He recalled:[12]

"After we had lived together very happily for 25 years, I imagined that a meeting after 8 years (apart), which we had spent in danger of our lives and which we had luckily survived, would be overwhelming. But I soon became aware that our marriage had not withstood the long separation."

Top: Irma's registration card. (Courtesy of Manx National Heritage)

Above: Irma's green ticket (top) and hand-made permit to visit Hanns. (Courtesy of Manx National Heritage)

However, Walter soon moved to England where he founded the furrier business Walter Lange Ltd, which his son Hanns took over on the death of his father in 1953. Mother and son remained in Purley and only returned to Germany to visit. Hanns married Edna Hayes, from Purley, in 1962. Irma died in Purley on 14th Feb 1986, aged 94 years; Hanns in October 2007 and his wife in February 2009.

Renate Olins – a Jewish refugee from Hitler's Germany

Renate and her family left Germany in 1937 for Amsterdam. Her father travelled back and forth to England to prepare the necessary paperwork and they arrived in England in 1938, when Renate was six years old. 'You didn't let on you were German Jewish and tried desperately to become part of the community in which you lived.'[13] Renate could not speak any English and was sent to nursery

Renate Olins (right) aged about 7 with her friend, October 1939. (Courtesy of Manx National Heritage)

school to begin her education. By the time war broke out, she spoke good English without a hint of an accent. They were all aware of the possibility of England losing the war and this was the cloud they lived under.

In 1939 Renate was now attending Kensington High School and education was her parent's absolute priority for her. When war broke out, German Jewish refugees, by virtue of the fact that they were German, became enemy aliens and because Hitler didn't want them they were deprived of German citizenship and so became stateless, a double insecurity. In 1940, her parents were taken before a tribunal and classified in Category B. Internment came soon after for her father. Weeks of misery followed as they could not gain any news of her father's whereabouts. Two months later her mother was arrested and Renate insisted on going with her rather than stay with a relative. They were taken from the

Harrow Road police station to a barracks and slept in camp beds. Renate was suffering from flu. The following morning they were herded onto a train for Liverpool and embarked on a boat to the Isle of Man.

When they arrived at St Catherine's Church Hall the internees were dragooned into groups and marched off to the various hotels and boarding houses to which they were allocated in Port Erin. Renate and her mother were billeted in the Seaview Hotel on Port Erin and Renate remembers it was run by a man called Mr Barber, who had a great bulbous red nose and was never sober! Jobs in the boarding house were shared between the women, Tuesday peeling potatoes, Wednesday help with the washing and sheets and so on. One woman was a fortune teller, but not from tea leaves: she would melt down toothpaste tubes and, because they were made of lead, they would be dropped into water and the shape they made would tell your fortune. Summer was spent playing on the beach, in rock pools and walking along the edge of the cliff. Renate observed that she never lived in such a lovely place before or since.

Renate Olins. (Courtesy of Manx National Heritage)

Internee Minna Specht set up a wonderful school and, once organised, Renate went every day. She recalled that Minna was very strict and if she arrived late, she was sent home. They received a letter from her father shortly after they had arrived and found he was interned in one of the male camps in Douglas. Many months later they were reunited in a church hall for an hour and a half.

In 1941, a married camp was set up in Port St Mary, but they were only there for about three months as in late summer 1941 they received their release. Renate considered it had been a kind of bittersweet existence. She wasn't confined and the beach was wonderful. In those days it was totally unpolluted and she learned to swim there. But it wasn't quite real life, because they weren't connected to their usual attachments.

Rosemarie Dalheim – Babes behind barbed wire

It was a beautiful morning, that first day of May 1942, when I set off to take up my very first job. I was sweet 17 and interned with my parents, brother and two sisters in the married aliens' camp at Port St Mary. I had been offered the job of helping at the camp kindergarten, the wages being the princely sum of five shillings a week. Some months previously, much to my own great, and, no doubt everyone else's surprise, I had matriculated. Taking the examination and passing it after two years of more or less non-existent schooling was, indeed, quite an achievement. So, now the Office and my parents thought it might be a good thing if I were usefully employed. I was not so sure! I was perfectly happy reading all the books the library could offer, knitting, going for walks within the camp with our landlady's dog, Jock, and weather permitting, spending long leisurely days on the beach. However, the job was mornings only and five shillings a week was an enormous amount.

The Dalheim family on the Isle of Man, autumn 1942. (Courtesy of Rosemarie Dalheim)

My brother, who went on the archaeological digs with Dr Bersu, only received three shillings and sixpence a week. It was a short walk down The Promenade from 'Blair Atholl' where we lived to the kindergarten, which was held in a large room at the back of Cowley's Café. Beyond that was the barbed-wire boundary. The children were in the enclosed garden playing a ring game and what a merry little group they were! German-born, British-born, Jew and Gentile happily holding hands with each other. The kindergarten was bilingual and some enterprising soul had translated German jingles into English. These were idyllic days and I thoroughly enjoyed myself playing with the little ones.

When the 'married' camp moved to Bradda, we joined the Port Erin kindergarten, which was held in the little golf club house at Rowany. This being in the women's camp, every weekday would see me going through the barrier between the camps with my little retinue of toddlers. Staff changes were constant as women were released and for one glorious week, being the 'oldest' inhabitant, I was head of the kindergarten. Then a trained woman was installed and my reign as head teacher was over. When peace was restored to Europe, I went to college and trained as a primary school teacher.

Anita Dalheim – Internment camp school days 1940–1943

Nostalgia

Looking back on my school days in Port Erin and Port St Mary during the war, I am filled with nostalgia. Being so unorthodox, as were the teachers too, they taught us more than we could have learned in a 'normal' classroom. It was hard to adapt to a school routine after that first hot summer of camp life. We'd had such freedom, spending our days dashing from 'Sunset View', on Port Erin promenade down to the fascinating life of beach and rock pools below. But our classes were never dull, all the teachers being drawn from all walks of life. As

Last photo before the camera was confiscated. August 1939. (Image courtesy of Rosemarie Dalheim)

some could not even master the English language, many classes were held in German – a very strange thing for me, having only been to English schools. Being taught the workings of 'ze hydraulic-press' in gutteral English was quite a laugh. Mrs Diehl, our Biology teacher, used to take us to the Biological Station and we loved staring at the giant squids and octopuses. Mrs Kneen taught us to love poetry and also encouraged us to write our own. I remember writing an 'epic' poem on an orange, after seeing Spaldrick Bay strewn with a cargo of oranges – it was great fun.

Diverse curriculum

As our school was in a terrace of houses, up a slope from Port Erin lower promenade, the barbed wire ran close by. Needless to say, the temptation to climb through it was too great for us! We did, and were caught and reprimanded. When our school in the Port Mary camp was opened in Cowley's Café (full of lovely corners in which to hide from our teachers), we missed our wonderful train rides to Port Erin. But, once again, the diversity of lessons and teachers made school life interesting. Learning Pitman's shorthand, advanced German Literature in German, mathematics and science way above our heads and German bookkeeping (when I didn't even understand *English* bookkeeping) were all in a day's work. At least the rough, tough games and gymnastics on the beach, and in all weathers, were a great outlet for our vast store of energy (our teacher being a German army instructor). This was in contrast to the lady-like PT (physical training) classes given by a dancer in Dandy Hill Chapel in Port Erin.

How we loved reading Shakespeare on the 'brows' and even put on the playlet of *A Midsummer Night's Dream* to the public! The internees were very grateful for *any* kind of entertainment. In spite of a teacher who loved his lavender hair oil – and I didn't – we read and loved Bernard Shaw. Our Scripture lessons were divided between our own Lutheran Pastor, Pastor Diehl, the Anglican Vicar and the Methodist Minister, Harry Johnson. The Catholic children had their own visiting priest, while the Jewish children had their regular lessons with the Rabbi. I remember no problems there.

Life is greater than learning

Back in Port Erin again, with less children and less staff – internees being 'released' periodically – our classes were very small. I became the only pupil in the 'matriculation class'. I was mostly left alone with a thick mathematics book. I would have been sunk without the answers at the back of it! However, something must have sunk in as I went to high school in Leeds once our family was released. I never felt that I'd lost three years of formal education. Far more, I felt that I had *gained*.

Later, when I was at Darlington Training College, our motto really struck home '*Vita magis Quam literis*' – 'Life is greater than learning' – which is what I had gained in the camp.

STORIES OF LOCAL PERSONALITIES

Keith McArd – call out the guard!

Keith McArd was a local Port Erin boy, born in 1936. He and his forefathers were builders who constructed much of Rushen and beyond. In 1940 he and his family were living at 'Crofton', Bayview Road, on the corner with Bridson Street.

When interviewed, Keith at first claimed to remember little of the impact of internees on his life because he was so young, nevertheless the stories below soon came pouring forth.

Keith's grandparents built and ran Windsor House, which was occupied by internees with strong German Nationalist sympathies. One of the internees taught Keith's mother German. Another was their house help and she was escorted from the barrier to the end of the road by a policewoman, from where young Keith escorted her to the house.

Call Out The Home Guard – Boy Missing!

Keith would sometimes play with Peter von Flugel, the son of a wealthy internee, a Baroness. She had her own accommodation in Port Erin, complete with servants, and sent Peter to King William's College, the Island's private school

Top: Keith McArd. (Courtesy of Keith McArd)

Left: Keith with his nanny on Port Erin Promenade. (Courtesy of Keith McArd)

CHAPTER THIRTEEN

for boys. Keith also went to school there. At first Keith was wary of Peter because he was German, but they became friends later despite the two-year age difference.

One day, during their games, Keith shut Peter in their rabbit hutch. Keith's family kept rabbits, as many people did to supplement food in wartime. At the internee roll-call, there was a big hue and cry when it was realised a boy was missing. The Home Guard was called out. It was then that Keith remembered where Peter was. Keith was in 'Very Big Trouble' with his dad, but, according to Keith, Peter seemed none the worse for his ordeal when released.

Keith and his friends used to watch the Home Guard (which was much like *Dad's Army* on TV) as they drilled and practised using ARP (air-raid precautions) pumps in the plot behind the Snaefell Hotel. To get to and from school, children had to have a pass to get through the barbed-wire barriers. Sometimes the gateway was supervised by the Home Guard and at other times by a policeman. No pass meant literally 'no pass' and if Keith forgot it, he'd have to cycle back for it.

The Dandelion Lady

The McArd rabbits were also an attraction for one of the internee women. She would gather bunches of dandelion leaves to share with them: internees were resourceful and keen to avail themselves of whatever food and vitamins were available. Dandelion tea is regarded as a traditional remedy for many things, including kidney problems, iron-deficiency anaemia, liver damage and constipation.

A Rook's Revenge

Keith also recalled they had a gardener from the camp – Keith's father said he was Russian – and one day this man was given the task of moving the position of the rabbit hutch. He was told to wait for help. Instead the 'Russian' smashed it to bits. Presumably for easier transportation? Keith felt sure there had probably been some confusion in the instructions, due to language difficulties, but at the time everyone was very upset. No doubt the 'dandelion lady' particularly so.

Later the Russian gardener's bald head suffered an attack from a rook, which drew blood. This was 'divine retribution', according to Keith's father.

The Cat Woman

Keith recalled an internee, called Miss Fischer, who bred cats in their builder's yard. Eventually it was overrun with the animals – but at least there were no 'longtails' (Manx alternative to rats). By the end of the war 40 cats still resided there. Something had to be done. The cats could not be rehomed – only Miss Fischer could catch them – so they were humanely despatched by Kermodes the Chemist.

[Note: this is probably the same Elisabeth Fischer, whom Betty Kelly remembers, and who corresponded with Betty's mother after release. Elisabeth's picture is on page 60 of *The Illustrated Roll-Call*, and she lived at the Golf Links Hotel, now the Princess Apartments.]

Keith remembered that another internee was allowed to have some spare quarry tiles from the McArd's yard and she made intricate handicrafts from them.

Shenanigans?

As our conversation drew to its end, Keith suddenly recalled a fine story his dad told about one of his masons. They were taking out fireplaces from one of the boarding houses occupied by internees and the mason observed a young woman lying on the bed as he came in to set about his work.

'Be friends with me?' the young woman said, invitingly, as he prepared to go.

'Oh no,' said the mason, 'I must get home for my tea – my wife will have it all ready.'

'Will you come back later?' the young woman asked.

We feel fairy sure he didn't, considering his stated priorities at the time.

Tradesmen often had access to the internee houses, and Keith suspects there were some shenanigans because of the number and frequency of plumbers, electricians and handymen required to attend to these houses.

It is known that one house in particular housed a contingent of 'ladies of the night' from Germany who had the misfortune to be in England seeking better earnings, when internment was put into force.

Irene Jackson – a passport for the teddy bear

Irene was born in 1928, in St Marys Rd, Port Erin, so was about 12 when the women internees arrived at Port Erin Station in May 1940. Her father, Mr Maddrell, managed a grocery shop in Castletown, was in civil defence with the Rushen Brigade, and her mother looked after the house. Irene said the early strategy with internees was to first get them placed in accommodation, then to sort them out later.

Internees

Irene's house had six bedrooms, and her parents slept in one. They had been allocated eight or nine internees plus two children, who were about the same age as Irene. So, it was about two people per room, the rate was one guinea per week. All internees had ration books.

Most internees only stayed for a few months before they were released. They liked the offal cuts of meat, which Irene and her family would have given to their dogs (this seems in line with the French/German appetite for offal as a delicacy), and they also made salads from dandelions.

Irene got on well with the internees. Each house had an internee who was selected as the leader, and had to report any incidents and help resolve any issues. The internee 'boss' at her house was training to be a doctor at Edinburgh University.

Occasionally, an internee would become ill and the Deaconesses would come to the house. There was little trouble but they had to be watched, since some had Nazi sympathies. Irene said there was one incident. Internees had to do housework assignments and two Austrian Jewish women with children were arguing about this. One threatened the other that if she did not do the housework chores for both of them, she would report her to Hitler, with dire consequences for her relatives remaining in Austria.

Nets and Knitting

Most of their internees spoke good English. One statement that amused the family, referring to the full dustbins was: 'The dustbins are overcrowded.' Irene played with the two internee children, mainly in the house and the garden. The internees taught her how to make string bags and nets for fishing. They also knitted a lot, using untreated Manx wool. They sold their goods in Port Erin and made some pocket money.

When the internees left, some swastikas were found, drawn on the landing and also on tablecloths.

German Aircraft

Irene remembers the sirens going, and her family and the internees all crowding under the stairs. They could hear the German bombers overhead, on their way to or back from Belfast. You could tell whether they were going or coming back by the engine noise: if they were on their way to Belfast they would be laden with fuel and bombs, and the sound was a heavy droning. On their way back, sometimes pursued, the sound was much lighter. Drew Herdman, who was also a child in Port Erin at the time, remembers these different sounds too.

Irene's mother came originally from Stockport, and her relatives endured much bombing. Her mother felt the German/Austrian internees had a very easy time compared to her relatives 'across' (in the UK).

School and a Passport for Teddy

After she passed her 11 plus, Irene attended Park Road High School for Girls in Douglas, since Castle Rushen High School was not built until after WWII. Where Castle Rushen High School is now, was then covered by Nissan huts for the navy. Irene would leave on the 7 a.m. train to Douglas and get back home by train at 6 p.m. She had to have an identity disc, 'in case I got blown to pieces' – and still has it.

There was no ID inspection on the train. Friends from Douglas had to obtain a permit to visit Port Erin, and one of the children asked for, and was given, a passport for her teddy bear.

Irene said that once many of the internees had been released, the size of the wired-in camp area diminished. The barrier was then moved from St Mary's Road in Port Erin to St George's Crescent. There was a small sentry hut manned by local civilian men.

Irene worked at the shoe shop in Port Erin until, in 1945, she was old enough to go to work at Noble's Hospital. When her mother died, Irene left Noble's to look after her dad. She got married in 1951, and was married for 57 years, until her husband died in 2008.

Mona Quillin – after 2001

Mona was born at the Four Roads in Port St Mary on the 26th March 1915. She had one sister, Mary, and they lived at the Four Roads for 16 years, before moving to Cronk Wyllin on the promenade in Port St Mary in 1932. They worked in Cronk Wyllin guest house and in 1940 were advised by government representatives that they would be receiving internees. They were given the option of leaving or staying in the guest house with the internees.

May 1940, when the internees arrived, was a glorious summer. They were accompanied by Lutheran Quakers. Many of their internees were from Stroud in Gloucester and there were twenty-three women including five children. Some had been teaching in a school in Stroud. Internee Mrs Pinchoff, her three children and sister Florette had been put on a train from Holloway Prison in London to Liverpool, ferried to Douglas on the boat, put on a train in Douglas to Port Erin, registered at St Catherine's Hall, put back on the train to Port St Mary and finally walked from the railway station to Cronk Wyllin.

There were various nationalities: German, Austrian, Czechoslovakian, even a Scottish woman who was married to a German. Mona would receive the rations for the internees from the government – she would send a form detailing

Photo taken on the steps of Cronk Wyllin. Back: Florence Bracon (Scottish); Mrs Hetty Pinchoff (Austrian); Teresa? (German); Mary Quillin Middle: Mona Quillin; Rita? (Austrian); Monica Demola (Bavarian); Paula, sister of Rita (Austrian) Front: Hetty Pinchoffs' children. (Courtesy of Mona Quillin)

the number of internees and would receive the goods from the grocer, butcher and fishmonger. Fuel (coal) was allocated and they were able to obtain and burn coke from the local gas station.

Landladies of the boarding houses were paid 21 shillings (one guinea) per adult and 12 shillings for a child weekly – the internees were given the nick name 'guinea pigs' because of this.

Lutheran Quakers who came from England would run a clinic for the internees at the Methodist Church in the High Street in Port St Mary. Illnesses were rare; the worst problem Mona recalls was that some of the internees arrived infested with lice – this would entail the whole household being treated at the clinic for lice infestations.

Internees would teach at schools (café/community centre) and they also did a lot of knitting and sewing, and created a drama class to keep occupied. The internees were able to use the beach, but it was partitioned so they swam separately from the locals.

Mona's father used to go to Gansey and collect local eating crabs. One day he caught a large conger eel and brought it back to the house. Mona and Mary could not face it – the Pinchoff sisters took it with delight, prepared it and made an eel soup – they did not waste a morsel. The sisters also cooked a potato dish, which was eaten by all and was delicious – Mona could not recall what they had called it or how it was cooked, but thought it was lovely. Another speciality made by the internees and was first introduced to Mona was Stöllen cake, when they were able to get the ingredients – a real treat.

Although Islanders did not experience full rationing, they would prepare lamb/beef stews, with mostly turnips and potatoes; occasionally there would be some rashers of bacon left over from the daily round of Tom Moore, the local butcher, and he would call round to the boarding houses in his van to sell what he had left over (in his horse and cart before he purchased his van). The landladies would buy any left-over meat, bacon or sausages and this would be a great treat.

Mona recalls one Nazi internee saying 'Hitler will be in the Tower of London in a week'. Another internee called Monica was from Bavaria and was engaged to a man in Dorset. She would do the cooking and kept in touch with Mona and Mary after leaving the Island. All her internees spoke fluent English.

Mona and Mary could not leave the house unattended and one or the other stayed in. They would lock their own rooms, which contained radios, and had to lock the food cupboards. The curfew was Mona's responsibility and she remembers her Scottish internee, Nancy Bloom, who was married to a German. She tried to escape on an Irish fishing boat in Port St Mary Harbour – she was arrested by Constable Arthur Cowin and put into the cells at Port Erin police station; she was subsequently returned to England and placed in Holloway Prison.

Mona recalls one Sunday evening about 6 p.m. in the summer. She looked out of the window and down below she saw a group of Nazi women parading up and down goose-stepping, saluting 'Heil Hitler' and shaking hands and embracing one another.

Mona recalled they had a shared bathroom with the internees. One day she went into the bathroom after the 'Isla' girls had been in for their bath (allowed twice weekly), and she noticed that a swastika had been drawn on the steamed up mirror. Shocking to think they all lived together – refugees, locals and Nazi sympathisers.

Mona recalled her father, Frederick, working at RAF Jurby airfield seven days a week during these war times, carrying out repairs, relaying and maintaining the runways. He was sworn to secrecy as the RAF were training pilots there. He left the house by 7 a.m. each day and they would make sure he had a full breakfast before he left, so it was an early start for them all. He would catch the train from Port St Mary to Douglas, take a further train to St Johns and then catch a bus to Jurby, making the same return journey at the end of the day and arriving home at around 7 p.m. Frederick was a widower and it was therefore Mona's job to make him up sandwiches and put hot water into a flagon, and tea and sugar into small Oxo tins each morning prior to his long journey.

Locals and internees worked alongside each other at Jurby airfield and Mona recalled the internees started to complain that when it was wet and cold they suffered, and requested a large shed/hut be built so they could eat their meals under cover. A shed was built for them as requested. No sooner had it been done, Charlie Gill (father of Tommy Gill) was so incensed about this, as the locals had not been given a hut, that he called all the local workmen out on strike and told the powers that be, as their work was of national importance, the authorities had better provide them with the same – an additional hut was quickly built for the locals.

Soon the women internees were moved to Port Erin and Port St Mary became a married camp for couples. Again, Cronk Wyllin housed a number of couples, as in May 1941 the promenade formed the married camp. The first internees were a Jewish family. The family had a tailor shop where they made clothes, shoes and sandals.

There had been trouble in another house where there were Nazis, but the householders had to take them on and be tough with them. The male internees generally went to work on the farms.

These internees went to Port Erin and Mona said that she did not have the pleasure of seeing it going bad for them and Hitler's downfall, but had the tables been turned they would have been very nasty with them. By Christmas 1941 the news was not good, but they just hoped for the best. If the news was bad, it was never discussed. There were rumours that Hess was in the Nunnery – no one would say much – walls have ears.

In one family, named Hatlander, there were two brothers who were sent by the British government from Guernsey to the Island. One was very Prussian-looking and had a white beard and a hearing aid, which used to make a noise and he was nick-named 'tinny whiskers', the other was vegetarian and was very tiresome. Mona would sometimes cook for them as they used to quarrel over the meals. The vegetarian would be fed rice, cheese and pancakes. Mona considered them real Nazis. Mostly, the women internees did the cooking. One of the brothers' sons was with his wife who was English and they were all wealthy people. They used to receive 'German money' from Switzerland and would drink heavily: they would order and arrange delivery of the booze from Darnill's in Port Erin at 6 p.m. in the evening and would always smell like publicans.

All were to be back in their respective billets by 9 p.m. (later during the summer months and lighter nights) and sometimes it was a struggle to get some of the bolder internees back by the curfew. Tensions occasionally built up, but it was generally quieter in Port St Mary than in Port Erin, owing to more men being interned in Port Erin. Internees did celebrate Christmas and put on concerts in various church halls: many of the internees were very talented artists and musicians, and the locals attended and enjoyed these concerts too.

Iris Burton, Port Erin artist

Iris Burton was born in 1925 and brought up at 'Chatsworth', a boarding house in Bayview Road, Port Erin, run by her mother (who died aged 66 in 1968). She and her husband, Jim, have been married for well over 70 years. They opened and ran 'Trend', a shop still operating successfully in Port Erin, from 1968 to 1988. Their speciality was distinctive Danish furniture, lighting, and decorative items purchased direct from the makers, and otherwise unobtainable in the Isle of Man.

Iris is an outstanding local artist and her paintings are in many homes, and she has been a particularly active member of the Erin Arts Centre, often painting scenery or decorative boards as background for theatrical or musical performances.

'Chatsworth' in WWII

In mid 1940, Inspectors visited 'Chatsworth' and went into every room. They counted the number of people who could be accommodated. 'Chatsworth' had a capacity of 16 people, and three rooms had two double beds, so that was four to a room. Most rooms had double beds, so that was two to a bed.

Iris was 15 years old, and at Douglas High School at the time. The rumour was that evacuees would be arriving from Liverpool, and Iris's mother was not told that the occupants would be internees.

They heard the train arrive, and saw women walking along the upper promenade with suitcases. Some of the women had children in tow. They were all placed in Port Erin hotels or boarding houses, initially Jews mixed with Nazis.

24 Hours' Notice

Iris and her mother learned that in England the women were given only 24 hours to pack a suitcase, leave home and report to Holloway Prison. Some were pregnant. They had no time to make plans, and, after time spent locked up in Holloway, they faced a long journey to the Isle of Man by train, then a four-hour boat crossing. Most were stunned.

No Fraternising! but be Kind …

There was chaos at first. But the women realised there was no escape, and that they had to adapt. It was a difficult situation for boarding house keepers, because some had sons or husbands in the British army, fighting the Germans. They were given one guinea (21 shillings) per week per internee and had to provide full board and lodging with this.

Hotel and boarding house keepers were advised 'not to fraternise – yet treat the internees with understanding in the hope that our own in a similar plight, would be treated as well in Germany'. Iris's mother decided they should be treated as she would want her own family to be treated.

Even the Budgie Spoke German!

Iris's mother wished to learn German and saw this as a chance of a lifetime. So she said 'No English is to be spoken in the kitchen.' An Irish woman who taught German at Oxford, and was interned, taught her, and she picked it up quickly. Iris's mother could identify and understand all the German dialects, and even the budgerigar, Chimpy, spoke German!

The budgies were out of their cage all day long; the other budgie, Dopey, spoke English. Iris's grandma was very deaf. Dopey knew this, and would sit on her shoulder, put his beak right inside her ear and say 'Harry is on the bus', and 'Iris is at school'.

Opposite 'Chatsworth' was 'Mona House'. Many of its internees were Nazis, and there was sometimes trouble. 'Mona House' was run by two spinsters, and they brought up Brenda Watterson (who sadly passed away in August this year).

Iris and her parents lived on the ground floor of 'Chatsworth', the internees on the floors above. The latter had a rota for cleaning, stairs, kitchen, etc.

Standing Up for the National Anthem

After some months, 'Chatsworth' was mainly occupied by nice people – German ladies who had married Englishmen many years before the war. There was a lovely atmosphere in the house, and they would listen to the 9 p.m. BBC Radio News together.

One evening, Iris's dad, Harry, was sitting in his chair, with 8 to 10 internee women in a circle. Iris and her mother were in the kitchen. Harry put the wireless on, and the British national anthem was played before the news. He stood up, and one by one the women in the circle got up too, till all were standing.

Iris and Christa, Ronaldsway 2005. (Courtesy of Mrs iris Burton)

He said, 'Thank you very much for standing up.'

They replied, 'We stood up in deference to you, not for the King.'

Harry later admitted to Iris, 'I only got up to look for a cigarette!'

Iris's Internee Friend, Christa
(see Chapter 12)

Christa was 19 when she arrived as an internee on the Isle of

Man, and Iris was 15. They became lifelong friends.

Iris continued to keep in touch with Christa after WWII: they would exchange long letters at Christmas, and shorter ones in between. Christa visited the Isle of Man and stayed with Iris in 1986, and again in 2005, as part of the 'Wire & Wool' Event. They corresponded until January 2014, when Christa died, aged 94.

The Three Graces: Karin, Christa, and Iris

Another close friend of Iris and Christa was Karin, whom Christa first met at Holloway Prison. They were first interned on Port St Mary promenade, and worked in the kipper factory. When Karin was released, she met a Canadian, got married and moved to Toronto.

Beachcombers

One jeweller went to the beach every day, and picked up pieces of semi-precious stones, like quartz, according to Henry Moore (who later ran Tower Insurance and lived at Spaldrick). Henry wrote a book on internment later.

Another collector was a woman who dug for worms and sold them for 1d each. She soon discovered that if she divided the worms in half they remained alive, and in this way she doubled her profits.

Other Points on WWII Internment

Next door to 'Chatsworth', Nurse Gale lived on her own in a big house – her son was in the navy. Baroness Von Flugel was interned at the top of the house next door, with her own servants. Her son went to King William's College (see Keith McArd – Call out the Guard!).

There were two main barriers. One in Station Road, the other in St Mary's Road. There was also a barrier at Collinson's Café, and barbed wire round Rowany Golf Course – but only three feet high, so you could jump over it. In practice, residents and internees lived together. Residents had to use a pass to leave the area.

At peak, there were about 4,000 internees in Port Erin, and 1,500 in Port St Mary. Internees were allowed on the beach, harbour, golf course and could visit the shops. They were also permitted to go to Bradda Glen and the Marine Biological Station. Christa swam in the sea every day.

There was trouble at first, with Jews and Nazis, for example, having to share the same double bed, but as things got organised, the trouble subsided. Worst of all were the 18Bs – the British Fascists who tried to stir up trouble.

Piccadilly Lil and Her Ladies

There was a large intake of German prostitutes at the Imperial Hotel – 'Ladies of the Night' – and news of this soon got around the locality. Iris said that in Berlin there were rumours that pickings were better in London, so a number of Berlin prostitutes moved there, and later got interned. Their boss was called 'Piccadilly Lil'. The Imperial was the last major hotel to be built in Port Erin, in the late 1930s.

Addendum by Iris Burton

After reading the draft summary of our conversation, Iris added these thoughts in a letter:

The stories and facts of the Rushen Internment Camp are, in my mind, quite unique. The main fact being that the owners of the houses and hotels did not have to leave their property (like Hutchinson Square, Douglas and Douglas promenade).

The wonderment and marvel of it all, looking back, is that ordinary people, like my own mother, were given the responsibility of looking after other women (enemies or friendly) during WWII … some themselves with husbands, and family, in the forces, even wounded or killed, but still required to do this duty!

Joyce Corlett – in her own words

I've lived in Port Erin all my life and my memories are mainly of Bradda. I was born in 1938 and in 1942, when I was old enough and we were going to church on a Sunday night, I remember the barrier across the bottom of Tower Road and I had to have my own ID card. The fellow in the box was a neighbour, but I still had to show my card every time! We used to nip across the golf course from Bradda and no one would bat an eyelid.

I think we did very well during the war, because my grandma had a little shop and we had a market garden. We didn't feel threatened until we went to school. We were outside the boundary of the camp and went into the internment camp area to get to school; it felt special and an adventure.

Joyce Corlett. (Courtesy of Rushen Heritage Trust/Alison Graham)

Along with our market garden we had chickens and other produce and we'd send a box of items to my grandma in Douglas every Monday on the train, and she would send stuff back to us from the pork butchers on a Saturday. There were never any questions asked about what was in the boxes; this went on throughout the war.

I remember another barrier at Station Road Chapel and I had to remember to bring my ID card when I started school on a Friday; I got my pocket money and we went to Mrs Harrison's with pennies to get a few sweets before we went back up to Bradda. My father was an ARP Warden and in charge of the coastguard. The phone used to ring and he'd go charging out. I had no idea where he was going and when you're a child, you don't ask questions!

My friend's father had a shoe shop and I was jealous of her, because she had beautiful cardigans with flowers on the front, made by the internees. The internees were very creative. Several local people had internees and kept in touch for years, some had only one bedroom available and a couple of internees. Beatrice Qualtrough in Malmore, a boarding house on Port St Mary promenade, had internees and she did a programme for the BBC as some internees had come back to meet up with her.

I remember a few people; Iris Burton's parents had internees and they were different as about 90% didn't speak English. At first husbands and wives had been separated, which caused quite a bit of anguish in Port Erin at one time, but it settled down. Some of the internees have kept in touch with their landladies all these years. I didn't know anyone as I was only five when the war ended. I do remember them being called friendly aliens?

I can remember a bomb being dropped in Baldwin. I was staying at my grandmother's and heard the bomb going over. It fell on farmland and fortunately it didn't hit anyone.

As children, the war didn't make much difference to us in the Isle of Man, we still played, went to school. We had a very charmed wartime. I've still got my original ID card and my ration card.

An innocent accused – memories from Norah Lewis (née Young)

War

Norah at the age of 13 lived with her grandparents, the Quirks, at Burnside, Glen View Terrace, and remembers being in Victoria Road Methodist Church (now Erin Arts Centre) when the Vicar announced that war had broken out. After the initial shocked silence, she remembered hearing sounds of weeping in the congregation.

Norah was at home when the newly arrived Camp Commandant was going

The Young Family.
(Courtesy of Norah &
Ashton Lewis)

from house to house along the terrace, requisitioning rooms. Payment was arranged of one guinea (£1.1.0) a week for each internee. No discussion, and protestations ignored. Norah was adamant that the payment made was £1 and not one guinea.

The Quirks of Internment Life

Norah said the Belle Vue Hotel (later the Port Erin Royal Hotel) was a maternity hospital and also accommodated Jews and a group of prostitutes. At a Memory Tea in Port Erin one of the ladies next to Norah said that the prostitutes were actually very nice – and very popular. This latter statement created much amusement. Jack Quirk, Norah's uncle, however, had a difficult time with the internees that were billeted in his Glen Eagles Hotel. A number of them were prostitutes, the gold ankle bracelet a signal of their trade, and Dame Joanna had to send one persistent offender, who continued to offer services, back to jail in London (something she rarely had to resort to).

The Internees

Mrs Schroeder, Mrs Busse and her daughter Catherine were their internees. They were Salvation Army people. They lived as part of the family, they ate their meals together, and all got on very well. Every two weeks Mrs Schroeder's husband, who was interned in Douglas, was allowed to visit. When her brother was killed, the Commandant arranged for them to be repatriated by the Red Cross.

Mrs Busse was British but she had married a German and according to Norah was 'more German than a German'. Both her sons were in the German army but paradoxically her nephews were in the British army.

Also billeted nearby on Glen View were the Metropolitan police women, Sgt Pike and Miss Pole (who both stayed in the Island, both marrying local butchers). They seemed very stern to young Norah. She remembers sitting with her friends on a summer evening on the promenade and as it was at the 9 p.m. curfew time, they were ordered home. They protested that they were not internees and had every right to be there.

Air Raid Practice

Norah and her friend signed up to learn first aid skills in the event of air raids, so they could rescue survivors. When they eventually arrived at their practice venue to 'save' their victim he had gone. All they found was a terse note stating "bled to death, have gone home".

But for the majority of the summer of 1940 her recollection is of a holiday camp atmosphere for the internees. As time passed Norah recalled a friendly atmosphere in the village. Local young men were going out with internees. There were German residents (the Wessons) in Port Erin before the war, who lived by Cooil's farm (where the other barrier to the camp was located) and she wondered whether anyone told the authorities that they were German, as they had been popular residents for many years before the war.

Not Fair!

When Norah's auntie had a baby, Norah said a pram was unattainable – but, 'There were plenty of prams provided for the internees with no problem!'

Many internees spent the time knitting. Norah marvelled at the speed of the German technique, but never quite mastered it herself. Residents had to use their clothing coupons to purchase wool and fabric but the internees were free to purchase any goods, and profits were made by illegally selling internee purchases to residents. A neighbour had a three-piece suite re-covered by one of the internees. The Red Cross parcels also proved a bonus – many residents had a tin of salmon from the parcels as a payment.

Home Guard

There were, however, numerous complaints about the local Home Guard volunteers. They manned the barrier through which all residents had to pass from the internment camp. The guards knew most of the local residents but insisted that a photographic permit card was produced by all, internee and resident alike. One young worker had to walk all the way back to Colby, even though the guard *knew* she worked in the local café where he bought bread daily.

When Norah's aunt was marrying an RAF serviceman, he had to go back to Stockport to get a pass from his local police station in order to get to the venue, Victoria Road Church. A young well-known member of the Kelly family in his army uniform, briefly home on leave, was sent back to Douglas for a pass, and Norah's friend, Betty Vernon, who lived just doors away from the barrier, was made to wait in line despite the fact she was wearing her land girl uniform and the guards knew that she only had about an hour on Sunday with her family before having to catch the bus back to Knockaloe Farm in Peel.

Fraternising with the Enemy?

Norah still remembers vividly, when she was about 14 years old, being frightened of the barrier guards. Having passed through one morning she saw one of the internees, Mrs Busse, who had previously lived with them, so she stopped and shook hands with her as was their normal greeting.

Shortly afterwards Nora was called in to account for this suspicious behaviour by the police. What had she been handing to the German woman, they demanded to know. Norah protested her innocence and, after what was a gruelling experience for a young girl, she was allowed to go on her way.

John W. Qualtrough – local historian

During the early part of the war there were internees billeted in Port St Mary on The Promenade. The area was surrounded by barbed wire, with gates and barriers, and with guards who with uniforms and a little bit of authority were 'Little Hitlers'.

Early in the war, the first fire tender in Port St Mary was Collisters' coal lorry towing a trailer pump; the fire station was built by the Commissioners' store, now used for the bin lorry. Later they got a proper fire tender – Johnnie Hislop was Chief Officer and my father was First Officer. John Hislop, his son and I used to get a lift to Port Erin cinema in the fire tender when they were going for a practice. One night we got to the barrier of the internment camp in Station Road and one member of the crew did not have his identity card. They would not let the fire tender through.

At least one member of the Special Constables on the barrier could not read. On one occasion the manager of the Perwick Hotel forgot his identity card, but he had a menu card about the same size in his pocket. He showed that and they let him through.

The wartime was interesting for young boys, as the RAF personnel from Cregneish Radar Station were billeted at the Golf Links Hotel in Port St Mary (now Carrick Bay apartments) and there were some Canadians there. We used to sneak into the boiler room and get American comics put out to light the boiler.

The army was billeted at Ballaqueeney Royal Army Pay Corps Officer Cadets Training Unit. They had one of the Cronk Skybbilt Quarries as a rifle range, where we used to find 303 bullet heads in the sand.

There was a dummy training village built in the fields where Rhenwyllin Close is now. The buildings were made of square petrol tins fastened together. We found many items in this area: I still have a bayonet.

The live ammunition training ground was Spanish Head. We used to go out there on days when the red flag was not flying and find all sorts of live ammunition – bullets, mortar bombs and hand grenades. There was also army billeted at Perwick Hotel and WAAFs at Moorlands at the Four Roads.

John in 1944. (Courtesy of John Qualtrough)

Betty in the suit made for her by the internees. (Courtesy of Betty Vernon)

Betty Vernon (née Crellin) – The engine driver's daughter

Betty's father had been the engine driver taking internees to Knockaloe Camp, near Peel, during WWI. In May 1940 he found himself repeating the role, bringing women internees and children from Douglas to Port Erin and Port St Mary.

Betty did not have much contact with the Rushen camp internees, because she was in the Women's Land Army and stationed in Peel. However, knowing that through the Service Exchange the local people could pay to have clothes made for them by the internees, Betty used some of her clothing coupons to purchase some very smart black and white check material. She also had a jacket which was no longer in use, so she took the material and jacket to the shop next to what is now Manton's Card and Gift Shop, where orders could be placed.

Mary Eslick. (Courtesy of Alison Graham and Jane Saywell)

When she went to collect her completed order, she was thrilled to find a very smart and stylish suit waiting for her. An excellent purchase!

Mary and Joan Eslick

All of the Port St Mary promenade properties were designated for use as the first married camp, and many of the landladies had already housed single internees when the first arrivals came in May 1940. They had gradually learned to live with, and accommodate, the differing lifestyles and in many cases had formed long-lasting friendships, although many of the single female internees had by now been released back to England.

Mary Eslick, who had five of her own children, having accommodated around 30 female internees in the first year in her boarding house 'Southlands' on Port St Mary promenade, was now to receive married couples in the second year of the camps.

Mary Eslick's Early Life

Mary with a shell that she made in the munitions factory. (Courtesy of Alison Graham and Jane Saywell)

Mary known as May Eslick (née Brew) was born 26th May 1895 in Douglas. She had five sisters and two brothers.

During the first few months of WWI, when she was 19 years old, she travelled with three of her sisters to Coventry to work in a munitions factory. She met her future husband while in the UK and was married to James Henry Eslick on the Isle of Man in September 1919.

James had been invalided out of WWI with shrapnel injuries and the effects of being gassed in the trenches. They lived and worked in Douglas initially, where the only job James was able to manage was as a telephonist in the telephone exchange. The couple subsequently moved to Port St Mary, where Mary took over the running of a boarding house – Southlands, on Port St Mary promenade with a few of her relatives.

James died in 1934 as a result of his injuries, when Mary was 39, leaving her to bring up five children on her own.

Times were hard and when the Home Office seconded the hotels and boarding houses for female internees the situation was turned around as each adult internee earned her 21s per week.

The situation, although hard for both residents and internees, was a godsend and there was now a light at the end of the tunnel for Mary.

Needless to say, Joan, one of Mary's daughters (pictured below), wrote, they were 'convinced they would be murdered in their beds and were all very apprehensive on their arrival'. However, the internees were of great help to Mary, as Joan recalls. They would scrub down the stairs every week (all carpets were removed and stored as the Home Office advised, as these would not be replaced once the internees had left) and on bath night, with the help of the internees, the children would all be scrubbed hard.

Joan also recalled how Mary, on hearing a commotion from an upstairs room, confronted and threatened two of the internees who were cheering, after seeing the red skies over Liverpool from the German bombing raids.

Joan continued, 'As Manx residents living in the same house as the then perceived enemy, it could be described as a unique experience. We had German "nannies" taking care of our everyday needs, German language tuition and no shortage of clothes, such as knitted garments, since they were prolific knitters.'

Mary's relatives outside Malmore, Port St Mary Promenade. (Courtesy of Alison Graham and Jane Saywell)

Married Internees in Southlands

Mary had several married couples billeted in Southlands, many who became good friends, such as Dr Gerhard Bersu and his wife Maria, who were both archaeologists of high standing and who stayed in the Island after release to continue their archaeological work on the Viking ship discovery at Balladoole.

Joan remembers another couple, a Mr and Mrs Joester, who also became good friends with Mary. They had lived in Hull for almost 50 years, but had never taken out naturalisation papers to become British citizens. They were arrested as aliens and shipped to the Isle of Man, even though their sons were fighting Germany in the British army! Other internees consisted of Barons, Italian aristocracy, barristers, artists and architects, most of whom had been London domiciled. Joan summed up her experience, 'the majority of these internees were cultured, charming people and a privilege to know'.

Both Joan and her best friend Hesba Creer (Hesba had one single female internee for a short time in her house in Port St Mary, who only came downstairs to eat and spent most of her time in her room on the treadle sewing machine) joined up to the WAAF as soon as they were old

Joan Eslick, Mary's daughter. (Courtesy of Alison Graham and Jane Saywell)

enough and within six months or so the war was over. They both maintained that, as soon as Hitler heard Joan and Hesba had signed up, he gave up!

Brenda Watterson – Memories of a child during the war years in Port Erin

Without any choice, our boarding house was filled with internees – Austrians, Jews and Germans. To a child they weren't enemies, but kind ladies who had plenty of time to knit and sew and take you swimming – the summers were all hot and sunny – everybody as brown as berries. What was known as our 'Rag Bag' (a sailor's heavy canvas bag), kept in a big kitchen cupboard, was eagerly emptied by the internees and such things as ankle-length serge skirts from the early 1900s were turned into gymslips, skirts and shorts. Linen curtains with drawn thread-work borders were transformed into blouses with the edging making an attractive front decoration. With the help of dyes – all colours! – I think I must have been one of the best dressed little girls out of that 'Rag Bag'.

Christmas was always kept by them. A 12-foot Christmas tree was covered in home-made decorations – nearly always white – with real candles in holders clipped to the branches and lit on Christmas Day (what a fire hazard!). Nightlights decorated the mantelpiece, table and piano, sat in coloured paper in the shape of water lilies. There was cotton-wool snow everywhere. A Christmas present from them to me – a large doll's bed made for my new doll, made out of a cardboard box and covered in chintz cretonne (part of an old curtain) with four little wooden legs. There were pillows, sheets, an eiderdown and a nightdress for the doll, and one exactly the same for me! – with our names embroidered on it.

We had 12 Nazis at this time who had been segregated from the Austrians and Jews and 'placed' in our house. One woman's family had been close friends with Ribbentrop the German Ambassador in London and close to Hitler, and she often spoke about family outings with him.

One day they helped me to a huge portion of 'wild nettles' which they had cooked as a vegetable and assured me was 'very good for little girls' and waited until I had eaten every bit up. Despite shortages they always had enough of everything: they had to do their own catering with help from the householder and were sometimes wasteful. I remember my aunt once 'recovering' bread they had dumped, making it into a huge bread and butter pudding for them and how they ate up every scrap saying 'how good', what was the recipe? The laugh was on them.

One morning, when they were sorting out getting ready to leave, they invited some children to the house to give them some toys and games they had received in Red Cross parcels. When leaving, laden, one little lad said, 'Are you Germans?'

'Yes.'

'Well I feel sorry for you, for the "Reds" are coming down and they are going to get you!'

I remember going for a walk one day to Port St Mary and, on reaching the manned barrier at the Old Repeater Station, being sent home to get our identity cards, which we had forgotten to bring with us. Despite knowing the guards very well you still had to show your cards going out and on the return journey. I was always sent back for them as I could run faster!

Then the final farewell: waving from the railway gates, tears streaming down my face, coming home to the house which now felt very big and empty. Once the lump in the throat had gone and my eyes less red, there was the thrill of running all over place from room to room and the feeling of freedom and at last being able to do what we wanted in our own home.

Tea Time Tales

We invited groups of locals with memories of the internment period to join us in 'Memory Teas' in St Catherine's Church Hall. It provided a sociable way to garner more material for this book. It was a very enjoyable community initiative for all concerned.

"We had a cardboard cut-out of Churchill on the counter and the internees would knock him over when they came to the counter."
- Esme....Young shop assistant in the paper

"At the customs check getting off the boat in Liverpool, my mother gave me the two bags with eggs, butter, cheese, etc and I would duck under the table."
- Young smuggler Helen (now Vicar's wife).

"You could not hear the dialogue in the Strand Cinema because of the clicking of knitting needles, the internees and locals. The locals knitted gloves for Lowcocks glove manufacturer whose owner lived in Port Erin. I could knit the gloves from memory today."
- Betty.

"The internees that had babies got a new pram, but we had to beg and borrow a pram. My baby's pram had wheels worn down to the metal. The internee babies had special gas masks that covered the pram.
- N.

"I was the best dressed child in Port Erin, beautiful outfits made by our internees for me. They became my friends. I went to the railway station to see them leave and I cried all day when they left."

"Wanda gave me a book for my birthday. I still have it."
Brenda Watterson
Mona House

"We thought they were cannibals as they ate raw fish, but soon we were eating fish in vinegar and dandelion salads." - R.

"My father was seconded to fire fight on Liverpool docks."
- Phil.

"I was the camp messenger and rode my bike around both Port Erin and Port St Mary. The camp was well organised and I never saw any trouble. I wore navy blue wool trousers and one evening it started snowing on the way home. As my trousers became more sodden, I could not ride and hardly walk, and I staggered into my home. My trousers took ages to dry on the kitchen airer."
- Betty Corrin

"The Deaconesses look really sombre in their long black dresses."
"No," said Ruth. "The dresses were Navy blue with a small turquoise spot."
(A fact confirmed by Sister Gabriel Archivist, Bethel.)

Tea Time Tales (continued...)

"We had an Austrian governess. We kept in touch until she died and my sister is named after her."
- Anne.

"We had 14 Nazis in our house."
"How did you know they were Nazis?"
"They all spoke German!"
In the beginning of the Camp, it was thought that the German speakers were the enemy.

"The refugees received Red Cross parcels with cigarettes and tins of salmon. After the camp closed we took down a partition wall and found numerous tins of salmon stashed away inside."
- Paul C, builder.

"There were Germans living in the village before the war. The Wesson's lived by Cooils Farm. They just continued to live as before the war."
- Norah

There was a hollow space in the baby's pram. It would be filled with meat, butter, and eggs. Mum would pinch my baby sister as we went past the customs check in Liverpool - they always let us through. Food was very scarce in Liverpool."

We heard the Liverpool Alphabet joke:
Child: "M-N-O-P- Q."
Mummy: "Q is for Queen."
"No Mummy – Q is for an orange".
- *A Manx toddler in Liverpool after queueing for over an hour for one orange.*

"When the air raid sirens went the German women ran to get the Jewish children in our safe place under the stairs."
- Lillian.

"There was great excitement when twins were born at the Hydro. I was taken to see them."
- Brenda

RELIGION AND THE DEACONESSES

Religion in the Camp – an introduction

The internees were members of a range of faiths and denominations – Jewish, Lutheran, Catholic, Methodist, Salvation Army – but the local churches welcomed them into their services almost as soon as they arrived in the camp. Many of the internees were very grateful for this kindness shown to them and it helped them to begin to come to terms with the difficult situation in which they found themselves. The Jewish internees found it a little more difficult as some other internees were not so welcoming.

However, as time went on, a temporary synagogue was set up for the 1,200 to 1,500 Jewish internees in the Strand Cinema in Port Erin.

Regular services were held at St Mary's and Bay View Methodist Church in Port St Mary, and the Wesleyan Church in Victoria Square, St Catherine's Church and Station Road Methodist Church all in Port Erin. In addition to the Sunday church services, organ and song recitals were held at St Catherine's Church in Port Erin, and St Mary's in Port St Mary every Thursday and Friday.

Many of the internees took an active part in the church services in both Port Erin and Port St Mary. The Lutheran Deaconesses' choir regularly participated in the services, as did a choir led by Miss Eva Langantels. Regular soloists included Captain Catherine Busse (Salvation Army), Mrs Haefner-Peppler, Mrs Bea Hutton, Mrs Henny Spier, Johanna Metzger-Lichtenstern and Mrs Jeanette Simon. There were also a number of musicians who made their contributions by accompanying soloists, and with recitals: Miss Eva Bearwald (violin), Dr (Miss) Magda Kelber (organ) and Ruth Bischoff (piano and organ).

At Christmas time, a play performed in Port St Mary attempted to combine Chanukah with Christmas. The first part was taken from the Old Testament of the Bible and the second part was based on the Nativity. In Port Erin, Wanda Wehrhan, a Lutheran Pastor's wife, successfully petitioned for a

The Strand Cinema, Port Erin. (Courtesy of Manx National Heritage)

Bay View Road Methodist Church, Port St Mary. (isle-of-man.com)

CHAPTER FOURTEEN

Christmas communion in German for all those who did not understand the service in English.

On Friday 8th November 1940, *Isle of Man Examiner* reported that:

"The Lord Bishop conducted a confirmation service at St Catherine's Church, Port Erin, on Sunday afternoon and gave the customary addresses. He was assisted in the service by the Rev. C. A. Cannan, BA, and the Bishop's staff was borne by the Rev. G. W. H. Hulme. The following candidates (all of whom are women internees) were confirmed: – Margarete Teufl, Nellie May Northolt, Bertraud Franziska Saldschin and Eddy Sigrid Koenig. The church was crowded and the ceremony most impressive."[1]

Reverend J. Benson Harrison. (Courtesy of Manx National Heritage)

Reverend Benson Harrison – probationer under pressure

The local Methodist Minister, Reverend Joseph Benson Harrison, and the Reverend Harry Johnson, Vicar at Port St Mary, were very supportive of the internees and encouraged their participation in church services. Reverend Benson Harrison did an amazing job of caring for his congregation. He was 29 years old and a probationer at Station Road Methodist Church, Port Erin and, in addition to his regular church members, he was suddenly faced with about 4,000 extra souls of whom many were, not surprisingly, in considerable distress.

Internees have recalled the musical and theatrical events he organised, the Sunday school and the training for church membership, which encouraged several internees to become members of the Methodist Church. However, a number of the local congregation did feel that he had divided loyalties.

He came under considerable pressure both from his work and his commitment to supporting the internees, and in February 1941 he became ill and appears to have had a nervous breakdown. He did recover and returned to Port Erin in June 1941, but then he moved to the Peel circuit. In 1942, he became an Army Chaplain. After the war and his conversion to Anglicanism, Harrison returned to the Island as curate at Kirk Christ in Rushen from 1949 until 1952.

The *Isle of Man Examiner*, Friday, 13 May 1955 (left) took up the rest of his story.[2]

New Appointment for Vicar of Marown

VICAR of Marown since the end of 1953, 44-years-old the Rev. Joseph Benson Harrison is leaving after the summer to take up the full-time appointment of general secretary of the Church of England Temperance Society and National Police Court Mission.

In addition to temperance work, this organisation undertakes social rehabilitation all over the country through shelters near prisons and through remand homes. It publishes a quarterly journal "Church and Nation" and also literature to back up its work and spread its influence in the colonies.

Mr. Harrison will be in charge of the head office at Palace Gate, Kensington, London.

He is a former organising secretary of the Diocesan Youth Council in the Isle of Man and, having been a war-time chaplain, has been chaplain since the war to 515 Manx Regiment, the Army

Cadet Force and to the local branches of the British Legion.

Mr. Harrison was originally a Methodist minister. He was in the Castletown Circuit from 1939 until 1941, when he was transferred to the Peel Circuit. After a few months there he became an Army chaplain. He served for a considerable time in the Middle East.

Returning to the Island, he resumed duty at Peel in September 1947. Two years later he resigned from the Methodist Church to enter the Church of England.

Ordained deacon in August, 1949, he was appointed second curate in Rushen parish. In January, 1952, he moved to Douglas to be curate of St. George's with all Saints'. He left there on being appointed vicar of Marown towards the end of 1953.

Mr. Harrison is a native of Gloucestershire. His wife is a niece of the late Rev. James Doran. Methodist minister, and Mrs. Doran. They have three children.

Reverend J. Benson Harrison, having returned to the Island as an Anglican vicar, he once more left in 1952. (Courtesy of Manx National Heritage (*Isle of Man Examiner*, Friday, 13th May 1955, p.11))

Sister Emmeline Cheshire (1889–1968) – constant friend & valued adviser

Early Years

Born on 18th December 1889, Emmeline Cheshire entered the Wesley Deaconess College, in Ilkley, Yorkshire, in September 1921.

Sister Emmeline went to her first appointment at Roath Road (Splott Road), Cardiff, in November 1922. Subsequently she worked in London; principally in Wandsworth and Ilford. She worked principally in Wandsworth and Ilford before moving to Leeds, where, for some time, she was in charge of the Hanover Square Mission Church.

In August 1940, Sister Emmeline was deputed by the Home Mission Committee for work in the Isle of Man for work in the Isle of Man with the internee women and their children. She deputised for the local Methodist Minister, Reverend Benson Harrison, presiding over services in the local Methodist churches in both Port Erin and Port St Mary, gave talks for the women internees and worked with young people in Sunday school and Junior Christian Endeavour, giving on one occasion, according to the *Isle of Man Examiner*, 'an inspiring address on "Pencils".'[3]

Sister Emmeline Cheshire. (Courtesy of Manx National Heritage (*Isle of Man Examiner*, Friday, 6th September 1940, p. 11))

In December 1940, Sister Emmeline wrote to the Warden of the Wesley Deaconess Order:

"I have been invited to take an evening service at one of the hotels here on the first Friday in every month. I went on November 8th, and was given a wonderful greeting on behalf of the group of internees present from the German Pastor's wife who has been in charge of the services since May. It is just what I have longed to be able to do. Yet, for many reasons, I knew that I must wait for the invitation to come from within the hotel. Since that evening the news of my visit has travelled through the camp and I have been asked to go to two other hotels and to one of the smaller houses. The curfew is at 6 o'clock. Thus the evenings are so long and I know that many of the internees will welcome me to take a Bible Class or service for them."[4]

Sister Emmeline also asked if the Order could help those internees who might be released:

"Is it possible for you to get me any names and addresses of people who are willing to employ, as domestic helps, any of the internees who get their release? At present, there are only one or two ... but I expect to get more requests as time goes on. Some are not able to return to their former situations because of the 'protected area' restrictions, and no one can leave the Camp even with their release granted by the Home Office, unless they have some place to which they can go and some means of supporting themselves."

Mrs Johanna Rieger. (Courtesy of Manx National Heritage)

Mrs Johanna Rieger, the wife of a Pastor of the German Church and the internee who had invited Sister Emmeline to one of the hotels on 8th November 1940, paid the following tribute to Sister Emmeline (published in the *Isle of Man Examiner* 22nd November 1940):

"It is a great privilege as well as a great joy for me to welcome you, Sister Emmeline, on behalf of all of us in our midst today.

Since the middle of June, a certain number of us have met regularly every Friday to hear the word of God. But I take it as a

very good sign that we will have you amongst us at least once a month, because I firmly believe that the future of this world, and especially a world after this war where the walls of hate seem to be insurmountable, depends on (us) as Christians – the Christians all over the world.

It will depend largely on our common prayer: not on prayers for our own victory, but that we may forgive each other as God may forgive us our own sins.

When we first came here to this Island, the churches of all denominations opened at once their doors to us, and we were and still are very grateful for that. And I sincerely hope and believe that, wherever British people detained in Germany come into touch with the German Churches, they will be welcomed and cared for as well over there, and we were welcomed and comforted from the anxious days of May and up to today.

May God help us all and grant this world, after all these dark and sinful days, a peace that serves all nations best – a peace according to His will and not to our own will."[5]

On 29th August 1942, the *Isle of Man Examiner* reported that:

"At the summer school for Methodist Deaconesses held at Ilkley, Sister Emmeline Cheshire was one of the speakers at the Sunday evening service at Wells Road Church on the 17th inst., and again on the following Tuesday, when she told briefly of how God was working amongst the women of the internment camp in Port Erin. The convention, at which was discussed 'The plight of the world and the Gospel of Christ', was under the guidance of Dr Maltby, ex-President of the Conference."[6]

Sister Emmeline continued with this work until August 1942, when she:

"… conducted a farewell service at the Sisterhood in Port Erin …Tribute was paid to the devoted work of Sister Emmeline, particularly among the women internees, during the past two years; and as an expression of appreciation Miss Leslie presented her with a travelling rug and a small cheque".[7]

She was described as having 'proved a constant friend and valued adviser and helper to those with whom she was appointed to minister and in an ever-increasing degree has earned the confidence and appreciation of all'.[8]

Bishop George Bell in 1953. (Howard Coster)

Bishop George Bell of Chichester (1883–1958)

A man of moral courage and fighter against injustice

There is no doubt that Bishop Bell was a leading, if not THE leading, Church of England figure in the fight against Nazism. He was instrumental in the promotion of ecumenism, a friend of Dietrich Bonhoeffer, and a strong supporter of the anti-Nazi Confessing Church in Germany.

He was also an outspoken critic of the programme of mass internment, the basis for the camps in the Isle of Man, and the bombing of civilian populations by either side, later exemplified by the carpet bombing of cities like Dresden. These latter positions brought him into clear conflict with Churchill and the wartime government. He was an active agent of German Resistance privy to, and supportive of, the group which planned an unsuccessful assassination of Hitler in 1944. After WWII he was an opponent of the nuclear arms race. Bishop Bell was certainly not a Church 'careerist', since his outspoken positions on many topics made him unpopular with the political establishment, and may have cost him promotion to Archbishop of Canterbury, which many at the time and since think he deserved.

Early Years – never an 'establishment figure'

George Bell was the son of a Vicar, and gained scholarships to achieve a good education. He was a Queen's Scholar at Westminster School, and was awarded a scholarship to Christ Church Oxford. He gained a First in Classics and won the Newdigate Prize for poetry. Ordained a deacon in 1907, he ministered in the slums of Leeds. Alongside his admiration for the socialist William Temple, this experience was to shape his life. His political views were always left of centre, and his outlook was international.

As Chaplain to the Archbishop of Canterbury in 1914 he became actively involved in the World Alliance for International Friendship. Through Churches he became a close friend of the head of the Lutheran Church in Sweden and together they campaigned on such issues as disarmament, the treatment of racial minorities, conscientious objectors, refugees, and extensive peace education. He worked with the Lutherans in London and was on committees with Fritz Wehrhan, the senior Lutheran Cleric in London.

Promotion and Controversy

He married in 1918 and became Dean of Canterbury in 1924, bringing changes to the Cathedral that some objected to, the broadcasting of services and the performance of dramatic productions in the Cathedral. He continued these reforms when he became Bishop of Chichester, commissioning T S Elliott to write *Murder in the Cathedral*.

From 1933 Bell supported the German Confessing Church, which proclaimed that Christian belief and National Socialism were incompatible, condemned anti-Semitism, and worked actively to help refugees and Jewish Christians.

At the outbreak of war Bell's mission of peace became more intense. He was in contact with the German Resistance and propagated controversial views on how to re-establish friendly relations with the enemy. His opposition to the allied bombing of civilians made him unpopular with the government. The Foreign Secretary called him 'that pestilent priest' when, during the London Blitz, Bell openly called for negotiations between Churchill and Hitler to bring an end to the bombing. His support for the so-called 'enemy aliens' did nothing to enhance his image, but it is in this role that he had an impact on the life and the administration of the internees in the Rushen Camp.

Visit to the Isle of Man and false reports

The Lutheran Pastors' wives wrote to invite him to visit them in the camp. He came and met them and gave a sermon in St Catherine's Church, Port Erin, in 28th July 1940, meeting with the young Methodist Minister Benson Harrison, who had had thrust upon him the burden of ministering to 3,500 women, who in many cases were distressed, lonely and frightened: an onerous task for a 29-year-old probationer. He wrote, after meeting the experienced 57-year-old Bishop Bell:

"From the moment I saw you, I felt greatly cheered by the very fact of your presence on the Island."

Harrison felt relieved sharing some of the problems he was addressing with the Bishop – but was later disconcerted to discover that Bishop Bell used this information in his many speeches condemning Government policy. Later, a highly critical report of the Port Erin Camp was published by the Free German League of Culture, an organisation dedicated to preserving German culture until the emigrants could return to Germany. But it was said to have strong ties to the Communist party of Germany, the KPD, which was suppressed by the Nazis in 1933 but remained an active underground opposition movement. Bishop Bell was a patron of the League.

The report stated that:

Jews and Nazis were not being separated (but no internees came with paperwork to say they were Nazi); the local residents thought all who spoke German were Nazi; that women had to share a bed (most of the hotels only had double beds); that food and health care was poor (both untrue).[9]

One internee, Mrs Garimberti, wrote to *The Guardian* newspaper stating firmly that the report was incorrect:

"The two articles that were in the paper early this week concerning the life of the women internees in the Rushen Camp I want to answer and I am doing so in the name of most of us.

What was said in the first article about our life in Port Erin is perfectly untrue. Mistakes happen everywhere in the world, but if a mistake was made here it was corrected at once. The hygienic conditions are very satisfactory indeed – only a small percentage being ill. It is impossible to deal with such big numbers at once – you can never satisfy 4,000 people, but the committee, which is working overtime, is only out for our welfare, health and hygiene.

We have got a hospital, with a special maternity part. If there is a TB case it is separated at once when the committee learn about it. If two people sleep in one bed, we must not forget that the beds are very big double beds, for which we get clean sheets every fortnight. There are bathrooms and plenty of hot and cold water in each room. As to the food, I can only say it is more like pre-war food and one is certain that people had to pay a lot of money in peace time to have such a nice time and such a nice place with all its comforts.

One must never forget that, after all, there is a terrible war going on, where millions of innocent people have to sacrifice everything and we were sent to the safest and most beautiful part of Great Britain.

Mrs Renate de Garimberti. (Courtesy of Manx National Heritage)

We will never forget what Britain has done for us refugees.
RENATE DE GARIMBERTI.
Port Erin, Isle of Man
(Ramsey Courier, *15th November 1940*)"[10]

The publication of the report brought two reporters from UK national newspapers. Their stories described an Island with an abundance of food, butchers' shelves brimming with hams and beef, very little rationing, even of sweets – a land of milk and honey. They reported that the internees were enjoying a seaside holiday atmosphere with very few restrictions. This information caused dissatisfaction and antagonism, even questions in Parliament, regarding the comfortable life of the internees while London was suffering meagre food rationing and nightly bombing.

Friction between Dame Joanna and Bishop Bell

Dame Joanna had more serious worries about her charges. Churchill had already broadcast to the nation about the possibility of invasion and the Commandant thought the publication of the whereabouts of 3,500 mainly Jewish women in the National press, which she attributed to the actions of Bishop Bell, could result in catastrophic retribution by the enemy.

This normally calm, highly organised Commandant could not contain her fury when Rev. Benson Harrison had to inform her that the Methodist Deaconess, Sister Emmeline Cheshire, who was helping him manage the extra workload of his ministry, had been arrested and detained in Douglas Police Station. They were both questioned. This was the result of a meeting arranged by Bishop Bell with Eva Kolmer, a committed Communist and general secretary of the Austrian Centre, who was under active surveillance.

The combination of Bishop Bell's indirect connection with the false report by the Free German League of Culture, the publicity generated by his drive for justice for internees, and unintended link to the arrest of two colleagues, may have become a source of frustration to Dame Joanna, and led to her comment to Benson Harrison:

"Bishop Bell is a highly dangerous man. If he is given any official role by the Home Office, I shall walk out."[11]

Bertha Bracey.
(Wikipedia)

Bertha Bracey, OBE (1893–1989) – leading Quaker relief worker

The Quakers (members of the Religious Society of Friends) played a leading, but not generally well-known role in the international effort to save the lives of those, many of them Jews, persecuted by the Nazis. The Quakers were particularly effective in saving the lives of Jewish children. It is estimated that they were responsible for saving over 20,000 Jews from almost certain death at the hands of the Nazis.

Early Years

Bertha Lilian Bracey was born in 1893 to parents living in Bournville, the model village set up that year by George Cadbury for the employees of the chocolate company where her father worked. Like most of the founders of major British chocolate businesses, the Cadbury's were Quakers. At the age of 18, Bertha herself became a Quaker. She graduated from Birmingham University and trained as a teacher. In 1921 she went to live in Vienna serving as a relief worker at the Quaker Centre, mostly setting up youth clubs. Bertha then moved to Nuremberg, working there and in Berlin to help relieve the catastrophic hardships caused by the German hyperinflation. In 1929 she moved to the Quaker headquarters in London as Secretary to the committee responsible for relief operations in Holland and Germany.

In 1933, with Hitler's rise to power, Bertha became Secretary of the Quaker Germany Emergency Committee organising help for Jews being persecuted by the Nazis in Germany, Austria and Czechoslovakia. Fluent in German and with a large network of contacts, by 1938 she had a staff of 59. The following year the Jewish refugee organisations were combined to form the Friends' Committee for Refugees and Aliens, headquartered in Bloomsbury House with a staff of 80 and a caseload of 14,000.

In 1934 she helped establish the Stoatley Rough School for Jewish refugee children in Haslemere, becoming Chairman of the Governors from 1938–1945 (and remaining as a Governor until 1960), as well as a school in the castle at Eerde in Holland for 100 German Jewish children.

Helping the refugees

On 9th/10th November 1938 *('Kristallnacht')*, Jews in Germany and Austria were intimidated, attacked and killed, their homes and businesses ransacked and looted, and their synagogues burned to the ground, while neither the police nor the fire services took any action. Immediately afterwards, Bertha visited Germany as part of a British emergency delegation and returned to lobby the British government to urgently relax immigration requirements. Also that month she was one of the delegates to the Home Secretary, Sir Samuel Hoare (also a Quaker), that led to the establishment of the *Kindertransport*, which during the next nine months was instrumental in saving 10,000 Jewish children's lives.

With the German invasion of Poland and outbreak of WWII on 1st September 1939, the Friends became very concerned about the more than 60,000 Jewish refugees in Britain and set up training schemes to help them qualify for jobs. By 1945 some 95% of the refugees were self-supporting.

In 1940 Bertha Bracey was the first welfare worker to arrive in Port Erin to provide support to Dame Joanna Cruikshank and her staff of five. On Bertha's advice Dame Joanna invited two further volunteers from the Jewish Refugee Society and three from the Society of Friends. Once Dame Joanna's staff had risen to 25 the aid workers left, with the exception of Margaret Collyer, a Quaker attached to Bertha's team at the Germany Emergency Committee, who had worked in Berlin and Amsterdam and also spoke German. Margaret was supportive of the establishment of the 'Service Exchange' and was still at the camp at least a year later.

Bertha made a report on her findings and the progress made in the women's camp, which was published in *The Manchester Guardian* in December 1941.[12]

In 1942 Bertha Bracey was awarded the OBE for her work for refugees. In 1945, when 300 orphaned children were found to have survived in *Theresienstadt* concentration camp, Bertha arranged with Bomber Command to have them flown to Britain to a reception camp in the Lake District.

In 1946 she was appointed by the Allied Control Commission in Germany to handle refugee affairs, and was later put in charge of women's affairs in the British and American Zones until she retired in 1953.

Bertha suffered from Parkinson's Disease in later life and died in 1989 at the age of 95. On 9th March 2010, Bertha Bracey was one of 27 recipients of the 'British Hero of the Holocaust' award, of which 25 were awarded posthumously.

The Lutheran Deaconesses

There were many curious onlookers as Sister Anna Jochman (1887–1965), the Matron of the innovative Dalston Hospital in London, led her crocodile of 40 nurses to their billet at Ard Chreg. They were Lutheran Deaconesses and their distinctive uniforms had never before been seen in the Island: a floor-length navy-blue-spotted gown covered by a cloak, and on their heads the distinctive white starched bonnets tied under the chin with a bow.

The German-trained nurses had been arrested at the hospital – and so hastily that one Deaconess complained that she had to leave a patient she was bathing in the bath.

The German (Dalston) Hospital, London. (Courtesy of Bethel Archives)

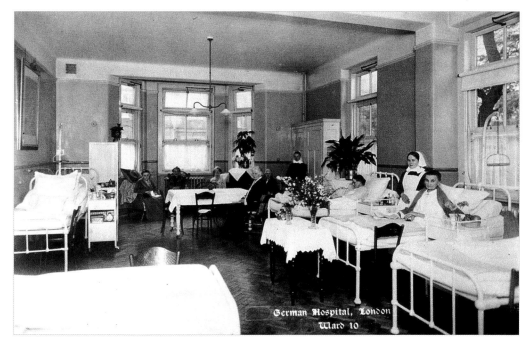

German Hospital, London
Ward 10

It was one of the few hospitals in London to have a kosher kitchen and catered for the large German and Jewish community in the area, as well as those in need in the local community.

Isolde Wehrhan, daughter of a Lutheran Pastor, but born in Britain, was one of the few nurses left to cope at the Dalston Hospital after the Deaconesses had been arrested and taken to Holloway Prison. They had to cope with a heavy influx of patients injured during the nightly bombing raids in London. Isolde's mother, Wanda, had worked with the Sisters in London, establishing a hostel for the homeless refugees, and when she became an internee she was billeted with the Sisters.

They were unfortunately one of the groups that were treated unkindly by the host hoteliers, even though the Deaconesses had been doing all the household laundry and looking after the sickly husband of the owner. After Wanda's letters of complaint to the Commandant about the treatment of the Sisters, they were all moved to the Windsor House.

The Lutheran Pastors' wives were concerned about the circumstances the Sisters found themselves in; Mrs Rieger writing to London to ask for funds to be sent to them and Wanda writing to the Commandant detailing the comfort, nursing and maternity care that the Sisters were providing and asking, 'Would it not be possible as a mark of their self sacrifice to allow a slight remuneration for their shoe leather?'[13]

Some tensions arose between Wanda and Sister Anna when Wanda lost the vote to be camp leader by just two votes. She thought Sister Anna was far too unworldly to make the demands required for the camp residents and continued to write letters of complaint almost daily to the Commandant. Sister Anna worked more closely with Dame Joanna who recognised her contribution to the smooth running of the camp – which led to the Commandant being criticised for 'working with Nazis' (in those days any German-speaking internee was considered by many to be a Nazi).

Sister Anna had been in the mother house, 'Sarepta', from the age of 15. The Deaconesses were committed to a life of dedication and prayer, combined with a commitment to help the disadvantaged, and it is doubtful if they knew anything of the politics in Germany then.

Sarepta, the motherhouse for the deaconesses. (Wikipedia)

The mother house, named Serepta, assisted Bethel, near Bielefeld, a Protestant institution for the healing and care of epileptics, and in 1940 2,000 trained nurses from Sarepta were deployed throughout the world on their missions of compassion.

The Lutheran Pastors' wives in Rushen Camp were all connected to Bethel. Pastors Wehrhan, Rieger and Dhiel had all been trained in the ministry at Bethel. Most of the Deaconesses had been in the convent-like atmosphere at the motherhouse of Sarepta from a very early age. They had dedicated their lives to Christian service and were trained in nursing and surgical skills at the nearby hospital and seminary of Bethel in Bielefeld. In 1940, 2,000 trained nurses from Sarepta were deployed throughout the world on their missions of compassion.

The Lutheran Pastors' wives in Rushen Camp had all been attached to Bethel, the institution founded by Pastor Bodelschwingh and it was his son who called a meeting to write a new confession of Faith. Dietrich Bonhoeffer was at the meeting. The Bethel Declaration clarified the resistance of the Lutherans to anti-Judaism and anti-Semitism. Hitler ordered the gassing of all the mentally ill patients being cared for at Bethel, but the Director resisted saying, 'You can put me in a concentration camp, but as long as I am free you do not touch any one of my patients.'

The Bethel Institute survived and to this day is a hospital for the disadvantaged.

During their internment, the Deaconesses looked after the children in the camp, teaching at Sunday school, providing maternity care, looking after the sick and even teaching basic nursing skills.

They were eventually repatriated and returned to the mother house at Bethel. Sister Anna continued to work as a Matron until 1958 aged 71.

Internee Birger Forell wrote in the diary that she kept during her time in the Isle of Man, 'We could not have found a better Camp Leader. She is calm, solid and clever and a mother to us all.'[14]

Sister Anna Jochmann (10th February 1887 – 12th October 1965)
She became a Deaconess in Lutheran Church in 1910. She was nursing during
WWI in London. Later she nursed at Bethel and Gevelserg and was Matron at
Hassche, Luedenscheld and Dalston hospitals. After internment, she nursed at
the Bethel Monastery and was Matron at the Gilead Hospital. (Image courtesy
of Bethel Archives)

MUSIC AND MUSICIANS

Music and the Musicians

A considerable amount has been written about the music in the men's camps in the Isle of Man during WWII and, indeed, there were many professional musicians interned there. However, there was as much musical prowess in the women's camp in Rushen in the south of the Island.

In most of the hotel lounges there were pianos, and the lounges themselves were large rooms designed for dances and concerts, so it was not long before a range of musical activities began to develop. It soon became apparent that many of the instrumental musicians had managed to bring their instruments with them and this added to the range of available activities. The church halls also became venues for events when larger audiences needed to be accommodated.

Else Haefner, a German organist operatic singer. She played a significant role at the services in St Mary's Church in Port St Mary. Her repertoire was mainly classical.

Bertha Huttenbach, a singer, known professionally as Bea Hutton, appeared in The Royal Variety Performance in 1935. She was the sister of the celebrated cellist Otto Huttenbach.

Joanna Metzger-Lichtenstern, a young soprano from Berlin, was the leading inspiration for musical activities in the camp (see Chapter 12).

Margarethe Schmid, born in Vienna and married to a German, was a music teacher. She would have assisted with lessons in the camp schools.

Dr Magda Kelber an educationalist and accomplished organist, she accompanied soloists, choral singing in the churches and also performed as a soloist.

Helga Krebs, born in 1916 in Berlin, was a professional pianist and played an important role in the camp. She was the Musical Director for many of the camp concerts, performed and also accompanied many of the soloists. She was a member of 'The Optimists'.

All photos courtesy of Manx National Heritage except Johanna Metzger-Lichtenstern, courtesy of Jewish Chronicle.

CHAPTER FIFTEEN

Olga Ritter, born in Hamburg in 1893, was a clever organiser and responsible for the arrangement and introduction of many of the concerts in the camp.

Jeanette Simon, a professional opera singer from Berlin, played leading roles in performances in the churches and was soloist at the service by Bishop Bell. She performed classical, operatic and folk songs.

Käte Boronow, born in 1894 in Strelno, was a pianist. She was the accompanist for several of the violinists in the camp entertainments.

Edith Lenar-Horowitz, known professionally as Edith Lenar, was an operatic soprano. Born in Vienna, she and her husband emigrated to the USA towards the end of the war and she applied to become a US citizen in 1946.

When **Ilse Wolffe** was interned, aged 19, she wanted to be a singer and received lessons from an unknown internee. After the war, she became a Leider singer specialising in the works of Schubert. She also taught singing in the UK.

Engel Lund, a Danish/Icelandic folk singer, made several visits to the camp to entertain the internees. It is believed that her visits were funded by the British Council's cultural provision for the internees, but it is also true that she was campaigning for the release of her professional partner, Ferdinand Rauter, interned in the Island in 1940.

Hildegard Luft was a professional pianist. She was responsible for the musical direction of an internee play called *The Seven Daughters* written by Minna Specht, which combined Chanukah and Christmas festivals.

Edith Bach-Kaczynski (1896–1975) – The Nightingale of Königs Wusterhausen

Edith Bach-Kaczynski. (Courtesy of Manx National Heritage)

Edith Bach was known as the 'Nightingale of Königs Wusterhausen'. She came from a musical family and was a coloratura soprano at the height of her powers in pre-war Berlin, performing all over Europe.

On 22nd December 1920, the first transmission of music and speech was made from the Königs Wusterhausen transmitter (built in 1915), which handled long-wave, medium-wave and short-wave broadcasts. Edith was a Director of the radio company and her singing was the first to be transmitted to England from Germany. Weekly concerts would be broadcast to the UK and Edith was noted regularly in the BBC radio supplement. The rise of Nazism, however, meant that by 1935 Edith was banned from performing, simply for being Jewish.

She had married into the Kaczynski family but, after *Kristallnacht*, her husband was arrested and transported to Sachsenhausen concentration camp. Edith escaped to England with her two small boys, William (aged four) and Edward (a baby). Edward had been damaged at birth by lack of medical attention.

They were fortunate in being able to obtain a work permit for her husband as a milliner and he was freed from the concentration camp. Reunited, they began a new life in England. Their reunion alas was brief. They were swept up in the paranoia of 'Collar the lot' and ended up in the Isle of Man, in separate internment camps. However, they were eventually reunited in Rushen Married Camp.

No records show Edith as having performed in the camp's music world, though she did give singing lessons as a diploma teacher and it is believed she taught Janette Simons and Ilse Wolff. When her injured baby son, Edward, first moved his paralyzed arm Edith was so overjoyed she had a message posted round the camp that she would now give singing lessons for free.

Edith's German passport marked 'J' for Jew. (Image by permission of W. Kaczynski)

After the war, when Edith was in her late 40s, she tried to restart her singing career by contacting the BBC, but it was not to be – there was no interest. She resigned herself to a role as wife and mother, helping her husband in his millinery business, and giving concerts for charity in her community. She still enjoyed her singing.

The family were sad that she had no recordings of her voice and none could be found, but her sons have recently been overjoyed to discover that a record does exist (*Der Rote Sarafan*) and have given a DVD to Rushen Heritage Trust, combined with a scrapbook of her appearances at the height of her fame. This will make the sound of the Nightingale of Königs Wusterhausen ring out once again.

A university house has been named after her, so her memory will now be perpetuated.

The musicians in the camp were prolific in their attempts to keep spirits up and fellow internees busy. There are too many to mention individually, but research has

identified the following people, who, in addition to those key players already identified, were also involved:

Rosy Hahn, Melitta Kratter, Henny Spier, Marta Koch, Else Frankel, Ingeborg Mendelsohn, Gertrud Zerner, Alex Eggerner, Margot Strauss, Dr Danziger, the Lutheran Deaconnesses, Eva Langentels, Sidi Stahl, Melitta Drucker.

Groups

At first the internees were not allowed to visit other hotels, so musical groups developed in a number of places and some overlapped when they rehearsed in church halls, etc. The groups included:

> Ira Rischowski's Golf Links Choir
> Else Franke's Round Song Choir
> Eva Langetels' Choir of Women Internees
> The Deaconesses' Choir
> The Camp School Orchestra
> Johanna Metzger-Lichtenstern's Camp Choir
> Bertha Huttenbach's Ladies' Choir
> Bradda Glen Sparrows
> The Optimists
> A small string orchestra in Port Erin

In addition to all of these groups there were two groups who were actors and musicians: the Youth Players, which incorporated a small choir and the Ailsa Craig Group of Entertainers.

Types of Music and Entertainment

Much of the music performed was by German and Austrian composers including Schubert, Strauss, Handel, Bach and Beethoven, but there were also performances of operas and hymns plus Manx and English folk songs.

In addition to these performances there were several Christmas events, puppet shows for the children, a Viennese evening, an evening of ballet and a number of variety shows written by the internees.

A programme for one such variety performance still exists (see right) and is in the safe keeping of the Isle of Man Collection at the Leo Baeck Institute in New York[1].

The programme was acquired by them as part of the effects of Martha Wolgast (Boschwitz). Martha was responsible for compiling the programme. She was a writer whose profile appears in Chapter 16.

Olga Ritter was responsible for the introduction and arrangement of the programme and Helga Krebs was responsible for the arrangement of the music.

It was an evening of songs, poems and music and what follows are details of some of the songs and poems and the people who were involved in the success of the evening on 6th July 1940, only five weeks after the internees arrived in Rushen:

Programme for musical evening. (Image courtesy of the Leo Baeck Institute, New York)

Item 1
This was a poem entitled 'Möwenschrei' (A Seagull's Cry) written by Martha Wolgast (Boschwitz) and set to music by Mrs Behrens.

Items 2 and 3
Viennese songs were very popular as many of the internees were Austrian, but 'Miss Ginger' has sadly not been identified and the Miss Cohn who played the accordion could have been Marianne or Margot!

Martha Wolgast and Mrs Behrens

Item 4
Unfortunately, it is not known which of the poems by Klabund (real name Alfred Henschke) was performed, but it was recited by Miss M Goldschmidt.

Item 5
The 'Dance Duet' was performed by the Misses Ortwein and Rodger, while the music was written by Mrs Larisch and arranged by Mrs Heilpern, who also sang the 'Cigarette Song' for Item 6. (No lyrics have been found.)

Miss M. Goldschmidt

Berta Ortwein

Eva Ann Rodger

Charlotte Heilpern

Dora Larisch

All portrait photos on this page courtesy of Manx National Heritage.

Johanna Metzger

Mrs Dora Lask

Mrs Steinfeld

Mrs Niczky

Miss Ellen Moses

Mrs Tilly Frank,

Item 6

'Cigarette Song' sung by Mrs Heilpern.

Item 7

This was a performance, by Johanna Metzger-Lichtenstern, of two Yiddish songs. Once again, there are no details as to which songs they were.

Item 8

This item consisted of poems by Wilhelm Busch and a poem, 'Sie sassen und tranken am Theetisch' (At Tea), by Heinrich Heine, recited by Mrs Dora Lask.

Item 9

Penny Thrillers, the title for this item, were also known as Penny Dreadfuls, Penny Awfuls, Penny Horribles and Penny Bloods. They were 19th century serial stories published in weekly parts, based on Gothic thrillers and stories about famous criminals and they could be bought for 1d.

The *Penny Thrillers,* in rhymes, were performed by Mrs Steinfeld, an actress, and Mrs Niczky.

Item 10

This is described as a *pot pourri* (songs) and is performed by Miss Ellen Moses, who was born in Stettin (Szczecin, Poland), in 1908 and was interned at the Ballaqueeney, in Port St Mary.

Item 11

The finale was a poem by Friedrich von Schiller entitled 'The Invincible Fleet' (Armada).

Johann Christoph Friedrich von Schiller, born 10th November 1759 in Marbach am Neckar, Germany, was a poet, philosopher, physician, historian and playwright. A friend of Goethe, his work was much admired by the likes of Beethoven, Brahms and Verdi, of whom many set his work to music. He died from tuberculosis in Weimar, Germany aged 45 in 1826.

There was an introduction in English by Mrs Tilly Frank, who was British by birth. It is possible that it was a choral recitation as the finale to the concert.

The poem is a description of the attack of the Spanish Armada, but the final 16 lines may have been drawn as a comparison with the conflict which was in progress at that time.

Friedrich von Schiller also wrote:

Friend and Foe

Dear is my friend – yet from my foe, as from my friend comes good; My friend shows what I can do, and my foe shows what I should.

Events and Venues

The churches, especially the Methodist church, had been very supportive of the internees' music programmes. Weekly events took place at the Methodist

Church in Station Road, Port Erin and St Mary's Church, Port St Mary, as well as at other churches including St Catherine's Church in Port Erin.

Conclusion

Music and entertainment played a huge and very important role in the lives of the internees and helped to sustain them through some very difficult times.

All photos on opposite page courtesy of Manx National Heritage except Johanna Metzger-Lichtenstern, courtesy of Jewish Chronicle.

SIGNIFICANT WRITERS

Boredom was a serious problem that the internees had to contend with and their enthusiastic musical activities helped them to address the issue, but, as well as the music, for some women creative writing was also a way of coming to terms with their situation.

Four such women were Livia Laurent, Lotte Moos, Ruth Michaelis-Jena and Marie Neurath.

'Livia Laurent' – Actress and Writer

This was the pen name of Eva Meyerhof (née Oppenheim), who was born on 6th October 1914 into a Jewish family in Frankfurt, Main. With her mother, Eva Oppenheim left Germany in 1933 for exile in Britain. She and her mother were carrying out unpaid domestic duties when she married Hartwig Meyerhof in Hendon, Middlesex in December 1935.

Little is known about her life in either Germany or Britain, but she seems to have worked as an actress and writer. At that time neither of these occupations was considered suitable for a respectable young woman, so this may have been partly responsible for her internment. However, Julie V. Gottlieb, in her book *Feminine Fascism: Women in Britain's Fascist Movement, 1923–45*, lists Eva as:[1]

"Interned in Holloway Prison and then in the Isle of Man under the category of 'hostile origins'. Published her poetry in the Poetry Review *in May–June 1941. She was not allowed to send any of her work from the internment camp and took on a legal adviser to settle the issue in June 1941. Permission for internees to write for publication while in internment was denied by the Secretary of State in August 1941. An application for her release was made by the Jewish Refugee Committee, Bloomsbury House, in 1941."*

Eva arrived in Port Erin on 10th September 1940 and was regarded as a 'refugee from Nazi oppression', although her tribunal had identified her as 'Category A'. Two months after attending a tribunal in Douglas, she returned to England on 22nd August 1941, released as a 'special case'.

After her return to England, Eva was persuaded by a journalist friend to write about her experiences in the Rushen internment camp. This resulted in her first book entitled *A Tale of Internment*, published in 1942.[2] Whereas many other writers were struggling to have their work published because of a paper shortage, Livia managed to get two books published that year, her second book being a collection of 'Poems'[3].

A number of critics have suggested that, in her poems, her use of English

The cover of Livia's book (published 1942).

was not always conventional, but then it was not her mother tongue. Others have described her work as 'fresh', 'unconventional' and 'sincere'.

After the publication of her own books, Eva, under her pseudonym, went on to translate several books from German to English for other writers, including Catherine Klein.

Lotte Moos (Née Jacoby) – Politically Active Poet and Playwright

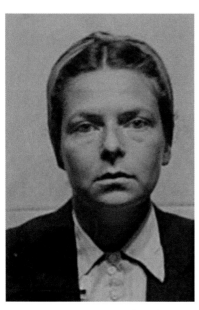

Lotte Moos. (Courtesy of Manx National Heritage)

Born Margarete Charlotte Jacoby in Berlin on 9th December 1909, Lotte was the third child of Samuel and Luise Jacoby. As a child, she was inspired by Charles Dickens's *A Christmas Carol* and she wrote short stories, fables and poems.

In 1919, aged ten, her first published work, in the *Berliner Tageblatt*, was an essay about eastern European refugees. On leaving school, she became a photographer's assistant in the left-wing Worker's Theatre. She went on to become a politically active poet and playwright.

In 1932 she married left-wing economist and poet Siegfried Moos and in 1933, with Hitler's rise to power, they were forced to move first to Paris and then London, where Lotte hoped to study at the London School of Economics (LSE). However, her German qualifications were not recognised and her plans were frustrated.

In 1936, having been refused leave to stay in Britain, she travelled to the Soviet Union to join her friend, Brian Goold-Verschoyle and to 'see what it was like'. She was quickly disillusioned by the Soviet system and she was allowed to return to Britain. In 1939 British authorities received information from a Soviet defector to say that she could be a spy, so she was arrested and interrogated by MI5 in Holloway Prison and then interned in the Isle of Man in June 1940.

At about this time she learned of the death of her sister in a Nazi hospital, but did not know of the deaths of her parents until after the war.

On her release from internment, in October 1940, she and her husband lived in Oxford where he was working at the Institute of Statistics. She worked as a nursemaid, translator, typist and teacher and wrote a column for the British German-language newspaper, *Die Zietung*, under the pseudonym Maria Lehmann.

After the war Lotte, her husband and young daughter moved to Durham when he was appointed as a lecturer at Durham University. Lotte took part in amateur dramatics and also wrote plays, still under her pseudonym, mostly for radio and television. Her play, *Come Back with Diamonds*, a comedy about a released political prisoner returning to Moscow, was performed at the Lyric Theatre, Hammersmith in 1964 – and was received with boos from the London communists in the audience.

Lotte wrote the following books of poetry:

Time to be Bold (1981).
A Heart in Transit (1992).
Collected Poems (1993).

Her daughter, Merilyn Moos, wrote a book about her father's life, which includes the search for details of the fate of her mother's Jewish parents in Nazi Germany, called *The Language of Silence* (2010).

Lotte died on 3rd January 2008, aged 98 and was survived by her daughter, Merilyn, her grandson, Joshua and her niece, Ruth Parker.

Ruth Michaelis-Jena (1905–1989) – Well Known in Scottish Literary Circles

Ruth Michaelis-Jena.
(Courtesy of Manx
National Heritage)

Ruth was born on 19th October 1905 in Detmold, Germany. Her family were Jewish and lived in Lippe, which was one of the last German principalities.

She was a writer and translator and had a particular interest in folklore. Ruth had begun her career in a bookshop where she thoroughly enjoyed the work and soon became department head. Shortly afterwards she opened her own bookshop, but one day in 1933 she found Nazi Stormtroopers outside her shop, the windows daubed with slogans and her customers stopped from entering.

Ruth decided she needed to leave and, in 1934, received permission to emigrate. Through her work she had made friends in Scotland and they gave her the support that she required when she arrived in August 1934. Her experience enabled her to find work in Thin's Edinburgh bookstore and, to supplement her income, she gave German lessons.

In January 1940 she was interviewed at a tribunal and subsequently interned in the Isle of Man on 1st July 1940. Like many of the internees she found the experience depressing, so it was with a grateful heart that she accepted the opportunity to use her skills to organise the books (given to the internees by local people and various charities) into a library.

She eventually left the Island on 4th July 1941, to return to her home in Edinburgh, where she joined a fire-fighting team as her contribution to the war effort.

In 1952 she married Arthur Radcliffe and they worked together on translating and editing material from the manuscripts of the Brothers Grimm and on research into the lives of the brothers.

Her husband died in 1960, but Ruth continued to produce a considerable volume of work, principally in the genre of folklore. She also gave lectures on the subject, including the Katharine Briggs' Lecture in 1973. She was an adventurous woman and was one of the first travellers from Britain to visit China.

In 1983 she wrote her autobiography, *Heritage of the Kaiser's Children*. She was well known in Scottish literary circles and was writing right up to the time of her death on 19th August 1989 aged 74.

Marie Riedermeister.
(Courtesy of Manx
National Heritage)

A diagram detailing the
manufacture of
cellulose acetate
powders and sheet.
(Courtesy of the
Isotype revisited
website)

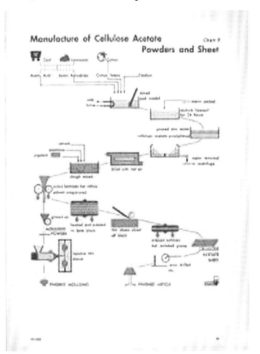

Marie Neurath (1898–1986) – the Isotype System and 'Railways Under London'

Born Marie Reidermeister on 27th May 1898 in Braunschweig, Germany, she went on to study mathematics and physics at the University of Göttingen from 1917 to 1924. Then, just before graduating, she met Otto Neurath (1882–1945) in Vienna.

In March 1925 Marie went to work as Otto's assistant in what had been a small museum of information about housing, but at the beginning of 1925 it had become the 'Social and Economic Museum of Vienna'. This was the start of her long career as a designer working with Neurath as part of a team making graphic displays of social information. Another important member of the Neurath group was German artist Gerd Arntz (1901–1988) who joined in 1928.

Marie worked at the museum in Vienna until there was a brief civil war in Austria in 1934. Then she, Neurath (who was a prominent Social Democrat) and Arntz (who had allegiances to radical-left groups) all left for The Hague. In 1935, they began to use the acronym Isotype (International System of TYpographical Picture Education) for their work.

When the Germans invaded the Netherlands in 1940, Reidermeister and Neurath escaped to England on the same boat as the Munzers (see Chapter 12 page 133), while Arntz stayed in The Hague.

In 1941, after release from internment, Marie and Otto were married and resumed work in Oxford, founding the Isotype Institute. They enjoyed living in Britain and helped the town council of Bilston, near Wolverhampton, to plan their post-war reconstruction.

After Otto's death in 1945, Marie continued their work with a small number of English assistants and in 1948 she moved to London. She dedicated her time to establishing a record of Otto's life and work, editing and translating his writings.

In 1971 Marie retired and gave all the work from their research project to the University Of Reading, where it can be found in the Department of Typography & Graphic Communication. It has been said in the journal for *Isotype Revisited* that the collection offers[4]:

"...excellent opportunities for scholars interested in European social history between the World Wars, inter-War modernism, the history of information design, and campaigns and initiatives that address social and economic planning, public health, housing and other dimensions of life."

And the collection will be:

"...equally valuable to anyone involved in the

graphic design of data, museum design, or the communication of complex issues to children, particularly in history and in the natural and physical sciences."

While Marie was in Rushen Internment Camp, she was one of a number of people teaching the children and running courses for the adults. After Otto's death, she developed the work of Isotype in a new and influential direction with her series of books, published by Max Parrish, which were based on a deep understanding of how children conceptualise the world. Many of you may recognise them from your classroom libraries of the 1950s and 1960s – today they are very collectable.

One series she wrote was called 'The Visual History of Mankind' and was intended to help young children to have a clearer picture of how different periods of history developed. One title, of many, was *They Lived Like This in Ancient Mexico*.

Other books explained how things worked that were not obvious to the naked eye, such as the workings and layout of the London Underground in *Railways Under London*.

Books about science (then known as 'nature studies') included *Too small to see* and *Strange Plants*.

Marie Neurath died in London on 10th October 1986, aged 88.

Above right: Otto Neurath.

Right: Marie in later life. (both courtesy of the Otto and Marie Neurath Isotype Collection, University of Reading)

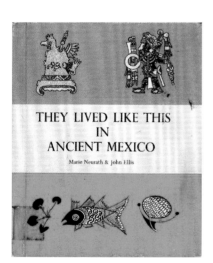

Above and right: One title in the series 'A Visual History of Mankind' – They Lived like this in Ancient Mexico. (http://isotyperevisited.org/isotype-collection/index.html)

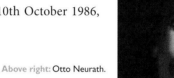

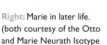

Mexico's capital, Mexico City, is on the plateau.
It was built on top of an ancient city. Guadalajara (say: gwah-dah-lah-HAH-rah) holds a yearly festival for a special kind of Mexican music, called mariachi (say: mah-ree-AH-chee).

Cancún (say: kahn-KOON) has some of the best beaches in the world.
Oaxaca (say: wah-HAH-kah) is home to colorful festivals and folk art.

Above and right: Books in 'nature studies' (science) series 'The Wonder World of Nature' – Strange Plants and Too Small to See. (http://isotyperevisited.org/isotype-collection/index.html)

Top right: 'Railways Under London' about the workings of the London Underground was part of a series explaining things that were not obvious to the naked eye. (http://isotyperevisited.org/isotype-collection/index.html)

Martha Boschwitz (née Wolgast) (1886–1959)

Martha Wolgast was born in Langenfeld, Germany in 1886. In 1911 she married Salli Boschwitz, a descendant of two significant Rabbis – Rabbi Chaim Weil and Rabbi Wolf Munk.

Salli died in 1915 and from then on Martha was referred to by both her married and maiden surnames. Martha was interned on 30th May 1940 after her tribunal at Bow Street and she was billeted in the Balmoral Hotel, Port Erin. Her internee registration card describes her as an 'artist/painter' and a brief report on page six of the *Isle of Man Examiner* for Friday, 15th November 1940 outlines a small exhibition of her work.

Martha had two children, Clarissa and Ulrich, who was a writer under the pen name of John Grane. He had lived in Norway and Luxembourg, and had several works published before moving to England in 1939. He was briefly interned and then shipped to Australia as an 'enemy alien' on the HMT *Dunera*. He was allowed to return to England in 1942, but the ship he was on, the MV *Obosso*, was torpedoed and he and 41 others returning were killed.

During her internment, Martha and Ulrich had collaborated on a children's story called 'König Winter's Geburtstag'. Ulrich had written the story and his mother had painted the watercolour illustrations. A bound copy of the handwritten story is in the Isle of Man Collection in the Leo Baeck Institute in New York, along with several signed copies of Martha's poems and a watercolour painting of the Station Hotel in Port Erin (opposite). Martha left the Island in May 1945 for Bloomsbury in London. She died in 1959.

Martha Boschwitz. (Courtesy of Manx National Heritage)

ART IN WOMEN'S INTERNMENT CAMP

Mme. Martha Wolgast, German artist, painter and writer, now interned in the Isle of Man, held a small, but remarkable exhibition of her portraits, painted during her internment at Port Erin. Some 25 paintings were on view.

(Courtesy of Manx National Heritage (*Isle of Man Examiner*, Friday, 15th November 1940, p.2)

The Station Hotel, Port Erin, watercolour by Martha Wolgast. (Courtesy of the Leo Baeck Institute, New York)

Margarete Klopfleisch:
Watercolour – Barbed
Wire (1941).
(Courtesy of Sonja
Grossner (née
Klopfleisch))

Margarete's internee registration card. (Courtesy of
Manx National Heritage)

ART AND ARTISTS

Very few professional artists have been identified among the over 4,000 women interned in the Rushen internment camp. This is in sharp contrast to the significant number of male artists interned in the Isle of Man in 1940, many of whom were assigned to the Hutchinson and Onchan camps, though others were certainly active in the Mooragh, Peveril, Palace, Central and Sefton camps.

Only three professional artists are known from among the Rushen women internees, namely:

> Margarete Klopfleisch (1911–1982)
> Pamina Liebert-Mahrenholz (1904–2004)
> Erna Nonnenmacher (1889–1980)

All three women were German, were primarily sculptors, and were interned initially in Holloway Prison before being transferred to the Isle of Man.[1] There may have been at least one other as, in her November 1940 interview with *The Manchester Guardian*, Dame Joanna Cruickshank, the Camp Commandant, noted: 'a talented Austrian sculptor holds clay modelling-classes and her pupils are doing good work'.[2] However, this may have been referring to Erna Nonnenmacher, as Dame Joanna may not have made a careful distinction between Austrian and German nationals.

By comparison it has been calculated that 8.6% of the roughly 1,500 internees in the Onchan camp were journalists, writers or artists. Whether this reflects gender bias in the early 20th century at a time when women artists were not taken seriously, whether for the most part women did not pursue fine and decorative arts as a profession in Germany and Austria, or some other factors is not clear.

A number of amateur artists are also recorded including: Martha Boschwitz (née Wolgast) (1886–1959); Lotte Salzburger, who produced a drawing of Ira Rischowski and painted the sets for the Golf Course Variety Show; and M. Sussmann, who is recorded as having painted pictures of animals and the frieze around the entrance hall in the Marine Biology Station (sadly all now lost).[3]

Margarete Klopfleisch (1911–1982)
'Birch Holme', Bradda Glen, Port Erin (internment address)

Margarete ('Gretel') Klopfleisch (née Grossner) was born in Dresden, Germany in 1911. Her father was a cabinetmaker and her mother an amateur opera singer. After serving in WWI her father struggled to make a living, so her mother had to work in a bottling factory. At age 14, following her mother's death, Gretel left school and took menial jobs as a maid or nanny.

Brought up with strong left-wing sympathies, she joined socialist worker youth groups and became politically active. She taught herself to play the violin and took lessons from a local violin teacher, before joining an 'agitprop' band in which she both played and sang. 'Agitprop' is highly politicised propaganda spread though popular media such as music, theatre, film and other art forms, especially communist propaganda used in Soviet Russia and that spread elsewhere in Europe and the USA in the 1920s. It is a contraction of the name: Department for Agitation and Propaganda.

From the age of 17 she became interested in art, especially sculpture, and modelled for life drawing classes run by Otto Dix (1891–1969)[4] at the Dresden Academy. Though never formally enrolled as a student, she asked Dix for advice on how to become an artist, to which he told her, 'Just take a pencil and paper and start'.

Through her membership of the communist *Rote Gewerkschafts-Internationale,* Gretel met Peter Klopfleisch (1902–1976), who was nine years her senior. When Hitler came to power on 30th January 1933, Peter was forced to go into hiding and in May fled to Prague. Gretel, too, soon had to hide, but when in November a warrant was issued for her arrest, her communist colleagues told her to emigrate. Joining Peter in Prague, they could not marry as a visit to the German Embassy for a licence would have led to arrest and shipment to a German concentration camp. Her brother, Hans, was arrested and imprisoned for anti-fascist activities.

Forbidden to work, they suffered extreme privation, eating only in soup kitchens. Notwithstanding, Gretel found an art teacher (a friend of internationally recognised artist, Käthe Kollwitz)[5] who in turn introduced her to a sculpture teacher from whom she learned stone carving. In 1937 she became a member of the prestigious Oskar Kokoschka Club, exhibiting her work with other fellow anti-fascist artists and eking out a living as a nanny. With Hitler's invasion of Czechoslovakia imminent, Gretel had to flee again. Around 4th March 1939 she left for England on the last train for women and children, travelling via Finland and Sweden and reaching England on 9th March.[6] Peter managed to escape via Poland and Sweden arriving in London on 15th May. Gretel was employed as a domestic help in Hampstead by artist Roland Penrose, who helped her further her studies. Peter and Gretel married in June, moving in October to a hostel in Maidenhead where Gretel attended sculpture classes at Reading University.

In May 1940 they were both interned, Gretel in Holloway Prison and then the Isle of Man. Gretel was by then pregnant, but suffered a miscarriage that led to a persistent haemorrhage from which she almost died and was saved only by an emergency operation while in Rushen camp. Little is known of her time in the camp, though there was at least one exhibition in which her sculpture 'Despair' was included.

Peter was sent initially to the Isle of Man, but was soon sent back to Liverpool for shipment to Australia on the infamous HMT *Dunera.*[7] There he spent nine months in Hay Camp, NSW, only to return to the Isle of Man for a further two months. Following their release, Gretel and Peter were reunited and in 1942 Sonja, the first of their two daughters, was born. Settling again in Maidenhead, Peter resumed his work as a compositor and Gretel resumed sculpting and painting, attending classes and exhibiting in London, Reading, Maidenhead, Cookham and elsewhere locally.

In 1950 they applied to the German Democratic Republic (DDR) to return, but the application was denied after a two-and-a-half-year delay. In 1956 they received an unexpected visit from Gretel's brother, who travelled to the UK illegally and cautioned them under no circumstances to return

"Despair" – IOM 1940.
(Courtesy of Leicester Arts & Museums Service)

to the DDR. Nevertheless, in 1960 Gretel took her two daughters to Dresden for a holiday, but once there the authorities confiscated her daughters' passports and replaced them with DDR ones, effectively forcing them to remain indefinitely. However, in Gretel's words, 'We were regarded with suspicion, mistrust and as spies by many people and eventually became victims of the Stasi secret police.'

The DDR authorities refused to acknowledge and accept Gretel's artistic abilities. Thus, she was compelled to work as a gardener, postwoman and scene painter for the Dresden State Theatre. In 1965 Gretel was awarded a compensatory pension as a victim of Nazi persecution, together with a larger flat, at which point Peter joined them from England. However, by then their marriage was over and they quickly divorced. Peter died in 1976. Gretel's younger daughter married around 1970, but Sonja continued to live with her

Pen drawing – "Mother and Child". (Courtesy of Sonja Grossner and the artist's estate)

mother. Beginning in 1971, they were subjected to unexplained thefts and damage to the contents of their home, especially artwork, and were placed under constant surveillance by the Stasi.

During the 1970s Gretel's health deteriorated and she died in 1982. One year before her death, she was at last accepted as a member of Dresden Artists' Union after a successful exhibition of her artwork at the Gallery Comenius in Dresden.

In December 1987 the John Denham Gallery in London held an exhibition of her work.[8]

Examples of her work are held in Moritzburg, Halle, the German Historical Museum, Berlin and the New Walk Museum & Art Gallery, Leicester.

Postscript: In 1984 Gretel's elder daughter, Sonja, a musician, who by then had regained her British passport, returned to the UK. Sonja believes that her mother, father and uncle, Hans, all died under uncertain circumstances.[9]

Sonja Grossner (Klopfleisch), kindly assisted with this profile.

Pamina Liebert-Mahrenholz (1904–2004)
'Gleneagles', Port Erin (internment address)

Pamina Liebert-Mahrenholz was born in Berlin where her father was a lawyer. He was also an opera lover and so chose to name his daughter after a character in Mozart's *Magic Flute*. After apprenticeship to a firm of milliners, she studied sculpture at the prestigious Berlin Royal Academy of Art under Professor Fritz Klimsch (1870–1960). In 1929 she married portrait photographer Rolf Mahrenholz (1902–1991).

Although awarded the Academy's *Priz de Rome* in 1932 as Klimsch's 'master student', the Nazis prevented her from accepting it on account of her being Jewish. Rolf emigrated to Britain in 1938, where he worked as a freelance photographer, followed by Pamina in June 1939.

On 10th June 1940, Pamina was interned in Holloway Prison. She used her bread ration to make sculpture in a similar creative vein to the 'porridge sculptures' of Kurt Schwitters in Hutchinson Camp.[10, 11]

She was transferred to the Isle of Man, arriving on 18th July and left two

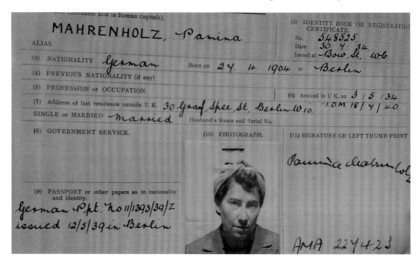

Pamina's internee registration card. (Courtesy of Manx National Heritage)

"White Doves".
(Courtesy of Ben Uri
Gallery & Museum)

"Two Female Nudes".
(Courtesy of Ben Uri
Gallery & Museum)

"Self-portrait".
(Courtesy of Ben Uri
Gallery & Museum)

"Reclining Nude".
(Courtesy of Ben Uri
Gallery & Museum)

years later in September 1942. Rolf Mahrenholz was also interned in the Isle of Man and eventually they were allowed to meet, once a month, in Collinson's Café in Port Erin.[12] Little is known of her internment; no work from the time appears to have survived and she is not recorded as a camp exhibitor.

After release, and unable to sculpt, she worked first in a lampshade factory and then batching kindling wood. Later she earned a living restoring china before turning again to sculpture and taking up painting and drawing in 1946.[13, 14]

She held several solo shows including: Camden Institute (1977), Ben Uri (1981), and Camden Art Centre (1983). In 2008 the Boundary Gallery held a joint exhibition with Berlin born ceramicist Margaret Marks.

Her work is represented in the Ben Uri Collection in London.

Erna Nonnenmacher (1889–1980)
'Carlton', Spaldrick, Port Erin
(internment address)

Erna Rosenberg was born in Berlin. After studying art there at the liberal (and Jewish-owned) Reimann Schule and the Kunstgewerbeschule, she attended the Technical School for Ceramics in Bunzlau and in 1919 she married fellow sculptor, Hermann Nonnenmacher (1892–1988).

Living in Berlin in the former studio of the artist Lyonel Feininger, Erna worked as a modeller for both the Fraureuth (1920–1924) and Rosenthal porcelain factories.[15]

Pressured by the Nazis, who classified the work of both artists as 'degenerate', in February 1938 Erna and Hermann emigrated to London, although Hermann, who was not Jewish, was invited to stay 'provided he divorced his wife', who was Jewish. By 1939 they were showing their work in gallery exhibitions in London with other exiled artists, including at the Wertheim Gallery, which hosted the first display under the auspices of the newly-founded Free German League of Culture, where Erna showed her typical feminine work while Herman was concerned with broader, more topical themes.

In 1940, both were interned. Hermann was sent to Onchan Camp[16] and Erna first to Holloway Prison and then Rushen Camp. She left the Isle of Man in February 1941. One clay tile from her internment, fired at Glenfaba Brickworks, Peel, survives in the Manx Museum.

In November 1941 Erna and Hermann exhibited in the AIA (Artists' International Association)/ Free German League of Culture exhibition in London. Her last exhibition was in 1978 at the Embassy of the Federal Republic of Germany as

Erna's internee registration card. (Courtesy of Manx National Heritage)

"Märchen" (Fairytale). (Courtesy of Germanisches National Museum)

Erna & Hermann
moving studio c.1940.
(Courtesy of Estate of
Inge King (1915-2016)
Australia)

one of 32 'London Artists from Germany'. Between 1948 and 1970 Erna assisted
Hermann, teaching modelling and pottery classes at Morley College of Adult
Education. She was nominated to the Royal Society of British Sculptors in 1964
and died in 1980.[17]

Below: "Maternity".
(Courtesy of Ben Uri
Gallery & Museum)

Her work is represented in the Ben Uri Collection, London, the
Germanisches National Museum (Nuremberg, Germany) and the Manx
Museum.

Bottom right: Calf of
Man: Crucifixion –
ceramic tile in the
Manx Museum.
(Courtesy of Manx
National Heritage)

PART 5: CLOSURE OF THE CAMP

FINAL YEARS OF THE CAMP

Local Reports on the Departure of the last Internees

As WWII raged on, the boundary and number of internees dwindled in camps W and Y in Port Erin and Port St. Mary. More and more internees were released and returned to England to either take part in the war effort in the ATS or in industry, or in some cases were repatriated back to Europe. There were a number of internees who were returned to internment in England.

The leaving of the remaining internees was reported in the local newspapers.

During the last year of the camp, 1944–1945, the majority of the internees left the Island. Aliens varying in age from a few months to over 70 were among the 580 who left the Island on board the *Rushen Castle* from Douglas on Wednesday evening, 5th September 1945[1]. Most of the internees were Germans or Italians, but included a few Japanese. Over 400 male internees came from Peel male camp, the remainder came from Port Erin, including many married couples. There were 70 men and 60 women in the party and also 27 children, of whom 11 were born in Port Erin. One baby, a few months old, arrived on the pier with its mother in a private car driven by one of the Home Office female staff. Two male stretcher cases arrived by the Local Government Board ambulance from Port Erin Camp Hospital. One, a German, had spinal trouble, the other a Japanese internee was suffering from rheumatoid arthritis. Another man who came in the Noble's Hospital ambulance was recovering from an operation for a duodenal ulcer. A number of RAMC personnel were there to look after the sick internees.

The internees, some of whom had been here over five years, nearly all looked well and most of them were quite well clothed, some noticeably so. Many smoked cigarettes, some of the men had pipes. Many of the internees carried big suitcases and the men from Peel marched along the North Quay from the railway station, the Port Erin party being conveyed from the station by bus. One of the married internees wore the ribbon of the 1939–45 Star, denoting that he had served in the British armed forces overseas.

An armed guard of about 40 members of the Pioneer Corps went with the internees and the whole party on board was in the charge of Inspector W. H. Howard of the Metropolitan Police, who wore the Military Medal ribbon in front of the three service ribbons of the last war. Among the officials who saw the internees off were Chief Inspector C. R. Cuthbert who had done a grand job as Commandant at Port Erin and Mr T. Angliss, Home Office Welfare Officer. The Island's Chief Constable Major J. W. Young and Superintendent Kelly were among the local police officials on the Edward Pier and Mr Alfred Teare and Mr Andrew Douglas, Manager and Assistant Manager respectively of the Steam Packet Co., were also on the job, with Captain Hugh Doran, Harbourmaster, and Mr Harold Matthews, Secretary of the Harbour Board.

If any evidence was necessary of the good treatment these internees had received from British camp officials, it was forthcoming when many were seen cordially shaking hands with the officials when saying goodbye.

For the local residents and towns' Local Authorities, post-war matters were

being discussed. When would the visiting industry be commenced? Rehabilitation of disabled service men and women would need to be considered and most importantly and biggest requirement, as minuted by the local Commissioners, would be the need for housing.

Enduring Friendships

Dalheim Family – *IOM Weekly Times*, 3rd June 1980

There were a number of internees who returned to the Island on a regular basis to visit the house owners with whom they had remained friends during their internment. Three daughters of one family, who were living in Hull at the time of the setting up of Rushen Internment Camp, returned to Port Erin many times for holidays.

Their story began when they were 'rounded up' with other aliens and shipped over to the Island on the 29th May 1940 aboard the *Josephine Charlotte*, the first ship to bring female internees to the Island. Their father, who had lived in England since 1909 was interned in Douglas Camp along with their brother Martin. The three girls were Rosemary, Anita and Erika Dalheim. Erika was a baby, but Rosemary and Anita who were quite a lot older recalled a long hot summer and initially the joy of no school for the first year. They were billeted in a boarding house on Port Erin Promenade called 'Sunset View'.

All the internees in the camp were given a job to do, the children also being given special chores. They remember a complete cross section and many nationalities. They eventually moved to Bradda Glen, which was still a holiday camp and their childhood memories of that time were nearly all happy. They recall meetings with their father and brother at Derby Castle once a month and made many friends with whom they had kept in touch.

The sisters were able to return to the Island in 1968 and have returned every summer since, when they often stayed with a Mrs Frances Maddrell. They returned again on the 40th anniversary to the day of their arrival, 29th May 1980. They stayed with a Mrs Kelly in Glen View Terrace. They reminisced about their five years spent on the Island, which had made a strong impression on them and who gained much from the experience, which could equally have had a detrimental effect on their future.

Rosemarie, Anita and Erika Dalheim. (Courtesy of Manx National Heritage (*Isle of Man Times*, 3rd June, 1980, p.2)

Later during their five years interned they were moved to Blair Athol in Port St. Mary and meetings with the menfolk taking place in the Ballaqueeney Hotel on the Promenade. Their school was located in Cowley's Café, later known as Manxonia fashion shop and currently owned by the Port St. Mary Commissioners and there was even a synagogue for the many Jewish internees located in the Town Hall.

The sisters had made the best of their childhood experiences, the best of which they felt is that they grew to know the Island, which drew them back each year to meet old friends and revisit places they loved.

Return of Internees

Mrs M. Wenz and M. Von T – *IOM Weekly Times*, 1980

A couple of internees who had read with great interest the newspaper article on the 3rd of June about the 40th anniversary trip of former internees (article about the Dalheim sisters) decided to write to the *Weekly Times*. They had also returned to 'celebrate' 40 years since they had been interned in Rushen.

Mrs Wenz met up with her friend in Liverpool, who had travelled all the way from South Africa. They travelled to the Island and stayed a night in Douglas and three nights in the Eagle Hotel in Port Erin. While they were here, they enjoyed re-visiting all the places that they used to know so well, many of the places wouldn't have changed so greatly since their internment.

They were interned in different locations, Mrs Wenz in one of the Bradda Glen holiday bungalows and M. von T in the Towers Hotel. As they walked around, they re-lived their time in Rushen in 1940. The bungalows at Bradda Glen had since gone and although they would have loved to have walked again up to Bradda Head, it would have been too much for them, both being in their 70th year. The Towers Hotel was still open and being run by the same family, which they found delightful to revisit.

The ladies enjoyed taking coffee at 'their old Bradda Glen', they enjoyed meals at Mr and Mrs Kennaugh's establishment (near the Railway Station), which included delicious gateaux with Mr K's lovely cream from their farm. They were even invited back to Mr and Mrs Kennaugh's house, where they all reminisced and re-lived time from 40 years before.

Reading the article certainly gave the impression that many of the internees accepted the situation and made the best that they could of it. Mrs Wenz went on to say that she never intended to return to her own country as she preferred England. She did not like what was going on and said she rather faced internment.

It says a lot for the internees' hosts and their conditions, when they can return, and want to return, to the place of their internment 40 years on and say: 'They were lovely memories we shall treasure as long as we live'.

Final Days

'Trail of Damage in Evacuated Houses'

After the repatriation of internees in 1944, the condition of some of the boarding houses in Port Erin, following inspections under the guidance of Mr H. Kearney, Chairman of the Port Erin Householders Committee, showed that they were in urgent need of repair before there could be any possible hope of restarting the visiting industry. It was going to take thousands of pounds to repair the enormous amount of damage done and to renew supplies of crockery, cutlery, bed linen, carpets and furniture and the 21/- allowed for each internee per week did not leave any margin for either renewals or renovations. Washhand basins had been used more as kitchen sinks, to the extent of washing vegetables, which they had grown in the allotments granted them, clogging up wastes. The matter would have to be taken up by the Householders Committee, Port Erin Commissioners and the Commandant.

'Save us from our Friends'

One local resident of Port Erin wrote to the *Isle of Man Examiner* in October 1944, following the large repatriation of internees back to Germany:
  "The day the barrier gate was taken away, allowing entry to all and sundry into Port Erin after the evacuation of the interned alien civilians, I happened to be in a confectioner's shop and saw and overheard the following, not so amusing to us, episode. A woman with a large shopping bag was being served and ordered three shilling cakes, then all the available pastry in the shop, which was only about six pieces. I heard her say that she was from Douglas, and said to the girl in the shop, 'You must be very pleased to see us back again after all this time?' and receiving an answer in the affirmative asked if there were any more pastry shops in Port Erin.

  Since our so-called 'liberation', we still have quite a considerable number of people here, and those from Bradda (and Spaldrick, areas forming the last married camp) come and shop in Port Erin three times a week and come down from half-past nine to half-past ten. In this time, the 'locusts' (a local term of endearment for the epidemic we have had) will have left practically nothing in the shops for the local residents, so can we honestly say we are really pleased to see our friends from Douglas who do their shopping here? I have, when I have been to Douglas, tried to buy fish in the morning and have often been refused as not being a resident there."
  "RESIDENT OF PORT ERIN"[2]

August – September 1945

Commandant Cyril Cuthbert remained on the Island until the closure of Rushen Camp in September 1945 and during the last few months he received correspondence from some of the internees, written by the internee appointed 'House Leaders' and 'Camp Speakers'. Two examples, one from Rushen Married Camp, Port Erin and one from an address in London seem to concur that the internees considered The Commandant as a fair man and many held him in high esteem.
  The final letter written by The Commissioners of Port Erin to the Home Office in London was sent in November, 1945.

Final Words

Having reflected on his time as the Camp Commandant, Inspector Cyril Cuthbert prepared a report dated 1947, covering his time in Rushen Camp. He wrote:
  "The regime there had been a humane one with Internees being treated in no way as suspected persons, but only as human beings, temporarily detained because

MAYFAIR 7127

78 Brook Street,
W.1

31st August 1945

Dear Mr. Cuthbert,

I should be failing in responsibility
if I were to omit giving expression to the
very high esteem which we Civilian Internees
of W and WY Camps had for you as our Commandant.

Your ever-ready helpfulness, your unfailing
kindness, often in most difficult circumstances
and your sympathetic treatment of the Internees must for ever remain in the memory of all
of us.

. . . if there was a Camp anywhere in
. . . whose Commandant has shown such
. . . e of justice together with a
. . . e welfare of the Interned as we
. . . enced from your hands, and it is
. . . feeling of gratitude that I
. . . letter to you.

. . . e,

Yours sincerely,

Wm. Fuhrhop,
Camp Speaker from April 1943
till July 1945.

. . . t, Esq.,
. . . rt Erin, I.o.M.

Dear Sir,

We, the undersigned Houseleaders of "WY" Camp,
beg you in the name of all the inmates of this camp to accept
the expression of our thanks for all you have done to make us
feel as comfortable as could be expected under the circumstances prevailing in the last years.

You have shown to everybody understanding for and
sympathy with his or her problems and troubles.

It is, therefore, not a small addition to our present
anxieties arising out of the fact of our going to be transferred
to another camp, that you are not to go with us, and though we
are confident that our new Commandant will do his best to help
us along, we feel sure that we shall miss your care very much.

So, please, let us say to you once more "Thank you",
and do us the favour of conveying our thanks to Mr. Coker and
the other members of your staff, with whom we have to part.

C.R. Cuthbert, Esq.,   Port Erin,
Commandant "WY" Camp,   Isle of Man,
Port Erin,   27th August 1945.
Isle of Man.

Dr. Conrad Bühring, representing "The Peveril".
The Waverley

Wm. M. von Wedel.

J. Guilfert, for Broada Piroste

M. Scholz   *The Imperial.*

K. Seppert.   *"Towers"*

Letters from internees
expressing their
appreciation of
Cuthbert's
management of the
camp. (Courtesy of
Manx National
Heritage)

of external circumstances, over which they had no control."

Further, he wrote:

"My earnest hope is that it will never be necessary to again effect an internment policy for women, children and families, but should it be necessary, Her Majesty's Government can do little better than repeat what was accomplished at Port Erin and Port St. Mary on the Isle of Man from 1940 to 1945."[3]

Many of the local residents who were effectively interned along with the 'alien internees' and many of the internees themselves would agree with Cuthbert's comments. Only after the end of the war would it become apparent how others were treated in Europe under Hitler's regime.

2

<u>COPY</u>

THE COMMISSIONERS OF PORT ERIN
COMMISSIONER'S OFFICE,
Port Erin,
Isle of Man.

A.G. Clague. Clerk.   22nd November,1945.

Sir,

I am directed by the Commissioners of Port Erin to transmit to you a copy of a Resolution unanimously passed by them at a Meeting held on the 21st instant,

"That this Board of Commissioners records on its Minutes appreciation of the excellent manner in which Mr. C.R. Cuthbert - Commandant of Port Erin Internment Camps - carried out his arduous and, at times, most difficult duties.   This Board, which he frequently consulted on matters connected with the Camp and which affected Port Erin, was at all times pleased with the most courteous and able manner in which he carried out his duties as Commandant and at the same time with consideration to the interests of the District of Port Erin in general."

As Mr.Cuthbert has now left this District I am instructed to respectfully request that a copy of the recorded appreciation be passed on to him.

I am, Sir,
Your obedient Servant,

(sgd) A.G. Clague,
Clerk.

The Home Secretary,
Home Office, Whitehall, S.W.1.

Letter from Port Erin Commissioners to the Home Secretary expressing their appreciation of Cuthbert's management of the camp. (Courtesy of Manx National Heritage)

APPENDICES

APPENDIX I – TRANSPORT

The British Government's decision in early 1940 to adopt a policy of mass internment and to house the majority of the internees in the Isle of Man had the benefit of putting them well out of harm's way. At its closest point at the Point of Ayr in the north, the Isle of Man lies 16 miles from Scotland. However, all the internees had to be transported by sea and the Island's main port of Douglas lies approximately 80 miles from Liverpool, which at the time was the main point of connection with the UK. In the case of the women and children housed in Rushen Camp, the journey was not finished when they landed in Douglas as they then had to transfer to Port St Mary or Port Erin in the south of the Island, a total distance of 15½ miles by train or by bus. Given the wartime shortage of petrol, the majority made the journey by steam train on the Island's narrow-gauge railway.[1]

The sea journey was not without hazard. By May 1940 German U-boats were seeking to control the Atlantic seaboard and the routes from Liverpool to America, so the mouth of the River Mersey had been mined for protection.

Arrivals

Traditionally the Isle of Man has been served by the Isle of Man Steam Packet Company; founded in 1830, it is the world's oldest surviving passenger shipping line. During WWII 10 of the company's 16 ships were commandeered for active service and four of these were lost to enemy action.

The retreat of the British army from Dunkirk following its defeat by superior German forces took place between 26th May and 4th June 1940. In the ensuing evacuation (Operation Dynamo) a total of 338,226 Allied troops were rescued by a fleet of 861 vessels of all shapes and sizes of which 243 were sunk during the operation.[2] Of those, 24,699 or 7% were carried in the eight ships provided by the Isle of Man Steam Packet Company.[3] Three of these vessels were lost: the *Fenella (II)*, the *Mona's Queen (III)* and the *King Orry (III)* between 29th and 3oth May.[4]

Consequently there was a severe shortage of suitable vessels to carry internees, starting on 27th May with the first shipment of male internees. To accommodate this a Belgian cross-Channel ferry, the *Princess Josephine Charlotte*, was taken into service. Over the course of the following four days she made three further crossings, the second on Wednesday 29th May and the third the next day, with 2,589 women internees and 259 children, a combined total of 2,848. Her final crossing was on 31st May. Thus Rushen Camp was the second internment camp to open, just two days after the men's camp on Mooragh Promenade in Ramsey, had opened on 27th May. No further shipment of women internees took place until 7th June, when the *Snaefell*, a Steam Packet Company ship, brought a further 267 women to Douglas[5]. Within just over a week a total of over 3,000 women and children had been transferred to the Island. Many of them came from London and the south of England and were interned first in Holloway Prison before making the train journey to Liverpool for onward passage to Douglas. One of the internees (Mrs Rieger) reported that her journey took a total of two-and-a-half days.[6]

After disembarking at the quay in Douglas, the women, in some case with their children, walked almost a mile along North Quay to Douglas railway station where steam trains were waiting to take them on the final leg of their journey to either Port St Mary or Port Erin on the southern tip of the Island.

After the initial influx, internee movements to and from the Island were accommodated via the Steam Packet Company's regular ferry services as shipping schedules began to return to a semblance of (wartime) normality. Internee numbers reached a peak in the second week of August when there were around 4,000 women and children in Rushen Camp.

Departures

The initial departures from the men's internment camps began almost as soon as they had arrived, with the allocation, willingly or unwillingly, of the internees to shipments from Liverpool to Canada and Australia in late June and early July 1940. The tragic sinking of the *Arandora Star* off the Irish coast by U-boat action on 2nd July, with the associated massive loss of life (a total of 682 internees, POWs, guards and crew were drowned), and the appalling and inhumane mistreatment of the internees on the *Dunera* during passage to Australia, together with the associated press outcry and challenges in Parliament, were factors in turning opinion in Britain against mass internment. The early releases, primarily from the men's camps, were initially those individuals (scientists, technologists, doctors and businessmen) who it was believed could contribute to the Allied war effort.

The women appear to have been rather less fortunate, perhaps because they were less well connected, less vocal, or less able to contribute demonstrably to the war effort than their male counterparts. By the end of 1940 a total of 849 women had been released. Transport for the women back to the UK mainland, and the release centres, was once again provided first by buses and trains. They retraced their steps from Port Erin and Port St Mary to Douglas and from there took the regular ferries of the Steam Packet Company. By the end of 1940, some 30% of the men had been released compared to 21% of the women.[7]

On 27th December 1940 the Steam Packet Company's passenger vessel, the *Victoria,* en route from Liverpool back to the Isle of Man, hit a mine. The ship was safely towed to land and there was no loss of life, but the decision was taken to switch to the port of Fleetwood, significantly reducing the distance and journey time. This route was served by the *Rushen Castle* and the *Snaefell*; the *Snaefell* was withdrawn in 1945, while the *Rushen Castle* continued until 1946. Following the mining of the *Victoria,* it was commandeered by the British Admiralty and later landed troops on Utah Beach during the 1944 Normandy landings.

The Gothenburg Exchange

Except for the exchange of 43 women in October 1941[8] and a few elderly women in 1943, it was not until the autumn of 1944 that the internees from Rushen Camp desiring to return to Germany were repatriated. As the war progressed, the position of British civilian internees in Germany was thought likely to deteriorate. Consequently, the Foreign Office made plans through the International Red Cross for a large-scale internee exchange on a one-to-one basis, leading to first the Lisbon and then to the Gothenburg Exchange.[9] Soon after midnight in the early hours of Friday 1st September 'rather more than 600 aliens … includ[ing] 470 women and 25 children' from Rushen and 'c. 100 men from the men's camps' sailed from Douglas on the *Rushen Castle* to Liverpool. There they were transferred to the Swedish America Line's *Drottningholm*[10] and departed later that day for Gothenburg. By 8th September they had safely reached their destination where they were exchanged for a like number of returning British POWs and internees.[11]

After the transfer of internees from the Isle of Man to Sweden the women's and married sections of the camp were merged. By February 1945 the remaining camp population was 269 adults and 70 children. In September 1945 the remaining 137 adults and children were transferred to the UK mainland to the Canon's Park Alien Reception Centre in Middlesex from where they were repatriated or released.[12]

The *Rushen Castle* seen here in Liverpool.

SS *Snaefell* (IV).

Princess Josephine Charlotte.

TSS Victoria.

Drottninholm in her repariation livery.

PASSENGER SHIP DETAILS					
	S.S. Rushen Castle	*S.S. Snaefell (IV)*	*S.S. Victoria*	*TS Josephine Charlotte (I)*	*S.S. Drottningholm*
Date built	1898	1905	1907	1930	1904
Shipyard	Vickers Sons & Maxim	Fairfield	William Denny & Brothers	Cockerills	Alex. Stephen
Location	Barrow in Furness	Govan	Dumbarton	Hoboken	Glasgow
Original name	*Duke of Cornwall*	*Viper*			*Virginian*
Original operator	London North Western Railway	G & J Burns	South Eastern & Chatham Railway	Belgian Marine	Allen Line
Tonnage (GRT)	1724	1713	1641	2950	10757
Length	315' (96.0 m)	315' (96.0 m)	311' (94.8 m)	347' (105.8 m)	538' (160.9 m)
Beam	37' 1" (11.3 m)	39' 6" (12.1 m)	40' 1" (12.2 m)	46' 2" (14.1 m)	60' (18.3 m)
Depth	16' 6" (5.0 m)	16' 6" (5.0 m)	16' 6" (5.0 m)	22' 8" (6.9 m)	38' (11.6 m)
Service speed (knots)	17.5	21	22	23.5	18
Passengers	1052	1700	1536	1400	1712
Crewe	52	61	41		
Bought (year)	IOMSPC (1928)	IOMSPC (1920)	IOMSPC (1928)	Swedish America Line (1920)	
Withdrawn/sold	1946	1945	1956		1948
Scrapped	1947	1948	1957	1950	1955

APPENDIX 2 – GERMANY'S DESPAIR

My father, Julius Rieger, a minister of religion at one of the German churches in London, came to Britain in 1930, at the age of 29, to stand in for the deceased pastor of St George's German Lutheran Church in London. Shortly after arrival he was asked by the journal *GOOD WILL, A Review of International Friendship*, to comment on the current economic and political situation in Germany. His short paper entitled 'Germany's Despair' appeared in January 1932, exactly a year before Hitler's ascent to power.

Dr Hans Christoph Rieger

GERMANY'S DESPAIR
By Pastor Dr. J. RIEGER

I have been asked to write of the present economic and political situation in Germany. I shall say nothing of the present position of Germany in regard to the rest of Europe. That is a matter which belongs to the Foreign Offices of the several States, and I shall therefore only deal with political questions so far as they touch the internal situation of Germany to-day.

The great problems of the present time, and especially of this winter, are not political, but economic. The surprising result of the recent German elections—of the General Election in September 1930 and of the state and municipal elections of the last few months—is the latest consequence of the terrible economic position which seems to hold out no hopeful prospects of any kind. The centre of men's thoughts this winter are not the great questions of high politics, but the old question with a new face: What shall we eat? What shall we drink?

My own opinion is necessarily coloured by my personal outlook and my own conviction and must be therefore altogether subjective. I am not a professor of National Economy; I am only a layman who sees and tries to understand what has happened and what will happen. This attitude may be disappointing, but you must remember that the bulk of a nation is not usually composed of professors, learned men and experts, even in Germany. The voice of a representative of the common people may be more acceptable than the academic explanations of a specialist.

I.   The experiences of the last five years have created two impressions about the special character of the present depression. First of all, the present crisis of Germany is not a crisis of Germany alone. It is a crisis which concerns the whole civilised world. Perhaps the centre of the present depression is to be found in Germany itself; perhaps you will find it somewhere else. But the main fact is that Germany does not stand alone. We cannot say, Germany is wrong. We must say, the world is wrong. The fanaticism of the German youth, both Communists and Hitlerites, has a common motive: when we alter Germany, we alter the world. Secondly, the present crisis of the world is not a temporary one like the crisis of 1873 or of 1900–01. The present crisis is a crisis of capitalism as a system. The capitalist period is finished, at least it is dying. The whole relation between supply and demand is disturbed. Large quantities of foodstuffs, raw materials and manufactured goods are lying in the warehouses of the world; goods of nearly every kind are cheaper than ever, but no one can buy them. In 1920 we had a record harvest; at the same time at least four millions of people in Russia died of hunger. The wheat crop of 1928, the largest for many years, could not be sold and much of it was of necessity left to rot. Cocoa has been burned in the Gold Coast, coffee thrown into the sea in Brazil. In the world of to-day a good harvest is not a blessing from God, but a curse; prices are the most important thing, not produce itself. Before the war the United States was an import country; now it has a high export figure. Japan, Russia, India, South Africa, which before the war were import countries, have already erected their own factories or are on the point of establishing their own independent industries.

The system of private capitalism, which had its great significance m the last century, could not satisfy the requirements of the post-war time. Never again can capitalism give work to the over twenty-five millions of workless people in the world, which include no less than five and a half millions in Germany alone. Rates of interest at ten, fifteen or even more per cent, are the ruin both of farm and factory. The capital invested in machinery means high interest, and fifty per cent, of all machinery in Germany is out of use. Therefore any price, even the lowest, at which goods can be sold, helps to reduce the burden of interest. Better to sell at a loss than to keep goods in stock. Hence the dumping of German goods. It is an export of hunger and despair, the great clearance sale of Germany.

Thus the opinion is growing up that what we are living to see in Germany is the tragedy of the world. What Germany is suffering to-day is the difficulty of the world to-morrow. This explains the activity of the radical parties of both political wings. A revolution can only alter an absurd system and will destroy only what deserves to be destroyed. On this point both the radical parties are agreed. But the differences between them are certainly greater than the likenesses; the ideal worlds of Communism and Fascism are as different as fire and water, and the tension between them becomes greater every day. Here lies the special danger of this winter. When the number of workless people reaches an astronomic figure, when the budget of the Reich cannot be balanced, when wages must be cut once more, civil war will destroy the last column of a tottering house. The name of this house is not only the German Government, but Christian culture and especially Protestant civilisation.

II. The real reason of all the difficulties in present-day Germany is the increasing discontent which is the fruit of this abnormal economic situation. It seems that all economic events have had the same tendency and the same effect, namely, of making the German people a nation of proletarians. The social situation is worse than ever. You must remember that the middle classes in Germany have nearly disappeared. The period of inflation of 1923 wiped out the value of the War Loans to which they had subscribed. The total amount of the War Loans, seven thousand five hundred million gold-pounds, in 1923 had a real value of twopence.

We have sixty-four million inhabitants, of whom thirty-two and a half million are working people, about the same proportion as in England. Ninety per cent of them have an income of under £10 a month; only ten per cent have an income of between £10 and £150 a month. The middle classes, which are usually the largest taxpayers and ratepayers, who are in England twenty-five per cent of the population, in Germany are only ten per cent. Of the other ninety per cent, seven and a half million earn between £6 5 s. and £10 a month, six millions between £5 and £6 5s. and sixteen million less than £5. One half of the working people do not earn the official minimum of existence.

Some of you may have an opportunity sooner or later of visiting Germany. My advice to you would be, do not take your information of Germany from the pamphlets of the Enquiry Offices. They never give a real picture of the presentday Germany. Germany has not only won the blue riband of the Atlantic; she has not only built Zeppelins; she is not only the leader of Continental post-war architecture and the pioneer of American standardisation. That is only one side of the picture; the living population shows you the other. The condition of the working classes is bad. For example, a sailor earns under £5 a month; the rent of a house for his family absorbs about £2, and there remains £3 for their subsistence. You can find similar conditions among all factory workers. But do not forget those who work in home industries all over the country; the craftsmen and basket-makers of the Frankenwald, the weavers of Silesia, the toy-makers of the Erzgebirge and the glass-blowers of Thuringia. The suffering of this part of the population is very often greater than that of the factory workers; wages of 1¼d., 2d. or 2½d. an hour are not exceptional.

The problem of unemployment is the hardest task of the present Government. The difficulties are enormous. We have learnt that the dole alone is not sufficient to fight this evil. Attempts are made to hold special meetings of many kinds for the unemployed. Christian organisations, such as Bethel, special societies and the Protestant Church as a whole, are looking for ways of alleviating the greatest difficulties. But the Church alone, Christian movements alone, cannot do very much. We only see that the solution of this unemployment problem is for us the most urgent matter. It is not a religious problem, but the great German Churches, both Protestant and Catholic, must create an atmosphere where an alteration of the present situation, that is, an alteration of the present capitalist system, is possible.

In the meantime the unemployment problem is a problem of the cure of souls. You can find in Germany three types of unemployed persons: (i) those who owned their own business or small factory and were independent; (ii) those who had a job as officials or workmen and were dependent; (iii) those who before had never worked. It is necessary to distinguish these three types. The degree of internal reaction, the degree of despair, the various kinds of temptation, of homelessness, of lack of food, of indifference to many things of culture, are dependent on the fact to which type the unemployed person belongs. Indifference and anxiety may very often develop a disgust of life. Then, again, industry does not want workmen; it has enough already. Richard

Euringer, in a recent novel on the unemployed, *Die Arbeitlosen*, represents the employers as saying: "You cannot come near the factory anymore; you cannot enter. We do not stretch a highly-charged electric wire around it; the gatekeeper at the pit-head does not use a gun. But you cannot enter. We have learned not to use you again; we have enough gumption *(Gruetze)* to get on without manual labour. We don't need you any longer."

Everything, of course, helps, especially the Winter Relief Society, an organisation which includes all independent social associations without regard to any religion or creed and which covers the whole country. All this is good and necessary, but all the goodwill we may show and all the sacrifices we can make are not enough to prevent the enormous sufferings of the army of unemployed. The outlook for the future is very bad and most depressing.

III. In writing about the present economic situation of Germany, I cannot pass over the problem of reparations. A new generation has grown up which knows nothing of the war from its own experience. This generation is not willing to pay one penny for the sins of an older generation which took part in the Great War, leaving aside the question of where these sinners must be sought for.[1] The number of those who will not any longer pay the annuities under the Young Plan is very large and increasing.

The post-war period has shown them that the loans which have been made to Germany by Great Britain and the United States have almost equalled the amount which has been paid in reparations. Private loans were necessary for the overhauling and re-starting of German industry, but an equal sum has been necessary for the payment of reparations. The whole problem is an endless circle with the only result that the interest upon these loans increases enormously every year. The German people raised seven thousand five hundred million pounds sterling in War Loans to carry on the war. They have paid nearly half as much as tribute. Including the value of her lost colonies Germany has paid the sum of £10,363,000,000. The interest on the foreign private and official loans will go on increasing, for new loans must be raised and thus the interest on them in a few years' time will reach the height of the Young Plan annuities themselves. Even supposing that at this moment all war-debts were cancelled, Germany would still have to pay the same amount of interest on her foreign loans. There would be only one difference: the political debts would have been changed into private debts, and that would be even more terrible There is no hopeful outlook of any kind for the future.

If you ask me why the radical parties in Germany have had so great a success and––for this is certain––will have further success, a large part of the German people, especially the youth of Germany will give you these answers: The capitalist position of Germany within Europe makes a radical alteration necessary; unemployment cannot be reduced by the old methods; the problem of reparation payments gives no outlook of hope for the future. Finally, let me repeat what the Very Rev. C. E. Warr of St. Giles's Cathedral, Edinburgh, said in his last Armistice Day message: The sands are running out.

APPENDIX 3 – LOCATIONS

Port Erin Promenade in
the 1930s and 1940s.
(old postcard)

LOCATION MAP FOR PORT ERIN

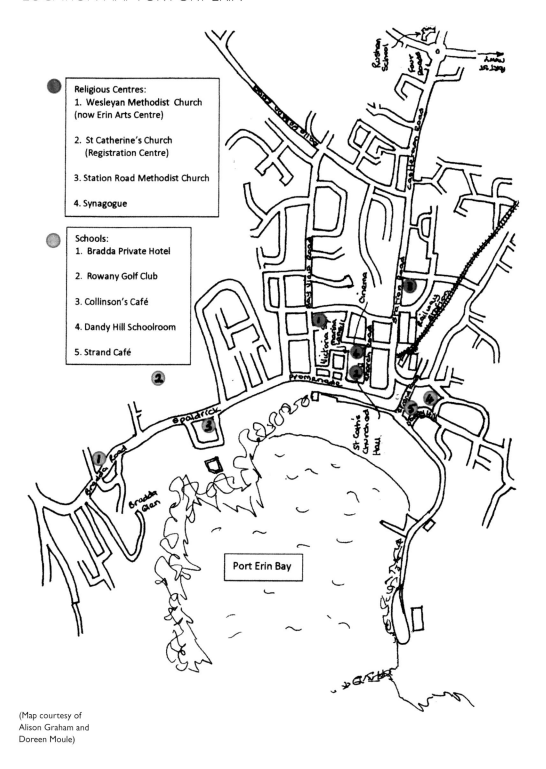

Religious Centres:
1. Wesleyan Methodist Church (now Erin Arts Centre)

2. St Catherine's Church (Registration Centre)

3. Station Road Methodist Church

4. Synagogue

Schools:
1. Bradda Private Hotel

2. Rowany Golf Club

3. Collinson's Café

4. Dandy Hill Schoolroom

5. Strand Café

Port Erin Bay

(Map courtesy of
Alison Graham and
Doreen Moule)

LOCATION MAP FOR PORT ST MARY

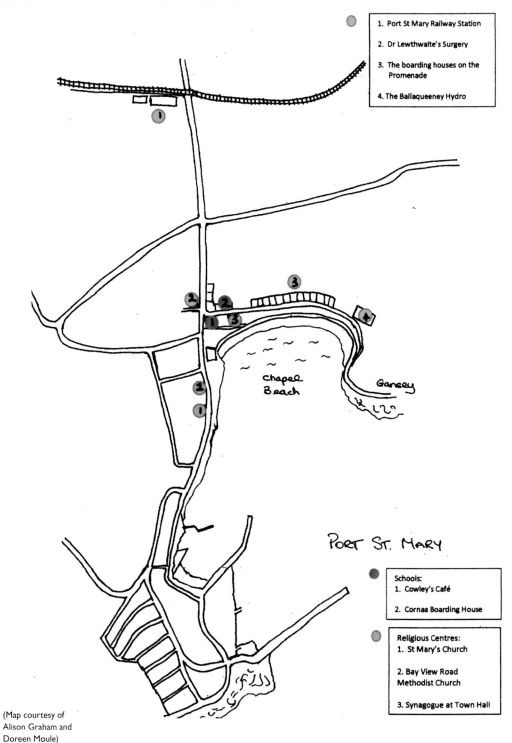

1. Port St Mary Railway Station
2. Dr Lewthwaite's Surgery
3. The boarding houses on the Promenade
4. The Ballaqueeney Hydro

Chapel Beach

Ganeey

PORT ST. MARY

Schools:
1. Cowley's Café
2. Cornaa Boarding House

Religious Centres:
1. St Mary's Church
2. Bay View Road Methodist Church
3. Synagogue at Town Hall

(Map courtesy of Alison Graham and Doreen Moule)

BIBLIOGRAPHY

Agenda (The), December 1940, pp. 5, 6.

Association of Jewish Refugees Journal, vol. 49, October 1994, p. 15.

BBC History: WWII People's War, *Fact File: Civilian Internment 1939–1945*, online, available at:
https://www.bbc.co.uk/history/ww2peopleswar/timeline/factfiles/nonflash/a6651858.shtml

Bracey, Bertha, 'Isle of Man Internment Camps: The Great Improvement Made in Six Months', *The Manchester Guardian,* 21st February 1941.

Bracey, Bertha, information online, available at:
http://www.quaker.org.uk/holocaust

Bracey, Bertha, information online, available at:
http://www.quaker.org.uk/eric-bramsted-tribute-bertha-bracey

Bracey, Bertha, information online, available at:
https://en.wikipedia.org/wiki/Bertha_Bracey

Brinson, Charmian, A. Mueller-Haerlin, and J. Winckler, *His Majesty's Loyal Internee: Fred Uhlman in Captivity,* London: Vallentine Mitchell, 2009.

Brinson, Charmian, 'A Woman's Place?: German-speaking Women in Exile in Britain 1933–1945', *German Life and Letters*, vol. 51, no. 2, April 1998, p. 208.

Brinson, Charmian, 'In the exile of internment or 'Von Versuchen, aus einer Not eine Tugend zu machen: German-speaking women interned by the British during the Second World War', in *Politics and culture in twentieth-century Germany*, Jordan Niven (ed.) , Rochester, N.Y.: Camden House, 2003.

Brinson, Charmian, 'Keine verlorene Zeit': Musik im britischen Fraueninternierungslager Rushen', in Rhode-Juchtern and Kublitz-Kramer (eds.), *Echolos*, Bielefeld: Aisthesis-Verlag, 2004, pp. 243–264.

Brinson, Charmian, 'Loyal to the Reich', in Richard Dove (ed.), *Totally Un-English: Britain's Internment of Enemy Aliens in Two World Wars*, The Yearbook of the Research Centre for German and Austrian Exile Studies, vol. 7, London: University of London, 2005.

Brinson, Charmian '"Please tell the Bishop of Chichester": George Bell and the Interment Crisis of 1940', *Kirchliche Zeitgeschichte,* vol. 21, no. 2, George K. A. Bell (1883–1958) – Bridgebuilding in Desperate Times (2008), pp. 287–299.

Brinson, Charmian, *AJR Information,* April 2000 – Search Notices, p. 5.

Brockerick, George, online, available at: www.george-broderick.de/files/rushen_camp

Ceserani, David and Tony Kushner (eds.), *The Internment of Aliens in 20th Century Britain*, London: Frank Cass, 1993.

Chappell, Connery, *Island of Barbed Wire*, London: Robert Hale Ltd., 1984.

Cleverly, Vicky interview with Mona Quillin, 2001.

Collins' English Dictionary (definition of 'enemy aliens'), available online at:
https://www.collinsdictionary.com/

Creswell, Yvonne, *Living with the Wire*, Manx National Heritage, 1994.

Cruikshank, Joanna, 'Dame Joanna's letter to Port Erin commissioners dated 29th May 1941', Port Erin Commissioners minutes (private documents).

Cuthbert, C., papers, Internee Lists, iMuseum.

Cuthbert, Cyril Roy Mitchell, *Science and the Detection of Crime,* Hutchinson, 1958.

Daily Herald, 'Women police "snooping"', Manchester, 7th Aug 1941.

Daily Mail, 6th October 1941.

Dalheim, Rosemarie, *The Sunny Hours,* New Generation Publishing, 2011, p. 258–256.

'Dame Joanna's Report – extracts', *Mona's Herald,* 3rd December 1940, p. 4.

Davidson, Hugh, conversation with Iris Burton, Port Erin artist, 20th July 2014.

Davidson, Hugh, interview with Irene Jackson, 10th May 2016.

Davidson, Hugh, interviews with Betty Kelly, 2014 and 2015.

Davidson, Sandra, interview with Keith McArd.

Dearden, Steven and Ken Hassell, *Ships of the Isle of Man Steam Packet Company,* Ochiltree, Ayrshire: Stenlake Publishing, 1999.

Deutsche National Bibliothek, private collection.

Dickson, R., S. MacDougall et al., *Forced Journeys, Artists in exile in Britain c. 1933–45,* London: Ben Uri Gallery, 2009.

Dickson, R., unpublished paper, 2016.

F.O., Manx Cat

Forell's, Birger, diary, unpublished.

Franklin, Alan, 'Second World War Internee Records for the Isle of Man', *AJR Journal,* February 2008.

Genealogy of the Meyerhof family from Hoof, Wolfhagen and Kassel.

'German Exile Archives 1933–1945', German National Library.

Gottlieb, Julie V., *Feminine Fascism: Women in Britain's Fascist Movement, 1923–45,* London: I.B. Tauris, 2000.

Grossner, S., *The Troubles to Greet Beauty,* Loughborough, 2011.

'Guarded German Women Wait in London Garden', *The Star,* 8th Oct 1941.

The Guardian, 'Lotte Moos obituary', Tuesday 15th January 2008.

Hinrichsen, Klaus E., 'Visual art behind the Wire' in D. Cesarani, D and T. Kushner (eds.), *The Internment of Aliens in 20th Century Britain,* Abingdon, 1993, p. 190.

Information Board at Dunkirk Memorial, Port St Mary.

International Co-operative Women's Guild, *Report on Women's Internment Camp,* 1941.

Internee Registration Cards, courtesy of Manx Museum.

Isle of Man Examiner, 'Passport Humbug', 15th September 1939, p. 1.

Isle of Man Examiner, 'Permit System Dead', 6th October 1939, p. 1.

Isle of Man Examiner, 31st May 1940.

Isle of Man Examiner, 31st May 1940, p. 5.

Isle of Man Examiner, August 1940.

Isle of Man Examiner, 18th October 1940.

Isle of Man Examiner, 18th October 1940, Front page.

Isle of Man Examiner, 8th November 1940, p. 6.

Isle of Man Examiner, 22nd November 1940.

Isle of Man Examiner, 22nd November 1940, p. 6.

Isle of Man Examiner, 28th August 1942, p. 8.

Isle of Man Examiner, 29th August 1942, p. 7.

Isle of Man Examiner, 10th September 1943.

Isle of Man Examiner, October 1944.

Isle of Man Examiner, Friday 7th September 1945.

Isle of Man Examiner, 13th May 1955, p. 11.

Isle of Man Times, 27th December 1941.

Isle of Man Times, 4th January 1941, p. 4.

Isle of Man Weekly Times, 'Staff changes', 8th Feb 1941.

Isle of Man Weekly Times, 1st March 1941.

Isle of Man Weekly Times, 3rd June 1980.

Isotype Revisited, collection introduction, available online at: http://isotyperevisited.org/2009/09/intro-for-collection.html

Jackson, Alan, interview with Joyce Corlett, 25th April 2015.

Kushner, Tony, 'An Alien Occupation: Jewish Refugees and Domestic Service in Britain, 1933–1948' in Werner E. Moss (ed.) *Second Chance: Two Centuries of German-speaking Jews in the United Kingdom, Tubingen: J.C.B. Mohr (Paul Siebeck), 1991.* p. 569.

Lange, Irma, unpublished autobiography, provided by Deutsche National Bibliotek, private collection.

Laurent, Livia, *a tale of Internment*, London: George Allen & Unwin Ltd, 1942.

Laurent, Livia, *Poems*, London: Favil Press, 1942

Lewis, Norah (née Young), memories.

MacDougall, S., *Creativity behind barbed wire*, Conference, March 2010, Abstract: A Vitalising Impulse – Sculptors behind the wire.

Mackie, Mary, *Wards in the Sky – The RAF's Remarkable Nursing Service*, (2nd ed.) Stroud: The History Press, 2014.

Manchester Guardian, 'Women Internees in Isle of Man: Interview with Dame Joanna Criuickshank', 23rd November 1940.

Manchester Guardian, 29th August 1942.

Margarete Klopfleisch (1911–1982): An Exhibition of Sculpture and Works on Paper, Catalogue, London: John Denham Gallery, December 1987.

Metropolitan Women's Police Service documents

Mona's Herald, 21st August 1942.

Mona's Herald, 'Shock for newlyweds', March 1942.

National Archives, *Collar the Lot! Britain's policy of internment during the Second World War*, online, available at: https://blog.nationalarchives.gov.uk/blog/collar-lot-britains-policy-internment-second-world-war/

National Archives, 'Internment', talk by Roger Kershaw, 21st September 2009, Archives Media Player [Audio], online, available at: https://media.nationalarchives.gov.uk/index.php/author/roger-kershaw/

Neuzugang in der Keramiksammlung – Kulturgut 49.II, Berlin: Germanisches National Museum, 2016.

News Chronicle, 'Women Aliens in Isle of Man Underfed', 15th October 1940.

Olins, Renate, *Daily Telegraph magazine,* 1995, iMuseum, accession no. M26462.

Onchan Pioneer (The), Manx National Heritage, Manx Museum Archive, Douglas: iMuseum.

Peto, Miss OBE., unpublished memoirs, The Metropolitan Women's Police Service.

Port Erin Commissioners minutes (private documents).

Port St Mary Commissioners minutes (private documents).

Port St Mary Commissioners minutes (private documents), 13th January 1941.

Port St Mary Commissioners minutes (private documents), letter dated 24th April 1941.

Ramsey Courier, 15th November 1940.

Registration Cards, Manx Museum

Report of the Port Erin camp, Free German League of Culture.

Rieger, Dr Chris, talk, 6th August 2016.

Rieger, Eva, *Friedelind Wagner: Richard Wagner's Rebellious Granddaughter,* Boydell Press, 2013.

Rieger, Mrs, Private communication.

Rodgers, Kate (ed.) *Our Heritage Memories of the Past in Rushen: Book 2,* no publication date.

Rushen internment camp rules.

Saywell, Jane and Ali Graham, transcript of meeting with Mona Quillin, 10th February 2015.

Sheffield Telegraph, 'Nurses on their way back to Germany', 8th Oct 1941.

Smith, Lynn, interview with Ira Rischowski, Imperial War Museum, February 1979.

Smith, Lynn, interview with Dr Erna Simion, Imperial War Museum, February 1979.

Spartacus Educational, online, available at: http://spartacus-educational.com/2WWgermansBR.htm

Sunday Express, 5th October 1941.

*The Protected Areas (Port Erin and Rushen and Arbory) Orders (*revised orders 9th September 1944), reproduced by permission of the Treasury of the Isle of Man. © Crown copyright reserved.

Thompson, Julian, *Dunkirk: Retreat to Victory,* New York: Arcade, 2011, p. 306.

United States Holocaust Memorial Museum, *Holocaust Encyclopaedia (German Jewish Refugees 1933–1939),* online, available at: www.ushmm.org

Walters, Rosemary, interview with Mrs Alice Kellett, 1994.

Walters, Rosemary, interview with Mrs Alice Kellett, Manx Heritage Foundation (now Culture Vannin), 20th September 1996.

'War Cabinet meeting held on the 24th May 1940 in Downing Street', War Cabinet Papers nos. 137 (40) May 1940, pp. 244–246; 207 (40), pp. 125–126, Imperial War Museum.

Wehrhan, Wanda, letters to the Commandant.

NOTES AND REFERENCES

CD of photos and newspaper cuttings and sections of Ivy Baxter – all courtesy of Friends of Metropolitan Police Collection and Reproduced by permission of The Mayor's Office for Policing and Crime (Heritage Centre)

Chapter 1 – From Friend to Foe

1. Spartacus Educational, online, available at: http://spartacus-educational.com/2WWgermansBR.htm
2. Connery Chappell, *Island of Barbed Wire*, London: Robert Hale Ltd., 1984, p. 39.
3. National Archives, *Collar the Lot! Britain's policy of internment during the Second World War*, online, available at: https://blog.nationalarchives.gov.uk/blog/collar-lot-britains-policy-internment-second-world-war/
4. Chappell, *Barbed Wire*, p. 19.
5. *Information Board at Dunkirk Memorial, Port St Mary.*
6. Chappell, *Barbed Wire*, p. 29.

General references:
United States Holocaust Memorial Museum, *Holocaust Encyclopaedia (German Jewish Refugees 1933–1939)*, online, available at: www.ushmm.org
Collins' English Dictionary (definition of 'enemy aliens'), available online at: https://www.collinsdictionary.com/
BBC History: WWII people's War, *Fact File: Civilian Internment 1939–1945*, online, available at: https://www.bbc.co.uk/history/ww2peopleswar/timeline/factfiles/nonflash/a6651858.shtml
National Archives: Archives Media Player, Audio, 'Internment', talk by Roger Kershaw, 21st September 2009, online, available at: https://media.nationalarchives.gov.uk/index.php/author/roger-kershaw/
1st photo of Hitler – Getty Images.

Chapter 2 – The Arrival of the Women Internees

1. 'The Passport Humbug', *Isle of Man Examiner*, 15th September 1939, p. 1.; 'Permit System Dead', *Isle of Man Examiner*, 6th October 1939, p. 1.
2. *Isle of Man Examiner,* Friday 31st May 1940, p. 5.
3. Tony Kushner, 'An Alien Occupation : Jewish Refugees and Domestic Service in Britain, 1933–1948' in Werner E. Moss (ed.) *Second Chance: Two Centuries of German-speaking Jews in the United Kingdom, Tubingen: J.C.B. Mohr (Paul Siebeck), 1991.* p. 569.

4. Charmian Brinson, 'A Woman's Place?: German-speaking Women in Exile in Britain 1933–1945', *German Life and Letters*, vol. 51, no. 2, April 1998, p. 208.

5. Brinson A Woman's Place, p. 210; Kushner, Alien Occupation, p. 572.

Chapter 3 – How the Camps Evolved

Maps from Public Records Office IOM

1. *The Protected Areas (Port Erin and Rushen and Arbory) Orders* (revised orders 9th September 1944), reproduced by permission of the Treasury of the Isle of Man. © Crown copyright reserved.

Chapter 4 – Two Very Different Commandants

DAME JOANNA CRUIKSHANK
1. Mary Mackie, *Wards in the Sky – The RAF's Remarkable Nursing Service*, (2nd ed.) Stroud: The History Press, 2014.
2. By merger of the Royal Flying Corps and the Royal Naval Air Service.
3. Mackie, *Wards in the Sky.*
4. Between 1st December 1938 and 1st September 1939 some 10,000 German and Austrian Jewish children under the age of 17 were saved from almost certain death through the work of an interdenominational group, the Movement for the Care of Children from Germany, in which the Quakers were very active. This was facilitated through an accelerated immigration programme approved by the then Home Secretary, Sir Samuel Hoare.
5. The children were not strictly internees as that category was restricted to ages 16–60. However, many accompanied their mothers into internment. It is not known how many children were interned in Rushen. A figure of 300 is given as the number of internees pregnant in November 1940.
6. 'Women Internees in Isle of Man: Interview with Dame Joanna Cruickshank', *Manchester Guardian*, 23rd November 1940.
CYRIL CUTHBERT
1. Cyril Roy Mitchell Cuthbert, *Science and the Detection of Crime,* Hutchinson, 1958.
2. Obituary, courtesy of Manx National Heritage.

General references:
1. Mary Mackie, *Wards in the Sky – The RAF's Remarkable Nursing Service*, (2nd ed.) Stroud: The History Press, 2014.
2. Connery Chappell, *Island of Barbed Wire*, London: Robert Hale Ltd., 1984, 2005
3. David Ceserani and Tony Kushner (eds.), *The Internment of Aliens in 20th Century Britain*, London: Frank Cass, 1993.
4. Charmian Brinson C, 'In the exile of internment or 'Von Versuchen, aus einer Not eine Tugend zu machen': German-speaking women interned by the British during the Second World War', in *Politics and culture in*

twentieth-century Germany, Jordan Niven (ed.) , Rochester, N.Y.: Camden House, 2003.

Chapter 5 – Married Camp

1. Port St Mary Commissioners minutes (private documents), 13th January 1941.
2. Dame Joanna's letter to Port Erin commissioners dated 29th May 1941, Port Erin Commissioners minutes (private documents).
3. Port St Mary Commissioners minutes (private documents), letter dated 24th April 1941.
4. *The Onchan Pioneer* – iMuseum, Manx National Heritage, (*The Onchan Pioneer*, a compilation of documents and drawings held in the iMuseum, Douglas).
5. *Isle of Man Weekly Times,* 8th Feb 1941.
6. *Isle of Man Weekly Times,* 1st March 1941.
7. *Isle of Man Times,* 27th December 1941.
8. 'Shock for newlyweds', *Mona's Herald,* March 1942.
9. 'Staff changes', *Isle of Man Times*, Friday 22nd January 1943, p. 8.
10. Online, available at: www.george-broderick.de/files/rushen_camp
11. *Mona's Herald*, 21st August 1942.
12. iMuseum – C. Cuthbert papers, Internee Lists.

Part 2

Chapter 6 – Internees Christmas Greetings

1. Rosemary Walters, interview with Mrs Alice Kellett, Manx Heritage Foundation (now Culture Vannin), 20th September 1996.
2. Hugh Davidson, interviews with Betty Kelly, 2014 and 2015.
3. Rosemary Walters, interview.
4. Lynn Smith, interview with Dr Erna Simion, Imperial War Museum, February 1979.
5. International Co-operative Women's Guild, *Report on Women's Internment Camp*, 1941.
6. Alan Franklin (of Manx National Heritage), 'Second World War Internee Records for the Isle of Man', *AJR Journal*, February 2008.
7. Lynn Smith, interview with Ira Rischowski, Imperial War Museum, February 1979.
8. Yvonne Creswell, *Living with the Wire*, Manx National Heritage, 1994. This accompanied the 1994 MNH Exhibition of the same name. It is an excellent book on WWI and WWII internment on the Isle of Man, and well illustrated.
9. Charmian Brinson, 'Loyal to the Reich', in Richard Dove (ed.), *Totally Un-English: Britain's Internment of Enemy Aliens in Two World Wars*, The Yearbook of the Research Centre for German and Austrian Exile Studies, vol. 7, London: University of London, 2005.

10. ibid.
11. Rosemary Walters, interview with Mrs Alice Kellett, 1994.

Part 3

Chapter 7 – Daily Life

1. Rushen internment camp rules.
2. Memories of a child during the war years in Port Erin, Brenda Watterson

Chapter 8 – The Service Exchange

1. Connery Chappell, *Island of Barbed Wire*, London: Robert Hale Ltd., 1984, p. 55.
2. *The Manchester Guardian*, 29th August 1942.

Chapter 9 – Health and Welfare of the Internees

1. *Isle of Man Examiner*, Friday 31st May 1940.
2. Dame Joanna's Report – extracts, *Mona's Herald,* 3rd December 1940, p. 4.
3. *News Chronicle,* 'Women Aliens in Isle of Man Underfed', 15th October 1940.
4. *Isle of Man Examiner*, 18th October 1940.
5. Alan Franklin, 'Second World War Internee Records for the Isle of Man', *AJR Journal*, March 2008.
6. *Isle of Man Examiner,* 10th September 1943.

Chapter 10 – Education for all

1. Charmian Brinson C, 'In the exile of internment or 'Von Versuchen, aus einer Not eine Tugend zu machen: German-speaking women interned by the British during the Second World War', in *Politics and culture in twentieth-century Germany*, Jordan Niven (ed.) , Rochester, N.Y.: Camden House, 2003, pp. 13–14.
2. ibid.
3. ibid.
4. Rosemarie Dalheim, *The Sunny Hours,* New Generation Publishing, 2011, p. 258–256.

General references:
Isle of Man Examiner, 22nd November 1940.

Chapter 11 – Role of the Constabulary

1. Retired Inspector Nicholson – verbally relayed to author

2. 'War Cabinet meeting held on the 24th May 1940 in Downing Street', War Cabinet Papers nos. 137 (40) May 1940, pp. 244–246; 207 (40), pp. 125–126, Imperial War Museum.
3. Miss Peto OBE., unpublished memoirs, The Metropolitan Women's Police Service.
4. ibid.
5. ibid.
6. Port Erin Commissioners minutes (private documents).
7. Port St Mary Commissioners minutes (private documents).
8. ibid.
9. ibid.
10. ibid.
11. *Isle of Man Times,* Saturday 4th January 1941, p. 4.
12. The Metropolitan Women's Police Service documents
13. ibid.
14. *Sunday Express*, 5th October 1941.
15. *Daily Mail*, 6th October 1941.
16. 'Women police "snooping"', *Daily Herald*, Manchester, 7th Aug 1941.
17. 'Guarded German Women Wait in London Garden', *The Star,* 8th Oct 1941.
18. 'Nurses on their way back to Germany', *Sheffield Telegraph*, 8th Oct 1941.

Chapter 12 – Internee Personalities

1. Brinson, Charmian, 'Loyal to the Reich', in Richard Dove (ed.), *Totally Un-English: Britain's Internment of Enemy Aliens in Two World Wars*, The Yearbook of the Research Centre for German and Austrian Exile Studies, vol. 7, London: University of London, 2005.
   Her reference is to an extract from a letter dated 10th July 1946, author unknown, from material gathered by Deborah Cherry as part of her on-going work on women detained under Defence Regulation 18B.
2. Interview with Charles Guard for Culture Vannin in 2005.
3. p109 The school was closed early in 1933, because Minna, as head teacher, 'would not conform to the Hitlerian principles
4. Dr Chris Rieger's talk, Saturday 6th August 2016.
5. p117 Manx Cat by F.O.
6. Eva Rieger, *Friedelind Wagner: Richard Wagner's Rebellious Granddaughter*, Boydell Press, 2013.
7. Irma Lange, unpublished autobiography, provided by Deutsche National Bibliotek, private collection
8. ibid.
9. He kept a diary for the entire period of his internment and one of his articles is recorded in 1941 in a book called the *Onchan Pioneer* with the title 'Onchan Camp Youth', which is held in the Manx Museum archive.
10. Irma Lange, unpublished autobiography, provided by Deutsche National Bibliotek, private collection.
11. ibid.

12. Deutsche National Bibliothek, private collection. Precise account in 'German Exile Archives 1933–1945', German National Library.
13. Renate Olins, *Daily Telegraph magazine*, 1995, iMuseum, accession no. M26462.

Chapter 13 – Stories of Local Personalities

Sandra Davidson interview with Keith McArd.
Hugh Davidson interview with Irene Jackson, 10th May 2016.
Jane Saywell and Ali Graham, transcript of meeting with Mona Quillin, 10th February 2015.
Hugh Davidson conversation with Iris Burton, Port Erin artist, 20th July 2014.
Alan Jackson interview with Joyce Corlett, 25th April 2015.
Memories from Norah Lewis (née Young).
John W. Qualtrough – local historian.
Betty Vernon (née Crellin).
Mary and Joan Eslick
'Our Heritage Memories of the Past in Rushen Book 2 edited by Kate Rodgers' no publication date.

Chapter 14 – Religion and the Deaconesses

1. *Isle of Man Examiner,* Friday 8th November 1940, p. 6.
2. *Isle of Man Examiner,* Friday, 13th May 1955, p. 11.
3. *Isle of Man Examiner,* August 1940.
4. Wesley Deaconess Order magazine *The Agenda*, December 1940, pp. 5, 6.
5. *Isle of Man Examiner,* 22nd November 1940, p. 6.
6. *Isle of Man Examiner,* 29th August 1942, p. 7.
7. *Isle of Man Examiner,* 28th August 1942, p. 8.
8. ibid.
9. Report of the Port Erin camp, published by the Free German League of Culture.
   Charmian Brinson '"Please tell the Bishop of Chichester": George Bell and the Interment Crisis of 1940', *Kirchliche Zeitgeschichte*, vol. 21, no. 2, George K. A. Bell (1883–1958) – Bridgebuilding in Desperate Times (2008), pp. 287–299,
   Her references are that the original report was in the *News Chronicle* but that the *Isle of Man Examiner* had replied on 25th October 1940 page 4. However, it was in the *IOM Examiner* earlier than that: *Isle of Man Examiner,* Friday 18th October 1940, Front page.
10. *Ramsey Courier*, 15th November 1940.
11. See Charmian Brinson, above.
12. Bertha Bracey, 'Isle of Man Internment Camps: The Great Improvement Made in Six Months', *The Manchester Guardian,* 21st February 1941.
13. Wanda Wehrhan's letters to the Commandant.
14. Birger Forell's diary, unpublished.

General references:
Bertha Bracey, information online, available at:
   http://www.quaker.org.uk/holocaust http://www.quaker.org.uk/eric-
   bramsted-tribute-bertha-bracey
   https://en.wikipedia.org/wiki/Bertha_Bracey
Sister Emmeline Cheshire – Deacon Josie Flute supplied information from
   the archives of the Wesley Diaconal Order.
Sister Emmeline Cheshire – quote from *'The Agenda'* (the Wesley Deaconess
   Order magazine), December 1940.

Chapter 15 – *Music and Musicians*

1. A programme for one such variety performance still exists and is in the
   safe keeping of the Isle of Man Collection at the Leo Baeck Institute in
   New York

General references:
Charmian Brinson, 'Keine verlorene Zeit': Musik im britischen
   Fraueninternierungslager Rushen', in Rhode-Juchtern and Kublitz-Kramer
   (eds.), *Echolos*, Bielefeld: Aisthesis-Verlag, 2004, pp. 243–264
Photos from Registration Cards courtesy of Manx Museum

Chapter 16 – *Significant Writers*

1. Julie V. Gottlieb, *Feminine Fascism: Women in Britain's Fascist Movement,
   1923–45*, London: I.B. Tauris, 2000.
2. Livia Laurent*, a tale of Internment*, London: George Allen & Unwin Ltd,
   1942.
3. Livia Laurent, *Poems*, London: Favil Press, 1942
4. *Isotype Revisited,* collection introduction, available online at:
   http://isotyperevisited.org/2009/09/intro-for-collection.html

General references:
Charmian Brinson, *AJR Information,* April 2000 – Search Notices, p. 5.
Livia Laurent, a *tale of internment,* London: George Allen & Unwin Ltd, 1942.
Internee Registration Cards courtesy of Man Museum.
Genealogy of the Meyerhof family from Hoof, Wolfhagen and Kassel.
Lotte Moos obituary in *The Guardian,* Tuesday 15th January 2008.

Chapter 17 – *Art and Artists*

1. Klaus E. Hinrichsen, 'Visual art behind the Wire' in D. Cesarani, D and T.
   Kushner (eds.), *The Internment of Aliens in 20th Century Britain*,
   Abingdon, 1993, p. 190.
2. 'Women Internees in Isle of Man: Interview with Dame Joanna
   Criuickshank,' *Manchester Guardian*, 23rd November 1940.

3. C. Brinson, 'In the exile of internment or 'Von Versuchen, aus einer Not eine Tugend zu machen: German-speaking women interned by the British during the Second World War', in *Politics and culture in twentieth-century Germany*, Jordan Niven (ed.) , Rochester, N.Y.: Camden House, 2003.f

4. Otto Dix (1891–1969) was a leading artist in pre-war Germany and was aligned to the *Dada* and *Neue Sachlichkeit* movements. Despite being condemned as 'degenerate' by the Nazis, who burned a number of his works, he remained in Germany throughout WWII.

5. Käthe Kollwitz (1867–1945) was a German printmaker and sculptor with an international reputation and was one of the most influential socialist artists in Germany before WWII. The Nazis despised her socialist inspired work, removing it from museums and threatening her with deportation to a concentration camp. The threat was not carried out due to her high profile.

6. Hitler annexed the Sudetenland (NE Czechoslovakia) in October 1938 and invaded the remainder of Czechoslovakia on 15 March 1939.

7. The HMT *Dunera* sailed on 10th July 1940 from Liverpool with 2,542 'enemy aliens' aboard. The appalling mistreatment of the prisoners by the British guards led to several court martials including the officer-in-charge, Lt. Col. William Scott, who was severely reprimanded. Connolly, Kate, *Sydney Morning Herald*, 'Britons finally learn the dark Dunera Secret', 19 May 2006.

8. *Margarete Klopfleisch (1911–1982): An Exhibition of Sculpture and Works on Paper*, Catalogue, London: John Denham Gallery, December 1987.

9. S. Grossner, *The Troubles to Greet Beauty*, Loughborough, 2011.

10. S. MacDougall, *Creativity behind barbed wire*, Conference, March 2010, Abstract: A Vitalising Impulse – Sculptors behind the wire.

11. C. Brinson, A. Mueller-Haerlin, and J. Winckler, *His Majesty's Loyal Internee: Fred Uhlman in Captivity,* London: Vallentine Mitchell, 2009.

12. Connery Chappell, *Island of Barbed Wire*, London: Robert Hale Ltd.,1984, p. 68

13. R. Dickson, S. MacDougall et al., *Forced Journeys, Artists in exile in Britain c. 1933–45*, London: Ben Uri Gallery, 2009.

14. *Association of Jewish Refugees Journal*, vol. 49, October 1994, p. 15.

15. Germanisches National Museum, *Neuzugang in der Keramiksammlung – Kulturgut 49.II*, Berlin: 2016.

16. Klaus E. Hinrichsen, 'Visual art behind the Wire' in D. Cesarani, D and T. Kushner (eds.), *The Internment of Aliens in 20th Century Britain*, Abingdon, 1993, p. 190.

17. R. Dickson, unpublished paper, 2016.

Chapter 18 – Closure of the Camp

1. *Isle of Man Examiner*, Friday 7th September 1945.

2. *Isle of Man Examiner*, October 1944.

3. iMuseum – C. Cuthbert papers.

General references
Isle of Man Weekly Times, 3rd June 1980.

Appendices

1. The Isle of Man Railways operates on the 'Manx Standard Gauge' of 3 foot (914 mm).
2. Julian Thompson, *Dunkirk: Retreat to Victory*, New York: Arcade, 2011, p. 306.
3. Connery Chappell, *Island Lifeline*, Prescot, T Stevenson & Sons, 1980.
4. Steven Dearden and Ken Hassell, *Ships of the Isle of Man Steam Packet Company*, Ochiltree, Ayrshire: Stenlake Publishing, 1999.
5. Alan Franklin, *Involuntary Guests*, Isle of Man, Lily Publications, 2017, p. 53.
6. Private communication with Mrs Rieger.
7. Chappell, *Barbed Wire*, p. 43, p. 83.
8. Chappell, *Barbed Wire*, p. 176.
9. Charmian Brinson, 'Loyal to the Reich', in Richard Dove (ed.), '*Totally Un-English?*': *Britain's Internment of Enemy Aliens in Two World Wars*, The Yearbook of the Research Centre for German and Austrian Exile Studies, vol. 7, University of London:, Rodopi, Amsterdam – New York, 2005, p. 112–3.
10. The *M.V. Drottningholm* and the *M.V. Gripsholm* were two passenger liners of the Swedish America Line that during WWII sailed under the auspices of the International Red Cross as exchange and repatriation ships. They were used to transfer POWs, diplomats and civilians in a series of exchanges. They were painted white, clearly marked 'Diplomat' and 'Freigleit – Protected' and sailed at night with full flood lighting.
11. Chappell, *Barbed Wire*, p. 177–9.
12. Charmian Brinson, *Loyal to the Reich*, p. 114–5

AUTHOR ATTRIBUTIONS

Preface: Sandra and Hugh Davidson

Part 1
Chapter 1:   Doreen Moule and Hugh Davidson
Chapter 2:   Doreen Moule
Chapter 3:   Doreen Moule
Chapter 4:   Dame Joanna – David Wertheim and Pamela Crowe
                    Cuthbert – Pamela Crowe and Alison Graham
Chapter 5:   Alison Graham

Part 2
Chapter 6:   Hugh Davidson

Part 3
Chapter 7:   Doreen Moule
Chapter 8:   David Wertheim
Chapter 9:   Alison Graham and Jane Saywell
Chapter 10:   Doreen Moule
Chapter 11:   Alison Graham

Part 4
Chapter 12:   Wehrhans – Pamela Crowe
                    Bersu – Pamela Crowe
                    Christa – Hugh Davidson
                    Jochanan – Sandra Davidson
                    Johanna Metzger – Alison Graham
                    William Kaczynski – Sandra Davidson
                    Munzers – Pamela Crowe
                    Ira – Doreen Moule/Hugh Davidson
                    Minna – Doreen Moule
                    Eva & Chris – Pamela Crowe/Sandra Davidson
                    Friedelind – Pamela Crowe
                    Irma Lange – Alison Graham
                    Renate Olins – Alison Graham
                    Rosemarie Dalheim – herself, taken from booklet by
                        Kate Rodgers
                    Anita Dalheim – herself, taken from booklet by
                        Kate Rodgers
Chapter 13:   Keith McArd – Sandra Davidson
                    Irene Jackson – Hugh Davidson
                    Mona Quillin – Alison Graham and Jane Saywell
                    Iris Burton – Hugh Davidson
                    Joyce Corlett – herself, taken from an interview with
                        Alan Jackson
                    Norah Lewis – Pamela Crowe

ACKNOWLEDGEMENTS

The publishers would like to acknowledge the following for their knowledge and assistance:

- Sonja Grossner (Klopfleisch) kindly assisted with the profile of her mother, Margarete (Gretel).
- Rachel Dickson, Head of Curatorial Services at the Ben Uri Gallery, kindly made information available for the profile of Erna Nonnenmacher.
- Inge King who made it possible to use the photograph of Erna and Hermann Nonnenmacher moving studios.
- The Metropolitan Women's Police Association
- The Mayor's Office for Policing and Crime. (Heritage Centre)
- Nina Miconi, daughter of Gisela Wehrhan Christian and granddaughter of Wanda Wehrhan, for the wonderful help and donation of letters.
- The Deaconess Museum for their support and material provided.
- Sister Gabriel the archivist at Bethel.
- Renate, Eva and Chris Rieger and Dagny Beidler for all the material and memories that they have shared.
- All the many local people who have shared memories, photographs and given their time and support in so many ways.
- Gough Ritchie Trust for their generous grant.
- Culture Vannin for their generous grant.
- The collections and staff at Manx National Heritage have been a crucial resource in the creation of this book and Rushen Heritage trust is most grateful for all the help provided. RHT is grateful to the Trustees of the Manx Museum and National Trust for permission to use the resulting material in this publication.
- Rosemarie Dalheim for her enthusiastic assistance in allowing the use of her material.
- Rob Clynes, cartographer, for all his help with the digitisation of the maps.
- A huge 'thank you' to Sara Donaldson, our editor and Ian Smith, our designer, for all the work they have done and their immense patience with a group of 'novice' writers.

INDEX